politics@media

DAVID D. PERLMUTTER, EDITOR

FREEING
THE PRESSES

THE FIRST AMENDMENT IN ACTION

EDITED BY TIMOTHY E. COOK

PUBLISHED IN COOPERATION WITH THE KEVIN P. REILLY
CENTER FOR MEDIA AND PUBLIC AFFAIRS

LOUISIANA STATE UNIVERSITY PRESS
BATON ROUGE

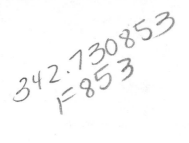

Copyright © 2005 by Louisiana State University Press

DESIGNER: Andrew Shurtz
TYPEFACES: Minion Pro, Trade Gothic
PRINTER AND BINDER: Thomson-Shore, Inc.

LIBRARY OF CONGRESS CATALOGING-IN-PUBLICATION DATA

Freeing the presses : the First Amendment in action / edited by Timothy E. Cook.
    p. cm. — (Politics@media)
  Includes bibliographical references and index.
  ISBN 0-8071-3077-X (cloth : alk. paper)
  1. Freedom of the press—United States. 2. Press law—United States. 3. Mass media policy—United States. 4. United States. Constitution. 1st Amendment. I. Cook, Timothy E., 1954– II. Series.
KF4774.F745 2005
342.7308'53—dc22

                  2005005656

CONTENTS

Preface   vii

Freeing the Presses: An Introductory Essay   1
TIMOTHY E. COOK

PART ONE:
FROM THE PAST

Introduction   29
CRAIG M. FREEMAN

The Press the Founders Knew   33
CHARLES E. CLARK

On the Relationship between Press Law and Press Content   51
FREDERICK SCHAUER

PART TWO:
AT PRESENT

Introduction   71
JACK M. WEISS

Why Democracies Need an Unlovable Press   73
MICHAEL SCHUDSON

Daily News and First Amendment Ideals   87
REGINA G. LAWRENCE

PART THREE:
TOWARD THE FUTURE

Introduction   109
RALPH IZARD

The Twilight of Mass Media News:
Markets, Citizenship, Technology, and the Future of Journalism   111
W. LANCE BENNETT

"New Media" and Contemporary Interpretations of Freedom of the Press   139
DIANA OWEN

Afterword   163
EMILY ERICKSON

Contributors   175

Index   177

PREFACE

Given all of the talk about freedom of the press and given all the research about the performance of the news media, it is remarkable that these two discussions rarely intersect. Those who discuss and apply principles of press freedom, including elected officials and justices of the Supreme Court, as well as lawyers and journalists, tend to talk in principled theoretical terms about the meaning of liberty and the role of the press in a democratic society. Their words are often distant from the real-world evidence of what the press does in practice. And while the study of political communication has developed a vast and sophisticated fund of knowledge about what the news media do, how they do it, and what effects the news has upon the public and upon the workings of the American political system, the normative conclusions that such scholars reach rarely touch upon the matters of freedom of the press that many take for granted in the world of political and journalistic practice.

The third annual John Breaux symposium, conducted at Louisiana State University in March of 2003, was designed to initiate a dialogue between the legal theory of freedom of the press and empirical examinations of the news media's performance. Under the auspices of the Reilly Center for Media and Public Affairs, six distinguished social scientists were commissioned to write papers addressing the meaning and condition of freedom of the press in the United States from their own expertise on what the press actually does. We then asked four noted experts in media law, the First Amendment, and media policy—all affiliated with the Manship School of Mass Communication at LSU—to serve as commentators. Over two days in Baton Rouge, we had far-reaching and fruitful discussions. The six authors have, since that time, revised their essays to reflect the discussion and each other's work. The commentators have written remarks to serve as introductions to each of the three sections or as an afterword for the collected works.

We are confident that the collection will serve as an initial foray into connecting together theories of freedom of the press with evidence about press performance. We hope that doing so will encourage scholars of the law and students of political communication to more thoroughly engage each other's literatures, contentions, and findings—with the result that both public policy on public information and scholarly research on the news media will be significantly enhanced.

As the organizer of the symposium and editor of this volume, my thanks go to the participants who wrote papers, commented on them, and came inside on a spectacular March day in Baton Rouge to enter into the discussion. But my foremost gratitude goes to those who funded my ideas and helped me brainstorm the conference, particularly Adrienne Moore, director of the Reilly Center, and Jack Hamilton, dean of the Manship School. Heather Herman provided indispensable help in arranging the details of the conference, ensuring the travel plans of the participants, and dealing with hundreds of logistical details. Finally, I am grateful to David Perlmutter, series editor of the politics@media series at LSU Press, and the staff of LSU Press for their encouragement and advice in transforming a set of papers into what we trust is a coherent and thought-provoking whole.

FREEING THE PRESSES

FREEING THE PRESSES

AN INTRODUCTORY ESSAY

TIMOTHY E. COOK

The opening years of the twenty-first century find Americans—and American media systems and political systems—at something of a crossroad. The political communication system that held sway for many years has eroded. The dominance of the three broadcast networks, which held until the early 1980s, has been eclipsed by the proliferation of cable channels. Readerships for that old standby, the metropolitan newspaper, are growing steadily older and smaller. New formats, such as radio talk shows, tabloidized news, reality television, and late-night variety shows have moved increasingly into the realm of politics. The rise of the Internet and the World Wide Web makes for political communication that does not simply erase previous boundaries of space and time but is more specialized, more customized to the individual, and full of new opportunities for interactivity.

This situation today resembles the era in the 1920s and 1930s leading up to the creation of the Federal Communications Commission (FCC), when decisions cemented a mass media system that lasted for many decades. The climactic establishment of the FCC ended up facilitating a limited number of commercial broadcasters rather than a wide range of diverse, nonprofit stations.[1] We could well expect a similarly substantial impact from policy decisions about the future development of and access to such forms of communication as cable, satellite broadcasting, and the Internet and Web.

Yet discussions about the public policies we should pursue in the United States to ensure the kind of political communication that we want as individuals and that we need as a society and polity are oddly incomplete. Part of the problem is undoubtedly, as media scholar Leo Bogart has written, the "crazy quilt of regulations that constitute our ad hoc national media policy, one that even its most dedicated interpreters find hard to make sense of, much less apply in any rational way."[2] Yet an enormous array of public policies deals with information. Media organizations have always benefited, and continue to benefit, from policies and practices in government that defray the cost of news gathering and news distribution and thereby subsidize the news.[3]

Some of these policies were decided by Congress. Publications have been sent through the mail by lower postal rates, or occasionally even for free, since before the American Revolution. The vast majority of media organizations are privately owned but prone to economic regulation, particularly for television and radio. But print media also have benefited from regulation that tends to discourage new competition and enhance the profitability of their enterprises. At the same time, media organizations often ask for and sometimes receive exemption from forms of regulation that apply to other business enterprises.

Other subsidies occur not by laws but through day-to-day practice. The public relations apparatus found in virtually every office at every level of American government underwrites the costs of journalists producing news. Any individuals who can document being "bona fide correspondents of good standing in their profession" have remarkable access to institutions, newsmakers, and information otherwise denied to the average citizen.

Finally, subsidies arise from judicial interpretations of "freedom of the press." Supreme Court decisions have made it difficult to win a conviction on the grounds of libel, narrowed the basis for prior restraint of publication, and struck down limitations on journalistic autonomy, such as state laws mandating a "right to reply" in newspapers. If news organizations do not get what they want out of the Court, Congress may deliver its own version of "freedom of the press," as in the Newspaper Protection Act, which exempts an economically endangered newspaper from the liability of antitrust legislation when it combines its physical plant with a competitor. Over the last forty years, the net effect has been to decrease governmental restrictions on news media, even while the reliance on subsidies, whether explicit or not, has increased.

The political communication system we have now in the United States is thus, at least in part, the result of public policy. Yet discussions of how to proceed have been truncated. Despite the portent of this moment, there is surprisingly little political or public attention to the prospect of how best to pursue a media system that fulfills the demands of a democratic polity. Why?

I argue that debate has been forestalled by a presumption that the First Amendment and the optimal public performance of journalism mandates a "hands-off" approach from government. Certainly, following the September 11 terrorist attacks, civil liberties have come under intense scrutiny with new practices and proposals from the Bush administration. Yet a hands-off interpretation of "freedom of the press" is not foreordained by the language of the First Amendment. One can easily lobby for civil liberties *and* a more concerted role for governmental policy at the same time.

As important, the hands-off approach (along with the assumptions underlying it) does not reflect the actual daily practice of how the news is made. Nor is it clear whether the hands-off understanding of the First Amendment has, in fact, achieved the goals that theorists have seen pursued. It is time to reexamine freedom of the press, both in theory and in practice.

FREEDOM OF THE PRESS IN THEORY

The First Amendment's injunction is crystal clear: "Congress shall make no law . . . abridging the freedom of speech, or of the press." Many writers see this as an absolute statement: no law means no law. Consequently, they prescribe a free press with minimal government intervention. This absolutist approach finds two commonly voiced rationales.

The first is *the marketplace of ideas*: it is necessary to restrict governmental intervention in the operations of the news media in order to encourage as wide a range of different viewpoints as possible. The foundation for this model is the 1964 Supreme Court case of *New York Times v. Sullivan,* and its majority opinion by Justice William Brennan.[4]

The second rationale is *the watchdog model,* which envisions the news media acting as an agent of the people, perhaps a fourth branch of government, checking abuses of power by the other branches. The watchdog model requires that the news media become independent of government to ensure that journalists can and do freely scrutinize and assess the actions and words of powerful officials, and thereby check abuses of power. If the Supreme Court itself did not enunciate a fully developed logic of the watchdog model, one of its members, Justice Potter Stewart, did so in a 1974 speech.

The marketplace of ideas and watchdog models both seek to enhance journalistic autonomy. And each model contains an implicit testable hypothesis: that increased autonomy leads to desired results, namely either an increase in the range of views expressed in the political system or an enhancement of critical scrutiny of government.

Such hypotheses, along with the description of widespread journalistic independence from government and other sources of power, would strike students of political communication as dubious. Instead, scholars agree that government and the press, far from being mutually self-reliant, are mutually dependent. Newsmaking and governing have interpenetrated each other, almost to the point of being indistinguishable. And this interdependence has *increased,* starting in the 1960s, the time period when the Supreme Court doctrine of freedom of the press became more self-consciously libertarian. To figure out this disconnect, let us begin by examining the central logic of the marketplace of ideas and watchdog models.

The *Sullivan* case transpired in 1960. L. B. Sullivan, the police commissioner of Montgomery, Alabama, sued the *New York Times* for carrying an advertisement signed by a variety of religious and civil rights leaders appealing for funds to defray the legal fees of Rev. Martin Luther King Jr. The ad included descriptions of the obstacles the African American civil rights movement was facing in the South. Sullivan cited one paragraph that referred vaguely to the Montgomery police as the basis for a libel case and pointed to several factual errors. The Alabama courts found against the *New York Times*. The Supreme Court, in a unanimous finding, reversed the judgment.

Justice Brennan granted that the advertisement contained several inaccuracies. However, given that the litigant was a public official, Brennan said that "compelling the critic of official conduct to guarantee the truth of all his factual assertions— and to do so on pain of libel judgments virtually unlimited in amount—leads to . . . 'self-censorship.'" Brennan's bugaboo was the era of the 1790s, when, under the Alien and Sedition Acts, President John Adams's administration prosecuted editors in the opposition camp for "seditious libel" that it alleged brought the government into disrepute and thereby undermined authority. So as to avoid the consequences of "the pall of fear and timidity imposed upon those who would give voice to public criticism," Brennan's opinion established a new limitation on libel: a public official cannot win a libel case without proving "actual malice."

New York Times v. Sullivan would have been a landmark had it done nothing but institute the most liberal libel laws in the world. But of equal importance is Brennan's rationale for this policy. His opinion assembles a Hall of Fame of quotes about freedom of expression: it is designed to gain "the widest possible dissemination of information from diverse and antagonistic sources" (Hugo Black in *Associated Press v. United States*); it is "fashioned to assure unfettered interchange of ideas for the bringing about of political and social changes desired by the people" (*Roth v. United States*); it "presupposes that right conclusions are more likely to be gathered out of a multitude of tongues, than through any kind of authoritative selection" (Judge Learned Hand in the D.C. circuit decision of the *AP* case). Brennan concluded from this panoply of quotes: "Thus we consider this case against the background of a profound national commitment to the principle that debate on public issues should be uninhibited, robust and wide-open, and that it may well include vehement, caustic, and sometimes unpleasantly sharp attacks on government and public officials."

Brennan envisioned an autonomous press. It requires protection from government intervention for two reasons: first, to be routinely critical of official performance, and second, to reflect a wide diversity of points of view and allow the public to receive the information it requires to participate in the political process.

THE WATCHDOG

Brennan's decision was not reached on the basis of a separate and distinct "freedom of the press." It is hard to imagine that Brennan's decision would have differed had it been a case of spoken slander, not printed libel. As Craig Freeman suggested during our discussions, the *Sullivan* case might also best be understood as one in a series of civil rights suits in the wake of *Brown v. Board of Education. Sullivan,* like most Court decisions and most Court watchers, does not distinguish between "freedom of speech" and "freedom of the press" under the rubric of "freedom of expression."

By contrast, the watchdog model agrees on the importance of press autonomy but prescribes a unique role for the press with a special status required by the Constitution. Speaking a few months after President Nixon's resignation, Justice Potter Stewart gave a speech at his alma mater, Yale Law School. Stewart began by noting how the Watergate case made many citizens "deeply disturbed by what they consider to be the illegitimate power of the organized press in the political structure of our society."[5] Stewart retorted that an adversarial relationship between government and the press was precisely what the First Amendment foresaw and was the goal of then-recent Supreme Court decisions.

"Freedom of the press," to Stewart, was not a straightforward extension of "freedom of speech." The two could not be consonant, he suggested, unless the founders were being redundant. Stewart made a distinction: freedom of speech accrues to individuals, but freedom of the press pertains to an institution. The freedom of the press clause is, "in essence, a *structural* provision of the Constitution. . . . The publishing business is, in short, the only organized private business that is given explicit constitutional protection."[6]

Stewart claimed the First Amendment was designed "to create a fourth institution outside the Government as an additional check on the three official branches." He interpreted the history of official repression prior to the Revolution as reflecting British authorities' awareness that "a free press was not just a neutral vehicle for the balanced discussion of diverse ideas. Instead, the free press meant organized, expert scrutiny of government." The Constitution, therefore, Stewart concluded, must seek the "institutional autonomy of the press."[7]

To Stewart's chagrin, his fellow justices never adopted his view that the "organized press"—"the daily newspapers and other established news media"—could claim particular rights and privileges derived from freedom of the press. For instance, over his (and often Brennan's) dissents, the Court concluded that freedom of the press neither grants reporters a constitutional right to refuse to disclose names of confidential sources nor establishes an "editorial privilege" around the news gathering process comparable to the "executive privilege" the Court had recognized for decision-making in the presidency.[8]

The statements of Brennan and Stewart represent different renditions of a particular version of "freedom of the press": a political theory that restricts the government's intervention in the news making process to allow for journalistic autonomy, whether to gain wide-ranging diversity of viewpoints or to maximize unfettered, professional criticism of officialdom.

FREE PRESS OR OPEN PRESS?

Brennan's enunciation of the marketplace of ideas model and Stewart's endorsement of the watchdog model were both handy for Supreme Court justices. Both approaches avoid the sticky question of measuring when the news media have performed their job of informing the people adequately enough to allow citizens to intervene productively into ongoing political processes. Neither approach requires the public to be engaged at all for the process to work. The marketplace of ideas can function by winnowing information and interpretation among activists and elites, possibly in the news itself, until a provisional consensus is reached, with or without public involvement. The watchdog model sees the news media acting as an agent of the people who need not be involved as long as the media are working on their behalf to maintain accountability and check official abuse.

But in spite of these advantages, there are two key drawbacks with the tradition staked out by Brennan and Stewart that favors a "hands-off" approach to the news media. One problem is theoretical; the other is empirical.

Absolutism is far from the only way to think about "freedom of the press." The First Amendment does not rule out all laws having to do with freedom of the press, only those that "abridge" such freedom. Law professor Lee Bollinger has acutely outlined that many Supreme Court decisions delineate a "secondary image" of a free press. This image underscores the rights of the listeners, readers, and viewers of the news and the obligations of news organizations to meet those needs.[9] These decisions most commonly apply to broadcast media, and more recently cable television, where the "scarcity" of the spectrum or the "bottleneck" control over cable lines furnishes a rationale for regulation that is less apt for print media. Yet the rhetoric, and implications, in some of these cases go considerably beyond broadcast and cable media.[10]

Consider the *Red Lion* case in 1969, when the Supreme Court unanimously upheld the constitutionality of the Fairness Doctrine (later abolished by the FCC in the 1980s), which required broadcasters to furnish reply time to political candidates or to those who had been personally attacked. Justice Byron White's opinion for the Court began with the scarcity rationale. But he went further: "[T]he people as a whole retain their interest in free speech by radio and their collective right to have the medium function consistently with the ends and purposes of the First Amendment. It is the right of the viewers and listeners, not the right of the broadcasters, which is paramount. . . . It is the right of the public to receive suitable access to social, political, esthetic, moral, and other ideas and experiences which is crucial here. That right may not be constitutionally abridged either by Congress or by the FCC."[11]

Though the Court was to hold back from extending the logic of a "right of reply" to newspapers in the 1974 case of *Miami Herald v. Tornillo*,[12] White's broad understanding of First Amendment rights of readers is found in cases referring to newspapers. A unanimous 1936 opinion invalidated a Louisiana tax on large newspapers, all of whom were critics of Senator Huey Long. Justice George Sutherland saw the tax as a "deliberate and calculated device . . . to limit the circulation of information to which the public is entitled in virtue of the constitutional guarantee."[13] In a 1976 case, the Court backed a public interest group that sought to overturn a Virginia law which prevented pharmacists from advertising prices of prescription drugs in newspapers. Justice Harry Blackmun's majority opinion concluded, "Freedom of speech presupposes a willing speaker. But where a speaker exists, . . . the protection afforded is to the communication, to its source and to its recipients both."[14]

In fact, there are two theoretical traditions to "freedom of the press" in United States history, best captured by two separate phrases in the state constitution adopted by Pennsylvania in 1776. In one section, it says, "[T]he people have a right to freedom of speech, and of writing, and publishing their sentiments; therefore the freedom of the press ought not to be restrained." In another, "The printing presses shall be free to every person who undertakes to examine the proceedings of the legislature, or any part of government."[15] The first section accentuates the people's right to "publish their sentiments" and values the press as a public forum open to all. The second highlights the watchdog function of "examining the proceedings of government." This doubling means that freedom of the press was designed to be granted to the citizenry as much as to printers.

The Pennsylvania Constitution was a fairly radical document. But recent work by political scientist Robert W. T. Martin suggests its duality was far from unusual in the eighteenth century, up to and including the drafting of the First Amendment.[16] Martin uncovers two distinct, if occasionally overlapping, approaches to the central meanings of "freedom of the press."

One is a "free press" model: the press should be free of state intervention so as to engage in criticism of government and thereby defend public liberty. The eighteenth century saw notable examples of crusading journalism, starting with James Franklin's campaign against smallpox inoculation in Boston in the 1720s. The free press model is the predecessor for Justice Stewart's rationale for the First Amendment whereby the people, in effect, delegate the job of criticism to the news media.

The other is an "open press" model: all individuals have a right to disseminate their viewpoints for general consideration. The history of colonial and revolutionary America presents many examples of this model in practice, with printers—largely for economic reasons—most often presenting themselves as impartial intermediaries passing along what was provided to them. The open press rendition of "freedom of the press" was most fully justified in a 1731 essay by Benjamin Franklin called "An Apology for Printers." Franklin claimed that "Printers are educated in the Belief, that when Men differ in Opinion, both Sides ought equally to have the Advantage of being heard by the Publick. . . . Hence they chearfully serve all contending Writers that pay them well, without regarding on which side they are of the Question in Dispute. Being thus continually employ'd in serving all Parties, Printers naturally acquire a vast Unconcernedness as to the right or wrong Opinions contain'd in what they print."[17] Franklin specifically rejected the free press rationale. He said it was "unreasonable. . . . That Printers ought not to print any Thing but what they approve. . . . An end would thereby be put to Free Writing, and the World would afterward have nothing to read but what happen'd to be the Opinions of Printers."[18]

The open press model was as much in the air as the free press approach when the First Amendment was adopted. Eighteenth-century observers did not often cleanly distinguish the two. But stressing an open press rather than a free press has starkly different consequences for printers (or their modern-day counterparts, journalists). In Martin's words, "The press was open to each individual's sentiments only because another individual's private property—a printer's press and his newspaper—was thought of as a communal good, something the printer was beholden to make available to the community as the primary institution of an expanding public sphere."[19]

Thus, the version of "freedom of the press" that underscores the autonomy of the news media from government is far from the only interpretation of the First

Amendment in the American tradition, whether in history or in jurisprudence. The "open press" approach alternated and sometimes merged with the "free press" doctrine throughout the eighteenth century. And the "secondary image" identified by Bollinger emulates the open press model in its understanding of obligations that the news media have toward the citizens at large. As Martin writes, the open press model was eclipsed by the debate in the late 1790s over the Alien and Sedition Acts (possibly because it was taken for granted by the then-common practice of competing partisan newspapers in most cities and towns). But it has never really gone away.

FREEDOM OF THE PRESS IN PRACTICE

Brennan's and Stewart's ringing statements also face some tough questions when they face empirical reality. It is not unusual for judicial philosophy to be out of sync with the application thereof. For example, one cannot help noting the irony that the Supreme Court in 1994 upheld regulation of cable television in order to protect vulnerable media outlets—even while being clear that the prime beneficiaries of the decision were local affiliates of broadcast networks, then among the most profitable media outlets in the business.[20] More pointedly, the *means* of an absolutist reading of freedom of the press seems to have been substituted for the *ends* of diversity and accountability that Brennan and Stewart set forth, despite little evidence that the goals are sought by the means defended.

We look here at two empirical sets of objections to equating freedom of the press with autonomy from government and politics. The first is historical. The vast majority of inquiries into the meaning of "freedom of the press" at the time of the Revolution and the drafting of the Constitution has been inspired by Leonard Levy's landmark 1960 book, *Legacy of Suppression*. Levy argued that, until the Alien and Sedition Acts, freedom of the press meant only that government could not prevent publication beforehand. To Levy, freedom of the press before 1800 said nothing about printers' facing legal charges thereafter.[21] Inspired by Levy's startling charges, the forty-plus years of scholarship following Levy have centered on the "ideology" or "theory" of freedom of the press, with occasional forays into the presence or absence of crusading journalists, such as James Franklin in Boston or John Peter Zenger in New York. The main evidence consists either of widely circulated political writings, or of attempts to prosecute or otherwise officially harass printers.[22]

Such inquiries into the meaning of freedom of the press only go so far. They rarely inquire about the political and social conditions that facilitate freedom of the press either in theory or in practice. Likewise, they too often focus on the precursors of today's journalism rather than examine the printer's work and the unstated assumptions that informed it in its own time. For example, crusading journalism in colonial periods was the exception. Indeed, this exception proved the rule: crusading journalism depended upon splits in the ruling elites that made it possible, if not necessary, for the printer to become a critic of the powerful.[23] Even legal theorists who urge attention to practice as well as theory in the eighteenth century elide this key point.[24]

As important, in addition to investigating the understanding of "freedom," we also have to inquire about the historical meaning of "the press." Then if we go back to the 1790s, Stewart's history seems doubtful. His expectation of "organized, expert scrutiny of government" is not borne out by the historical evidence. Through the eighteenth and much of the nineteenth centuries, all players tacitly accepted that newspapers and other publications would be sponsored by political factions, and later by political parties. The partisan press would be partially displaced by the rise of more commercial newspapers seeking larger audiences (and thereby downplaying politics and political points of view), beginning with the "penny press" of the 1830s. But the partisan press persisted through at least the turn of the twentieth century—particularly in rural areas, which, after all, were where most Americans lived.[25] Despite attempts of newspaper publishers to receive institutional protection in early foreshadowings of the watchdog model, the case law that dealt with freedom of the press at lower courts during the nineteenth century gave no priority to institutions above individuals.[26]

Nor does today's practice in the United States uphold Brennan's and Stewart's expectations for freedom of the press. Media scholar Thomas Patterson, in a pioneering comparison across countries, tellingly noted a central paradox: the United States press is formally freest of government intervention but exhibits the least diversity in the news of any western democracies.[27] A hands-off approach to the press may simply reinforce political actors who build on the economic, political, and social resources they already have, much like a libertarian approach to economics.[28]

Most scholars have found evidence upholding Lance Bennett's "indexing" hypothesis. In other words, the range of views expressed in the news reflects the extent of disagreement among political decision-makers.[29] Moreover, the topics in the news tend to be certified by governmental action and statements, as journalists gravitate toward "sources in a position to know," or in a position to act, most of whom tend to be officials. Without official commentary or action, topics may then (to use political scientist Daniel Hallin's terms) never leave the "sphere of consensus" and enter the "sphere of legitimate controversy."[30]

Brennan and Stewart might be gratified to see that overt pressure from officials upon journalists is relatively rare in the United States. But as sociologist and media scholar Herbert Gans recognized in the 1970s, journalists are reluctant to disrupt the routine process of news making, lest they jeopardize ready access to the information officials provide them. As a result, reporters engage in what Gans called "anticipatory avoidance of pressure."[31] Such tactics are most pronounced in newsbeats where reporters and officials in continuing relationships push toward symbiosis. Yet general assignment reporters, too, rely heavily on officialdom. If they do not face the same pressure to maintain a continuing relationship, they lack inside knowledge that would cause them to turn to anyone but designated spokespersons on a particular topic and/or from a particular institution.[32]

Government intervention and regulation are far from the only ways in which news can be and is shaped and channeled by officials. In the most ambitious cross-national attempt to date to compare and assess a variety of European and North American media systems, Daniel Hallin and Paolo Mancini make a crucial point about what they call the "Liberal" media systems, exemplified in their study by the United States, Canada, Britain, and Ireland:

> The relation between the state and the media is not solely a matter of regulation, subsidy and state ownership. It also involves the flow of information — including images, symbols and interpretive frames. And in this sphere, it is not at all clear that the media and the state are more separate in Liberal than in the other two systems studied here: though the rhetoric of the Liberal countries tends to stress an adversary relation between the media and the state, and though the state's formal role as regulator, funder and owner is more limited than in other systems, it is important to stress that this does not necessarily mean the state has less influence on the news-making process.[33]

In sum, to evaluate the current status and future prospects of freedom of the press at this critical juncture in political communication in the United States, we must test the agreed-upon logics best enunciated by Brennan and Stewart against historical and empirical reality. Doing so will allow us to have a clearer understanding of what freedom of the press means in theory as well as of its implications for the practices and policies the United States sets up to maximize it.

Our discussion proceeds in three parts. First is "From the Past," which considers evidence from history and law to see exactly how the historical commitments made to freedom of the press correspond with the performance of the press. Second is "At Present," which zeroes in on the current state of our knowledge about journalistic autonomy (or lack thereof), particularly from government. Third is "Toward the Future," which discusses the rise of new technologies and new formats of news that, at least on their surface, promise greater democratization and may well increase the extent to which political debate in the United States is "uninhibited, robust and wide-open."

PART ONE: FROM THE PAST

Any discussion of the meaning of freedom of the press in theory and practice must begin by considering the era of the American Revolution and the founding of the republic. I noted above that scholars have tended to zero in on the development of the principle of press freedom and to restrict their attention to the practice of official prosecution (if not persecution) of printers. Yet to follow up on the insight of Hallin and Mancini, we cannot understand freedom of the press without understanding the day-to-day operation of journalistic enterprises today—or of the press in the eighteenth century.

Historian Charles Clark, who has authored the definitive history of American newspapers prior to the American Revolution, critically considers the veracity of Stewart's claim that the founders expected the press to engage in "organized, expert scrutiny of government." Instead of delving into the contemporary understandings of "freedom," Clark deftly examines what the founders would have recognized as "the press." As he shows, by the time of the Bill of Rights, "the press" had become understood as an institution unto itself, organized through business and political linkages. But it is doubtful if it contributed "expert scrutiny."

In particular, while the founders may have experienced a press that was formally independent of government control, that press was anything but autonomous from political factions and the incipient political parties of the time. In some ways, contrary to Stewart's history lesson, the press of 1789 resembles less the gigantic, independent mass media organizations prevalent when Stewart spoke in 1974 than the emerging media mix of today that encompasses a wide variety of often ephemeral outlets. It is a subject of controversy whether the interpretation of "freedom of the press" should be bound by the original intent of the framers of the Constitution and the Bill of Rights. But surely Clark's revealing account of the "press the founders knew" can give us insight into what they experienced and what they envisioned.

The perspective of development over time can also help us examine the causal hypotheses implicit in Brennan's and Stewart's models, both of which posit, in the lingo of social science, a negative relationship between state intervention and the presence of the desired outcome (a wide range of public views to Brennan, scrutiny of government to Stewart). Yet with an N of 1 (the United States), it is hard to assess this hypothesis. We need either comparisons over time or across jurisdictions. Frederick Schauer, a renowned legal philosopher, has begun to examine the real-world application of legal doctrine. Schauer reports here some of his research comparing Australia and the United States, and gives a preview of ongoing work looking at the news media's performance in American states with different legal approaches toward the press.

Schauer concentrates on libel as the policy area offering the best chance for comparison across systems. He investigates a puzzle: less restrictive libel laws do not seem to make for either a greater range of views or less deference to government. Instead, the stringent libel laws of Australia coexist with a press that is at least as "uninhibited, robust and wide-open" as that of the United States. Schauer's analysis raises doubts about whether there is a simple and direct cause-and-effect relationship between "press law and press content." At the very least, the law is one (and not necessarily the most influential) of a number of political and economic influences upon press performance. Other inquiries, such as comparing news media content in states with and without "shield laws" that protect the confidentiality of reporters' sources from legal proceedings, are surely in order. Doing so would also help us figure out a key question: Does press law nurture a particular journalistic approach, or do news media already follow particular preferred practices and lobby for laws that will simply reinforce them?

PART TWO: AT PRESENT

We have already raised doubts about whether we can equate a low level of formal official intervention in the news media with either high autonomy on the part of journalists and journalism or wide diversity in the media content that is thereby produced.

Reporters are commonly thought of as authors of their stories. But they operate in a highly structured and hierarchical news organization and are answerable to superiors (editors, producers, publishers) who need not justify their decisions. Reporters' contacts and interactions with their sources give them advantages, such as authoritative, inside information, that they can use to their benefit in negotiating the news within the organization. But relying upon sources, especially powerful and thus newsworthy officials, places other restrictions on their autonomy. Finally, with the news media's accelerating profit-mindedness, reporters and news organizations overall may be less free from the constraints of the bottom line or pressures, actual or anticipated, from advertisers. Ironically, scholars point out that journalists are most autonomous from the poorly understood and infrequently consulted mass audience, raising doubts about their accountability to the public.[34]

Some factors can and do work to enhance journalistic autonomy from government. It is clear that reporters have become less deferential to officials over the last several decades. Witness the growing negativity of news assessments, the decreased deference of reporters' questions in White House press conferences, and the development of the twenty-four-hour news cycle that emphasizes endless dissection, discussion, and debate of official statements, misstatements, actions, and inactions.[35] Relations with government officials may become more adversarial as reporters increasingly shift from newsbeats to general assignment reporting. Sociologist Eric Klinenberg's recent ethnographic research at the *Chicago Tribune* shows that newsworkers work more and more within the confines of the newsroom in order to be "content providers" for a variety of modalities.[36] With the easy electronic availability of press releases and transcripts, reporters no longer need to be based physically at a strategic spot to get information—which downplays the vitality of informal contact and symbiosis. Access to Web-based information, such as press releases provided by political activists, further tends to level the playing field.[37]

Journalists—quite literally—do have the last word about whether and how something becomes news. A plaque on the desk of President Reagan's White House spokesperson, Larry Speakes, is both a joke and an accurate rendition of reality: "You don't tell us how to stage the news, and we won't tell you how to cover it." Reporters *start* with the material that authoritative sources suggest to them. But they rework it into a coherent, compelling narrative that meets journalistic standards of quality. These "news values," such as terseness, vividness, personalization, concreteness, conflict, and drama, are often at odds with the reasons that political actors seek political communication.[38]

At times, the definition of news eludes powerful sources. Harvey Molotch and Marilyn Lester's classic examination of the Santa Barbara oil spill in 1969 suggested that accidents—occurrences that are neither anticipated nor prescheduled by official sources—disrupt the standard newsmaking routines and provide a window of opportunity for unofficial sources. The news media's penchant for melodramatic and still-developing stories may cause continuing issues, neglected by officials, to break into the news and stay there for a while. Lance Bennett and Regina Lawrence found such a pattern with a "news icon," the garbage barge *Mobro,* which meandered around for days in the Atlantic looking for a place to dump its trash and served as a news peg for months about problems of garbage disposal and recycling. More fully, Lawrence has focused on the differences between "institutionally driven" and "event driven" news, and how the latter can and does inform the former, not just the other way around.[39]

But does this autonomy lead to wide diversity in sources, viewpoints, or interpretations in the news? Most scholarship suggests that it does not. Nobody knows what news is until it appears in a news outlet. Under such high uncertainty, newspersons under the crunch of the deadline rely upon each other—within the newsbeat and across news organizations—for cues and reinforcements about newsworthiness. If interpretations vary from one outlet to the next, there is considerable overlap in understandings of who makes news and why. To be sure, news processes and news contents are most alike among news outlets that have similar technologies, formats, and conceptions of their audiences; however, strong similarities across media and modalities point to a single "media answer" for how an event or official will be covered.[40]

We begin part two with an essay by Michael Schudson, a highly influential sociologist and historian of the news. Having just published an excellent overview of the sociological literature on how news gets made, he is deeply familiar with the conclusion that there are many constraints on journalists and journalism. The reliance on official sources, the norms of professionalism, and what Schudson terms "the constraints of conventional wisdom" in the limited social world of American journalists all push the press to be an establishment institution with limited autonomy and a constricted range of viewpoints. But Schudson suggests that other factors of American journalism can and do push in the opposite direction at the same time. In particular, newsworkers' convergence on breaking events, the emphasis on conflict, and the cynicism that goes along with being an outsider to power all enhance their autonomy and free expression.

As Schudson suggests, many observers deride this eventfulness, obsession with conflict, and cynicism. Evoking journalistic missions of social responsibility, they prefer discussion of deep, underlying issues. Schudson begs to differ. Somewhat to his surprise, he finds himself praising the same behaviors many find distasteful. He stresses the benefits to democracy of a cadre of journalist-outsiders, and seeks to figure out what could be done to prevent journalists from succumbing to the temptation to become insiders. He suggests steps in the education of journalists. One might also consider policies that might encourage a variety of news outlets, such as Weblogs, or that might facilitate greater access to unofficial sources of news.

Regina Lawrence, a political scientist who is well known for her discussion of "event-driven news" and its impact in politics, assesses much of the same scholarly literature as Schudson. Lawrence concurs with Schudson that reporters are not "lapdogs" to power. She critiques the body of work that suggests that the reliance of journalists, and of the news media as an institution, on more powerful political and economic actors inevitably makes the news media a mere extension of power.

But while Lawrence agrees with Schudson that news organizations do sometimes produce hard-hitting news and robust debate, she points out how conditional, almost fortuitous the process is. Her objection to Stewart's expectation of "organized, expert scrutiny of government" is that it results "by accident and circumstance." Moreover, even if the routines are broken by "event-driven news," the news media slowly return to business as usual, winnowing out possible storylines with the constant help of official sources.

To Lawrence, the access of powerful officials to the news is constant, but the ability of nonofficial voices to enter into the debate is highly variable and contingent. Thus, if the news expands public debates, it occurs less as a conscious decision by journalists to open up discussion than as a byproduct of increasing conflict among decision-making officials, or when political actors can be assessed by standards they themselves have suggested. Ironically, then, "uninhibited, robust and wide-open debate" occurs most often at the government's behest. But, as Lawrence adroitly points out, if the First Amendment provides protection against direct government censorship, it says nothing about the benefits of cooperation—if not collaboration—with powerful officials. She closes by refocusing the discussion on the First Amendment away from restricting powers to curb the press, and toward policies that address not simply the economic and political structure of the news media but the range and robustness of public debate.

PART THREE: TOWARD THE FUTURE

Brennan's and Stewart's theories of freedom of the press deserve reevaluation in light of the dramatic shifts in the news media since the 1960s and 1970s, when they enunciated their models. The mass media, along with the mass audience, have become fragmented. New technologies and new formats offer more information more quickly, more individual control by citizens over the information they obtain, and more decentralized, more interactive forms of political communication.[41]

The burgeoning quantity of sites of political communication at the very least poses practical problems for Stewart's emphasis upon a readily recognizable "organized press" and his call for special recognized privileges (and responsibilities) for the press and for journalists. The successful applications of self-employed Webloggers for access to the Democratic National Convention in 2004 are only the first signs of a shifting understanding of who journalists are and what journalism is. In 1972, Justice Byron White's side prevailed, rejecting Stewart's bid to accord journalists a special constitutional status. His warning may need to be updated for new technology but it surely seems justified: "It would be necessary to define those categories of newsmen who qualified for the privilege, a questionable procedure in light of the traditional doctrine that liberty of the press is the right of the lonely pamphleteer who uses carbon paper or a mimeograph just as much as of the large metropolitan publisher who utilizes the latest photocomposition methods."[42]

The new and varied formats would seem to presage a return to the earlier manifestations of the press, such as those Charles Clark described in the eighteenth century. But as long ago as the early 1990s, W. Russell Neuman astutely warned that technology was not destiny, noting contradictory impulses from the new media. Technologies enable communicators to narrowcast to ever more specialized audiences, and allow citizens to enter into a more interactive dialogue with each other and with their leaders. But the tendency of most citizens to use passive, routine forms of communication, and the political economy of the news media's concentrating enterprises, points away from democratization.[43]

Neuman's paradox—the growing opportunities for democratized news, and the seeming inability or unwillingness of citizens to avail themselves of those possibilities—is still before us. In particular, a proliferation of sites (Web and otherwise) of political information may or may not mean a proliferation of content. If audiences dwindle for any one news outlet, the news media can still pursue profit by rampant cost-cutting. Thus, news now relies increasingly on outside reports—whether pools of reporters or news services of one sort or another—to provide content that reporters remake into stories for their news outlets without ever having to leave the newsroom. John McManus's pioneering look at "market-driven journalism" at three California local television news stations concluded that fewer resources for reporters led to greater reactivity to the news (and to potential news sources) and more reliance on story suggestions of other news outlets, such as the local daily newspaper.[44] Even apart from the "synergy" encouraged by the consolidation of media empires, we see greater explicit and formal collaboration between journalists in the creation of news, when newsmagazine reporters appear as insider experts on cable political talk shows (and are paid extra by their employer to do so), when a PBS *Frontline* documentary serves as the basis for a series of investigative journalism on the front page of the *New York Times,* or when *Wall Street Journal* reporters have regular slots in the daily line-up of the all-business cable channel CNBC.

Since new technology is often understood in terms of the possible uses of technologies that preceded it, it is no surprise that the first studies of the Web and other new media in politics depicted old wine in new bottles.[45] But the history of new technologies is instructive. Consider radio. What we now think of as radio's great advantage—its potential to be broadcast to a whole range of listeners—was a pitfall for those, such as the U.S. Navy, who wanted to use it as a point-to-point form of "wireless" communication (whether radiotelegraphy or radiotelephony). Only after amateurs explored and demonstrated the possibilities of using radio as a broadcast medium did its huge economic potential become understood.[46]

If new technology fosters new forms of journalism, those forms coexist with, more than displace, the old. Thus, in the 1840s, the invention of the telegraph and its use for a new kind of news epitomized by the Associated Press dispatches did not wipe out the old reliance on long-winded "correspondents," whose letters were placed alongside terse AP bulletins.[47] In the case of the Web, the rise of Weblogs, electronically accessible diaries maintained by individuals, provides a new form of political discourse, if not journalism, that can and does sit aside the Web sites of news organizations that only slightly repackage their news (though they do so more frequently) for a new format.

The possibilities of the Web and other forms of narrowcasting for linking members of small, already politically activated communities are considerable. Ralph Izard points out in the introduction to part three that these technologies do not invent entirely new forms of political communication. Web sites aimed at distinct communities are new variants, for instance, of long-established publications for minority readers and viewers. Well before the latest technological revolution, the black press and Spanish-language television news combined traditional journalism and rather untraditional advocacy. They saw their readers and viewers both as constituents requiring service in the form of appropriate political communication and as audiences to be sold to advertisers.[48] In the process, they took news stories already circulating in the mainstream news and added on their own information and commentary far more than the other way around.[49] Similarly, in the media mix that contains traditional news media and new media, the latter may initiate news stories less frequently than they provide new bits of information for, and ways to interpret the news to, particular communities.

The multiplicity of voices, the greater linkage to already established political communities, the "networks" of like-minded political communicators, and the easy start-up costs for news outlets all take us back to the forms of news that Charles Clark described for the eighteenth century, albeit at exponentially greater speeds across distances far more vast. And the interactivity that is the hallmark of new media pushes political communication into new, relatively uncharted territory. The two essays in part three examine these new developments alongside the established twentieth-century models of freedom of the press exemplified by Justices Brennan and Stewart—and find them wanting.

Lance Bennett, whose career has been equally celebrated in the study of the politics of news media and of civic engagement, surveys the decline of the political communication system provided by the mass media and its displacement by a more varied media mix that includes, as he invaluably labels them, "micro media" and "middle media." Bennett, questioning Stewart's advocacy of a privileged position for the institutional press, catalogues many ways the protection of the First Amendment has been abused by mass media. Information useful to political engagement has been increasingly squeezed out by the growing emphasis of news media on the economic bottom line—without stemming the decline of news audiences and the eroding confidence of the public in the press and its products.

Bennett notes that Stewart's suggestions are even more poorly suited for the new media world of personal digital networks and the prospect of increased direct linkages between citizens. Extending privileged positions to journalists and journalism makes no sense when, as Bennett puts it, "anyone with a computer or a mobile phone is a potential reporter or publisher." The once-clear divergence between becoming informed about politics and engaging in politics is blurring. Under such circumstances, the definition and process of news becomes more democratized. In place of the application of journalistic standards and norms, the news may instead stem from algorithms that count Weblinks (as is done by Google.com); find ways for readers to rate information sources to endorse those that are generally of higher quality, utility, and dependability (as Amazon.com does for people who submit minireviews of books); and aggregate judgments across a wide range of citizens (as Zagat.com does for its city restaurant rankings). Ironically, as Bennett suggests, the evolving media system may come close to Brennan's goal of "uninhibited, robust and wide-open debate" without any of the policies Brennan saw as leading to that goal.

Diana Owen examines a yet broader range of "new media," including formats that were developed for other purposes but increasingly have been applied to politics. Her purview includes not only the possibilities that the Internet and Web make possible but also such formats as low-power FM stations, talk radio, and reality television. Owen's essay is especially intriguing since, as a prominent scholar of the new media and civic education, she has been skeptical of the prophecies of democratizing potential from the new media. But in returning to investigate the domain of the 1998 book she coauthored with Richard Davis, *New Media and Politics,* Owen finds that a new political communication system has evolved and matured.

In particular, the increased familiarity of Americans with new forms of technology—helped along by the coming of age of a new generation that grew up with them—has created a new class of what she insightfully terms "citizen news producers." Owen explains that the ever-accelerating news cycle has made "breaking news" into a commodity most news outlets could no longer claim as their own. Even in traditional forms of journalism, the definition of news has moved away from timely happenings to information and interpretations that citizens can use. Citizen news producers are able to enter into the mix with information that audiences find valid, reliable, and useful. The net result, she concludes, is to move the political information environment of citizens away from a "free press" model exemplified by Brennan and Stewart and more toward an "open press" tradition that has been submerged for decades.

FOR FURTHER CONSIDERATION

In sum, these authors raise many doubts about the validity in practice of the most hallowed presumptions of Supreme Court jurisprudence on freedom of the press. Potter Stewart's attempts to establish special constitutional protections for the institutional press are revealed as incomplete history to Charles Clark and all but impossible to apply in today's media world to Lance Bennett. William Brennan's presumption that less government regulation of the press makes for the expression of a wider range of viewpoints is questioned by Frederick Schauer and Regina Lawrence in different ways. Stewart and Brennan both stress the vital contributions of autonomous news media, a condition challenged by both Michael Schudson and Regina Lawrence—though these two do not agree on exactly how much autonomy is necessary for the news media to be doing their job well in a democracy. And even the centrality of a "free press" understanding of the First Amendment is challenged by the revival of an "open press" tradition, most explicitly by Diana Owen and implicitly by other authors as well.

Many questions, both theoretical and empirical, crop up from reading these stimulating essays. But surely the most vital is: What is to be done about all of this? For instance, media lawyer Jack Weiss suggests here that while the scholarly literature surely needs to be more familiar to those that make the law about freedom of the press, judges cannot be expected to operate so much by the findings of social science as by common sense. Weiss's point is even more telling if we realize that other policy-makers, such as Congress, the president, and the federal bureaucracy also make public policy on freedom of the press.

To a degree, I agree with Weiss. We cannot expect officials to become political communication scholars on top of everything else they do. And "common sense" suggests that, while Bennett and Owen may well be right that it is all but impossible to distinguish journalists from everyone else, we still need somehow to do so. If citizen news producers are now more evident in the media mix, we do not yet see, to recall a line of Schudson during the symposium, hackers at presidential press conferences. Something resembling today's mass media will probably find a niche for survival in the developing media mix. The mass media have simply become too important in the American political system—for setting the agenda for officials and the public alike, for framing issues and suggesting policy responses and other solutions, for helping to deliberate over options—to fade quickly away. And just as community presses have long relied upon large metropolitan dailies, the mass media may call attention to the topics of discussion over which more fragmented groups and populations, informed by middle and micro media, discuss and ruminate. Under such circumstances, we still need journalists—and we need ways for officials to recognize who is a journalist.

Our common sense need not be dictated by the findings of empirical social science, but it can still be informed by new considerations that the research reported here suggests. For instance, there are two contrasting visions of the marketplace of ideas. One envisions a news outlet as a forum that contains wide diversity within itself. It ensures equal representation by all legitimate points of view in order to lead over time to deliberation and decision. The model here would be the op-ed page for a national daily newspaper. But another suggests that the marketplace of ideas works well only across a variety of news outlets, each of which is linked to and speaks for a given political or social identity and thereby adds to the mix.

Our authors here raise serious doubts about the ability of a single news outlet to serve as a marketplace of ideas. So public policy could be turned to ensure a greater range and diversity of news outlets. The government can centrally safeguard freedom of the press in a proactive way or, more generally, it can ensure the adequate flow of information by means of public policy.[50] While the model suggested by broadcast regulation provides one basis for discussion, we could also think about encouraging forms of subsidies targeted to economically vulnerable outlets. Even Supreme Court justices such as Sandra Day O'Connor who doubt the continued constitutionality of regulation are quick to point out that governmental subsidies or tax breaks could be used toward such goals.[51]

At the very least, we need to raise questions about the dominant presumption that freedom of the press necessarily envisions a "hands-off" approach from government. The tendency to focus on the rights of the press underplays the rights of citizens to the information they require to intervene productively in the political process. Otherwise, "freedom *of* the press" risks being reduced to nothing more than "freedom *for* the press," with no guarantee of positive benefits for the citizenry or for society. While we may have images of downtrodden, sometimes disreputable litigants who have fought for First Amendment freedoms, we should remember that the First Amendment is nowadays frequently used for the advantage of the already powerful, such as by buttressing the profitability of huge media enterprises or protecting a candidate's right to spend as much money as she wants to win an election.

Realizing that "hands-off" is not necessarily better is particularly crucial nowadays because new opportunities for political communication might well be fragile. For example, there is no guarantee that search engines such as Google. com and Yahoo.com, vital to mastering the glut of information on line, will not skew their methods as they, like mass media organizations, are publicly traded and go after ever-higher profits. The wide-open nature of the Web may change, given the difficulty that many sites have encountered in trying to make money from advertising. If Web sites are then restricted to subscribers, public availability to valuable information is limited. Regulation of the Internet and the Web is surely on the horizon, after a series of devastating viruses and worms hit during the summer of 2003, and as consumers have become increasingly frustrated over the proliferation of spam (unwanted, unsolicited email) in their in-boxes. How that regulation works, and for whose interests, must surely include a broader understanding of how government can foster as well as imperil freedom of the press. For instance, imagine public policies to facilitate citizens' access to news they need. Just as public libraries provide books and magazines to facilitate access to a wide range of ideas, so a governmentally administered search engine could do the same.

Some may protest that visions of an open press aimed at "uninhibited, robust and wide-open debate" takes us too far from the public common. By this approach, accepting and even encouraging a more fragmented political information system removes us from the agreed-upon forum of the news, propels us to miniature communities where we get incomplete information, and makes it more difficult to imagine popular dialogue and deliberation. Yet while deliberation and discussion that occur within and across news outlets are valuable to the public for suggesting a range of ideas, too often that deliberation ends when the news reaches closure without including or even consulting the public on the matter.[52] Perhaps we would do well to redirect our attention away from deliberation in the news media and put it back where it belongs—in the political institutions.

NOTES

1. See especially Robert W. McChesney, *Telecommunications, Mass Media, and Democracy: The Battle for Control of U.S. Broadcasting, 1928–1935* (New York: Oxford Univ. Press, 1993).

2. Leo Bogart, "Shaping a New Media Policy," *The Nation* (July 12, 1993): 57–60, quote at 58.

3. For an overview of these subsidies, see Timothy E. Cook, *Governing with the News: The News Media as a Political Institution* (Chicago: Univ. of Chicago Press, 1998), chapter 3. A more ambitious history of how the communication system in the United States was centrally shaped by politics is Paul Starr, *The Creation of the Media: Political Origins of Modern Communication* (New York: Basic Books, 2004).

4. *New York Times v. Sullivan*, 376 U.S. 254 (1964). As Lee C. Bollinger puts it, "No Supreme Court case of this century is more important to our notion of what press freedom means. It was one of those rare decisions that provided a conceptual framework and an idiom for its time." Lee C. Bollinger, *Images of a Free Press* (Chicago: Univ. of Chicago Press, 1991), 2. See also Lucas A. Powe Jr., *The Fourth Estate and the Constitution: Freedom of the Press in America* (Berkeley: Univ. of California Press, 1991), ix.

5. Potter Stewart, "Or of the Press," *Hastings Law Journal* 26 (1975): 631–7, quote at 631.

6. Ibid., 633 (emphasis in original).

7. Ibid., 634.

8. Respectively, *Branzburg v. Hayes*, 408 US 665 (1972); and *Herbert v. Lando*, 441 US 153 (1979).

9. Bollinger, *Images of a Free Press*, chapter 4.

10. For an appreciation of the evolution of Justice Stephen Breyer's jurisprudence in this regard, see Owen Fiss, "The Censorship of Television," in *Eternally Vigilant: Free Speech in the Modern Era*, edited by Lee C. Bollinger and Geoffrey R. Stone (Chicago: Univ. of Chicago Press, 2002).

11. *Red Lion Broadcasting Company v. Federal Communications Commission*, 395 U.S. 367 (1969), quote at 390.

12. *Miami Herald v. Tornillo*, 418 U.S. 241 (1974).

13. *Grosjean v. American Press Company*, 297 U.S. 233 (1936), quote at 250.

14. *Virginia State Board of Pharmacy v. Virginia Citizens' Consumer Council*, 425 U.S. 748 (1976), quote at 756 and 757 n. 15.

15. David A. Anderson, "The Origins of the Press Clause," *UCLA Law Review* 30 (1983): 455–541, at 464–6; quotes at 465.

16. Robert W. T. Martin, *The Free and Open Press: The Founding of American Democratic Press Liberty, 1640–1800* (New York: New York Univ. Press, 2001).

17. Benjamin Franklin, "An Apology for Printers," in *The Political Thought of Benjamin Franklin*, edited by Ralph L. Ketcham (Indianapolis: Bobbs-Merrill, 1965), 20–4, quote at 21.

18. Ibid., 21–2 (emphasis in original omitted).

19. Martin, *Free and Open Press*, 163.

20. *Turner Broadcasting System v. Federal Communications Commission,* 512 U.S. 622 (1994).

21. Leonard Levy, *Legacy of Suppression: Freedom of Speech and Press in Early American History* (Cambridge, Mass.: Harvard Univ. Press, 1960).

22. See, for instance, Jeffery A. Smith, *Printers and Press Freedom: The Ideology of Early American Journalism* (New York: Oxford Univ. Press, 1988); Anderson, "Meaning of the Free Press Clause"; Martin, *Free and Open Press.*

23. The fullest and most revealing single account of the day-to-day work of printers in the eighteenth century is Charles E. Clark, *The Public Prints: The Newspaper in Anglo-American Culture, 1665–1740* (New York: Oxford Univ. Press, 1994). See also the thought-provoking essays of Stephen Botein, "'Meer Mechanics' and an Open Press: The Business and Political Strategies of Colonial American Printers," *Perspectives in American History* 9 (1975): 127–225, and "Printers and the American Revolution," in *The Press and the American Revolution,* edited by Bernard Bailyn and John B. Hench (Worcester, Mass.: American Antiquarian Society, 1980), 11–57. Other books that wonderfully put the early experience as a precursor for later journalism (and later politics) without the assumption of progress over time which mars so much of standard journalism history include Michael Schudson's *Discovering the News: A Social History of American Newspapers* (New York: Basic Books, 1978); Thomas E. Leonard's *The Power of the Press: The Birth of American Political Reporting* (New York: Oxford Univ. Press, 1986); and David Paul Nord, *Communities of Journalism: A History of American Newspapers and Their Readers* (Urbana: Univ. of Illinois Press, 2001).

24. For instance, law scholar Lucas Powe writes, "The pluralistic nature of politics in Philadelphia—where both Congress and the assembly were beset by internal factions—meant that a printer would have ready-made defenders of his actions." Powe, *The Fourth Estate and the Constitution,* 33–4. Powe seems not to have realized that such pluralism was not always to be found—in which case printers might well be reluctant to question authority.

25. Important revisionist readings of the benefits of the partisan press include Gerald J. Baldasty, *The Commercialization of the News in the Nineteenth Century* (Madison: Univ. of Wisconsin Press, 1992); and Jeffrey L. Paskey, *"The Tyranny of Printers": Newspaper Politics in the Early American Republic* (Charlottesville: Univ. Press of Virginia, 2001). To be sure, newspapers advertised their "independence" more and more in the nineteenth century, but this did not mean independence from partisanship so much as it meant that the paper was not economically dependent upon government contracts and subventions.

26. Timothy W. Gleason, *The Watchdog Concept: The Press and the Courts in Nineteenth-Century America* (Ames: Iowa State Univ. Press, 1990).

27. Thomas E. Patterson, "The Irony of a Free Press: Professional Journalism and News Diversity" (paper presented at the annual meeting of the American Political Science Association, Chicago, Ill., September 3–6, 1992).

28. Frederick Schauer, "The Political Incidence of the Free Speech Principle," *University of Colorado Law Review* 64 (1993): 935–57.

29. W. Lance Bennett, "Toward a Theory of Press-State Relations," *Journal of Communication* 40 (1990): 103–25.

30. Daniel C. Hallin, *The "Uncensored War": The Media and Vietnam* (New York: Oxford Univ. Press, 1986).

31. Herbert J. Gans, *Deciding What's News* (New York: Vintage, 1978), 270–6.

32. Ibid., chapter 4.

33. Daniel Hallin and Paolo Mancini, *Comparing Media Systems: Three Models of Media and Politics* (New York: Cambridge Univ. Press, 2004), 233.

34. An excellent introduction to this literature is Michael Schudson, *The Sociology of News* (New York: Norton, 2003).

35. See Thomas E. Patterson, *Out of Order* (New York: Knopf, 1993); Steven Clayman and John Heritage, "Questioning Presidents: Journalistic Deference and Adversarialness in the Press Conferences of U.S. Presidents Eisenhower and Reagan," *Journal of Communication* 52 (2002): 749–75; and the articles in a special section, "Framing," coedited by W. Lance Bennett and Steven Livingston in *Political Communication* 20 (2003), led off by Bennett and Livingston's introductory essay, "A Semi-Independent Press: Government Control and Journalistic Autonomy in the Political Construction of News," *Political Communication* 20 (2003): 359–62.

36. Eric Klinenberg, "Convergence: News Production in a Digital Age," *Annals of the American Academy of Political and Social Sciences* (2005), forthcoming.

37. See Sonora Jha Nambiar, "Social Protests, Asocial Media: Patterns of Press Coverage of Social Protests and the Influence of the Internet on Such Coverage" (Ph.D. diss., Louisiana State University, 2004).

38. I have written more fully on this point in Timothy E. Cook, "The Negotiation of Newsworthiness," in *The Psychology of Political Communication*, edited by Ann N. Crigler (Ann Arbor: Univ. of Michigan Press, 1996), 11–36; and Timothy E. Cook, "Reporters and Senators Revisited," in *Esteemed Colleagues*, edited by Burdett Loomis (Washington, D.C.: Brookings Institution Press, 2000), 164–93.

39. Harvey Molotch and Marilyn Lester, "Accidental News: The Great Oil Spill as Local Occurrence and as National Event," *American Journal of Sociology* 81 (1974): 235–60; W. Lance Bennett and Regina Lawrence, "News Icons and the Mainstreaming of Social Change," *Journal of Communication* 45, no. 3 (1995): 20–39; Regina Lawrence, *The Politics of Force: Media and the Construction of Police Brutality* (Berkeley: Univ. of California Press, 2000); Regina Lawrence, "Defining Events: Problem Definition in the Media Arena," in *Politics, Discourse, and American Society: New Agendas*, edited by Roderick P. Hart and Bartholomew H. Sparrow (Lanham, Md.: Rowman and Littlefield, 2001), 91–110.

40. For further discussion and related citations of evidence, see Cook, *Governing with the News*, 76–82.

41. Note this conceptualization does not rely necessarily upon the properties of the technology. Compare the similarity of this definition through the very different technologies discussed by Jeffrey Abramson, F. Christopher Arterton, and Gary Orren in *The Electronic Commonwealth: The Impact of New Media Technologies on Democratic Politics* (New York: Basic Books, 1988), and by Richard Davis and Diana Owen, *New Media and American Politics* (New York: Oxford Univ. Press, 1998).

42. *Branzburg v. Hayes*, quote at 704.

43. W. Russell Neuman, *The Future of the Mass Audience* (New York: Cambridge Univ. Press, 1991).

44. John H. McManus, *Market-Driven Journalism: Let the Citizen Beware?* (Thousand Oaks, Calif.: Sage Publications, 1994).

45. Davis and Owen, *New Media in American Politics*; Richard Davis, *The Web of Politics: The Internet's Impact on the American Political System* (New York: Oxford Univ. Press, 1999), chapter 2.

46. See Susan J. Douglas, *Inventing American Broadcasting, 1899–1922* (Baltimore: Johns Hopkins Univ. Press, 1987).

47. Richard B. Kielbowicz, "News Gathering by Mail in the Age of the Telegraph: Adapting to a New Technology," *Technology and Culture* 28, no. 1 (1987): 26–41.

48. For example, see Susan Herbst, *Politics at the Margin: Historical Studies of Public Expression Outside the Mainstream* (New York: Cambridge Univ. Press, 1994); Ronald N. Jacobs, *Race, Media and the Crisis of Civil Society: From Watts to Rodney King* (New York: Cambridge Univ. Press, 2000); and América Rodriguez, *Making Latino News: Race, Language, Class* (Thousand Oaks, Calif.: Sage Publications, 1999).

49. Jacobs, *Race, Media and the Crisis of Civil Society.*

50. For an important statement suggesting this approach, though more fully in the area of freedom of speech than freedom of the press, see Cass R. Sunstein, *Democracy and the Problem of Free Speech* (New York: Free Press, 1993).

51. "While the government may subsidize speakers that it thinks provide novel points of view, it may not restrict other speakers on the theory that what they say is more conventional." *Turner Broadcasting System v. Federal Communications Commission*, O'Connor, J. dissent; slip opinion, p. 7.

52. Marjorie Randon Hershey, "The Constructed Explanation: Interpreting Election Results in the 1984 Presidential Race," *Journal of Politics* 54 (1992): 943–76; Benjamin I. Page, *Who Deliberates? Mass Media in Modern Democracy* (Chicago: Univ. of Chicago Press, 1996).

PART ONE:
FROM THE PAST

INTRODUCTION

CRAIG M. FREEMAN

Our look to the future begins with a review of the past. For many legal scholars, this process is simple: it starts and ends with a review of case law. This process mirrors the process used by the courts, where new decisions are based on holdings from older cases. The process of standing by decided matters—stare decisis—leads to predictability and stability in the law. A dependence on stare decisis, however, occasionally forces the law into unfortunate corners. At times, courts are bound to free themselves from the constraints of the doctrine to correct a wayward drift in the law. Chief Justice William Rehnquist noted, "*stare decisis* is not an inexorable command; rather, it 'is a principle of policy and not a mechanical formula of adherence to the latest decision.'"[1] The same reasoning applies to our review of the history of press protection. By basing our review on the prevailing theories of the past, we run the risk of mechanically adhering to the latest research on the topic. Both Charles Clark and Frederick Schauer eschew notions of stare decisis. Each essay provides a fresh look at seemingly settled notions of press freedom.

Clark examines the characteristics of the press, "this great bulwark of liberty," to see if it possessed the qualities so often presumed in today's society, such as those Justice Potter Stewart famously listed in 1975: autonomy, organization, and expertise. His thorough investigation of "The Press the Founders Knew" challenges modern notions that the framers of the Constitution and Bill of Rights envisioned a press similar to our current news media institutions. While the press had been producing news for the colonists as early as 1690, an organized, collective press was fairly new to the founders, and autonomy from political power and expertise were not to be found at all.

Frederick Schauer's essay focuses on a more recent epoch in our legal history. A number of cases in the latter part of the twentieth century, including the Supreme Court's landmark decision in *New York Times v. Sullivan*,[2] provided heightened protection for the press. *Sullivan*'s defenders maintain that the threat of libel liability would unnecessarily fetter freedom of the press. The protection afforded by the Court, they argue, fosters the robust press debate that is at the core of our democratic system. Schauer, on the other hand, questions the empirical keystone of *New York Times v. Sullivan*'s arch. He uses Australian law and the Australian press to illustrate a system with less protection, yet more debate. By breaking away from the vacuum of American decisions, Schauer sheds light on a potential flaw in one of the cornerstones of press freedom in America.

Both Clark and Schauer serve to countervail strongly held beliefs on press freedom. Court decisions in the ten years following *Sullivan* endowed the press with unprecedented power. In addition to protecting the press against libel suits by public officials, the court granted the press limited immunity from suits by public figures (the linked cases of *Associated Press v. Walker* and *Curtis Publishing Co. v. Butts*[3]), shielded the press from the subpoena power of the courts (*Branzburg v. Hayes*[4]), and allowed the publication of classified documents despite objections by the government (*New York Times v. United States*[5]). While the full court never explicitly ascribed to Justice Stewart's views on an autonomous, organized, and expert press, the protection afforded to the modern press evinces the Court's desire to protect the institution's autonomy. Forty years later, most scholars take for granted that the Constitution's framers considered an organized institution when they included the press clause of the First Amendment. Clark's fresh examination of this seemingly settled subject forces readers to question the fundamental principles of the Brennan court and its progeny.

Schauer's essay also questions the validity of forty years of assumptions. The *Sullivan* decision invalidated a questionable verdict by a Montgomery jury during the height of the civil rights movement. The narrow holding of the *Sullivan* court—"the Constitution delimits a State's power to award damages for Libel in actions brought by public officials against critics of their official conduct"[6]—makes perfect sense when compared to a public official's absolute protection from liability for his libelous statements. The Court noted the parallel in its opinion, stating, "It would give public servants an unjustified preference over the public they serve, if critics of official conduct did not have a fair equivalent of the immunity granted to the officials themselves."[7] Just three years later, however, the court extended the protection to defamation against public figures.[8] The balance was destroyed, and the press was afforded the license to defame without consequence in the vast majority of cases. Schauer's essay forces us to reevaluate the propriety of this broad blanket of immunity for the press.

I admit resting too comfortably on a stare decisis approach to legal history. After reading these essays, I find myself questioning the foundations of other legal principles. The radical changes in American media systems over the last forty years demand a fresh look at entrenched doctrines. The following essays provide the perfect way to begin our reevaluation of the freedom of the press.

NOTES

1. *Payne v. Tennessee,* 501 U.S. 808, 828 (1991), quoting *Helvering v. Hallock,* 309 U.S. 106, 119 (1940).

2. *New York Times v. Sullivan,* 376 U.S. 254 (1964).

3. *Associated Press v. Walker* and *Curtis Publishing Co. v. Butts,* 388 U.S. 130 (1967).

4. *Branzburg v. Hayes,* 408 U.S. 665 (1972).

5. *New York Times v. United States,* 403 U.S. 713 (1971).

6. *New York Times v. Sullivan,* 376 U.S. 254 (1964), quote at 283.

7. Ibid., quote at 282–3.

8. *Curtis Publishing Co. v. Butts,* 388 U.S. 130 (1967).

THE PRESS THE FOUNDERS KNEW

CHARLES E. CLARK

Just thirteen days before the first ten amendments were proposed in Congress, an essay on the press by the aged Benjamin Franklin, then in the last year of his life, appeared in the daily Philadelphia newspaper the *Federal Gazette*. Like much of the writing Franklin had been doing nearly all of his long life, it contained a tongue-in-cheek solution to what he viewed as a serious problem. With his eye on the very liberal Pennsylvania Constitution of 1776, his title was "An Account of the Supremest Court of Judicature in Pennsylvania, viz. The Court of the Press."

An untrammeled press, wrote Franklin, can "judge, sentence and condemn to infamy" any private individual or public body it wishes without either the legitimate authority or the procedural rules of the official courts. He suggested that the "liberty of the press" provision of his state's constitution, in which he himself had played a role, might need some qualification. "If by the *liberty of the press* were understood merely the liberty of discussing the propriety of public measures and political opinions, let us have as much of it as you please. But if it means the liberty of affronting, calumniating and defaming one another, I . . . own myself willing to part with my share of it, . . . and shall chearfuly consent to exchange my *liberty* of abusing others for the *privilege* of not being abused myself." To adopt the useful distinction offered recently by Robert W. T. Martin, Franklin's concern here—despite his own terminology—was with the "open" press ideal as expressed in Article 12 of the Pennsylvania Bill of Rights, as distinct from the expressed purpose of a "free" press in Article 35 of the frame of government.[1]

In his quest for a "check" against the abuse of power by the court of the press, he offered a very Franklinian solution. Leave the liberty of the press untouched, he suggested wryly, but balance it with the "liberty of the Cudgel." Thus "if an impudent writer attacks your reputation, . . . you may go after him as openly and break his head." Knowing that Pennsylvanians were already discussing an altered state constitution that would be put into effect the next year, he ended by suggesting that it would be better for the public peace if legislators were to take up the question and explicitly set the extent and limits of both liberties.[2] What actually happened in 1790, as it turned out, was that the new constitution made some careful adjustments. Limits actually were set, recognizing in the first place one's responsibility for "the abuse of that liberty" when writing on any subject, and in the second place the possibility of prosecutions under a greatly modified version of the common-law doctrine of seditious libel whereby criticism of the government could be a crime.[3]

Aside from what Franklin's essay may suggest about the imperfect development of the laws of libel in 1789, and even about an unfinished dialogue about the liberty of expression and its limits, what interests me at the outset is his rather Platonic use of the phrase "the press." The term "liberty of the press," which was the earliest way in which the word "press" was used in a generalized sense, presumably could mean a liberty extended to (or a right enjoyed by) any one or all of innumerable individual printers. A meaning similar to this is implicit in the other First Amendment freedoms of speech, religion, and assembly. But when Franklin speaks of "the court of the press" and generalizes about its power, he is speaking of a collective entity, a presence, and a function in society that transcends its individual members.

"THE PRESS" AS INSTITUTION

Only recently had "the press" taken on this collective meaning, and even in Franklin's time relatively rarely. In the *Pennsylvania Gazette,* the electronic version of which can be searched, the word "press" (when it means printing press rather than a cider press or the impressment of sailors or some such thing) is used overwhelmingly in its most literal sense. Usually it refers to a particular printer's press, as in "ready for the press," "now in the press," "put to press," and the like. The first use of the term in a more general sense, more or less as it was used in the First Amendment, was in 1756, but then it was in connection with "restraint upon the Press" and, in the same year, "Liberty of the Press."[4] During the Stamp Act crisis and on successive anniversaries of its 1766 repeal, the phrase "Liberty of the Press" and "Freedom of the Press" is of course very much in evidence.[5] The first generalized use of "the press" that I have found other than in the context of freedom or restraint is on March 27, 1766, when a letter from London reports that "The Press daily gives something new on the Subject." That, by the way, was some thirty years before the earliest such usage noted by the *Oxford English Dictionary.* In 1770, in a letter copied from the *New-York Gazette,* "the press" in a generalized sense, in this instance an "open" press, is held up as essential to the right conduct of public affairs: "Publick grievances can never be redressed but by public complaints; and they cannot well be made without the PRESS."[6] I found "the press" used in this sense nine times between then and 1783, not including the many more numerous times it appeared in the explicit phrase "liberty," or "freedom" of the press. Once it was in the form of a couplet buried within a rather long poem that recognizes the problem of de facto limits on an "open press": "The free Enquirer hence finds hard Access / Where partial Influence awes a public Press."[7]

To get a sense of what the Revolutionary generation may have understood by "the press" and its function, why it seemed important to maintain its freedom, and of what that freedom consisted, it is not enough to visit the discussions of this topic in the founders' generation alone. Meanings of the crucial terms evolved, as did the practice of publishing on public matters, over the course of very nearly the entire eighteenth century. We need to explore that evolution—which included, by the way, a revolution.

One key point of departure for this collection of essays has been Justice Potter Stewart's characterization of the press as an autonomous institution, guaranteed that status by the First Amendment in order that it could carry out "organized, expert scrutiny of government." My job is to see how well eighteenth-century realities coincided with that twentieth-century description.

The limited evidence above does show that by 1790 there were those who had begun to think of "the press" as an institution, perhaps even as an "organized press" in the sense that Stewart used the term several times in his essay.[8] Article 35 of the Pennsylvania frame of government certainly was written with the idea of "scrutiny of government" in mind where it states, "The printing presses shall be free to every person who undertakes to examine the proceedings of the legislature, or any part of government." This is what Tim Cook calls in his introductory essay the "watchdog" model of press freedom. The same idea may be inferred in the Massachusetts Constitution of 1780, which justifies the guarantee of liberty of "the press" by declaring it "essential to the security of freedom in a state." The same phrase, with the same use of "the press," appears in the New Hampshire Constitution of 1783.[9] But was that institution "autonomous," and had any government in America on any level yet experienced a scrutiny that was both "organized" and "expert"?

A LIMITED AUTONOMY

If by "autonomous" we mean operating independently of outside influences, the evidence favoring such an interpretation of the eighteenth-century press at work is at best scattered. And even when we do find it, as in the case of James Franklin's New-England Courant in the 1720s, a cluster of politically conscious newspapers in New England in the 1740s and 1750s, and for a time perhaps the Pennsylvania Gazette itself, we find little basis for generalization.

Benjamin Harris thought he was being autonomous when he issued the first and only number of *Publick Occurrences* in 1690, exactly a century before the Bill of Rights, but soon found that the provisional government of Massachusetts thought otherwise. By official fiat, that was the end of the first attempt at a periodical newspaper in the American colonies. Autonomy never occurred to John Campbell, who started the first successful American newspaper in 1704. As postmaster of Boston, he tried to make his *Boston News-Letter* as close to an organ of government as a rather stingy legislature would permit. He got "approbation" from the governor for the contents of every weekly number, which was then proudly emblazoned "Published by Authority." William Brooker, Campbell's successor in the postmastership, operated his *Boston Gazette,* begun in 1719, under the same assumptions and with the same motto. In the same year, Andrew Bradford of Philadelphia became the first American printer to publish a newspaper on his own account. He could scarcely claim "autonomy" for his *American Weekly Mercury* even if he had wanted to, given that he held the official printing appointment for both the province government and the Society of Friends, Pennsylvania's governing elite. Some years later, Andrew Bradford's father, William, who had gone to New York on the invitation of the governor to become the province printer, began the *New-York Gazette.* In due course, much to his distaste, he would have to use it in a paper war with John Peter Zenger's upstart *New-York Weekly Journal,* which existed only because of its sponsorship by an opposition political faction.

These early examples set the pattern of newspaper publishing for much of the eighteenth century. Most often, the sole printer in the provincial capital had the government printing contract for laws and proclamations, did job printing for the community, contracted for small books and pamphlets, occasionally ran a bookshop or bindery or both, published a newspaper and perhaps an annual almanac, and after 1753 often served as postmaster.[10] Gradually, the larger seaport towns acquired one or more competing printers, and as the supply of printers expanded, some of them set up shop in smaller towns. Many of those newly served places, like Annapolis, Newport, Charleston, Williamsburg, and Portsmouth, New Hampshire, were also province capitals, and the pattern established early in Philadelphia and New York continued there. The press in other towns, most notably Germantown, Pennsylvania, with its German-language printer and newspaper, could perhaps truly claim to be "autonomous," but it was an autonomy of little or no significance to the conduct of public affairs. Competing printers in Philadelphia and New York, meanwhile, did not have a government connection but would have welcomed it if they had had it, and they sometimes competed for it. Boston, the earliest and by far the leading publishing town until rivaled by Philadelphia during the Revolution, was a case unto itself. Until 1741, the most important newspaper publishers there were not printers but either postmasters or, in one case, a teacher and literary figure who contracted with printers. The two exceptions, the *New-England Courant* and *New-England Weekly Journal*, published by the printers James Franklin and Samuel Kneeland, respectively, were atypical in that both began as attempts at literary journalism with "clubs" of writers as their main contributors. After that period of experimentation was over, the publishing pattern in Boston was essentially the same as it was everywhere else.[11]

The question of whether the press was "autonomous," to use Justice Stewart's term, becomes of most interest only after the newspapers began to pay more attention to political matters than had been the case in their early development. James Franklin's *New-England Courant* was an exceptionally early entry in the political (as well as the literary) arena, but its life was short. Moreover, its "autonomy" was very soon challenged by the Massachusetts Assembly, which took a sly remark as an insult and jailed the printer for a month in 1722. At the beginning of the next year, after some more direct attacks on both church and state, the General Court issued an order prohibiting Franklin from publishing without the supervision (a nice word for censorship) of the province secretary. The *Courant*, however, continued unsupervised, but over the name of James Franklin's teenage apprentice, Benjamin. The subterfuge continued until the end of the *Courant's* brief life in 1726, a good three years after young Benjamin Franklin had left Boston for more promising terrain. This extra-legal maneuver, by the way, circumvented what turned out to be the last serious official attempt in British America, despite continued royal instructions, to control the press by prior licensing.[12]

The next notable case in which a publisher was involved in political controversy and ran afoul of officialdom came a dozen years after the Franklin episode, in 1735. That, of course, was the celebrated trial in New York of John Peter Zenger. Since by "autonomy" Justice Stewart meant independence from governmental authority, then we can say that the *New-York Weekly Journal* was autonomous, or at least attempted to be. In the end, and at considerable cost to its printer-publisher, it maintained that autonomy. The paper and its publisher, however, were hardly independent from an outside influence of another kind, namely the powerful Lewis Morris political faction that hired Zenger to establish his paper in the first place and controlled the content that got him into trouble.[13] The Zenger episode raises the question, therefore, whether it is realistic to think of autonomy only as Stewart understood it, merely as the official absence of governmental authority.

In Boston, for example, all of the several newspapers in the first half of the century but the *New-England Courant* and after that the *Boston Evening-Post* were willing acolytes of both the royal governor and the established clergy, to whom they owed much of their patronage. This was true whether or not they professed to be "published by authority."

The politicization of the American newspaper took definitive shape during the 1750s. In part this development took the form of partisan wrangling. The young printers of the *New-York Mercury* and the *Independent Reflector* continued the earlier New York tradition as tools of the warring political factions that sponsored them. James Parker, however, one of the several former employees whom Benjamin Franklin set up in business, published his *New-York Weekly Post-Boy* in accordance with the "open press" ideal embraced by most pre-Revolutionary printers, but to his discomfort was buffeted from all sides for printing politically controversial articles. Most of Franklin's other partners who set up printing shops and newspapers in other towns, from Providence to Charleston, operated in accordance with the same ideal until drawn into the Revolutionary movement. Even though several of them were eventually appointed postmasters, they can be said to have operated largely "autonomous" presses. None of them, however, was immune from pressures from various directions and of various kinds, including political ones.[14] Nor do we find much if any "scrutiny" of government.

The movement of the American newspaper toward an emphasis on politics at the expense of the attempted genteel literary journalism of the 1730s was in part generational. One of James Parker's apprentices, for example, was William Goddard, who at the age of twenty-two set up his own printing shop and established the *Providence Gazette,* the first newspaper in that city, in 1762. He announced at the outset that his paper would be dedicated to "the Spirit of true *British* liberty."[15] Seven years earlier in Boston, Benjamin Edes and John Gill, having bought the *Boston Gazette* from Samuel Kneeland, abandoned the generalized ideal of "politeness" favored by their predecessor's generation to adopt the more sharply partisan rhetoric inspired by recent American reprints of the English Whig writers of the 1720s and embraced by the popular party in Massachusetts.[16] Unlike the most partisan of their New York contemporaries, however, neither Goddard nor the Edes and Gill partnership as far as we know operated as a paid tool of any faction. They took pride, in fact, in their independence and in an adherence to the open press ideal even though they took no pains to hide their political preferences. They were, in short, as far as we can see, as close to "autonomous" as we can expect to find in this part of the century. The same can be said for David Hall, Franklin's successor as publisher of the *Pennsylvania Gazette.* He kept his press open for controversy, but was more cautious than his younger New England colleagues about letting his own predispositions show through. Here again, however, openness to debate by opposing sides needs to be distinguished from the watchdog role that Stewart believed the First Amendment actually assigned to the press several decades later.

ORGANIZED FOR WHAT?

To the extent that the eighteenth-century printing trade was organized, so too could the printer-owned newspapers of the American colonies be said to have a kind of collective structure, resulting in pretty much a fundamental sameness. America had no formal guilds or associations such as London's powerful Company of Stationers, but business and family relationships among printers created strong webs of mutual influence, and in some cases dependency. Benjamin Franklin, to take the most dramatic example, dispatched former apprentices to set up printing houses with himself as partner in Charleston, Annapolis, New York, Newport, and Wilmington. James Parker, the Franklin associate who went to New York in 1741, did the same for several of his apprentices, as did David Hall, the Franklin partner who took over their joint printing enterprise in Philadelphia in 1748. The incredibly prolific and coherent printing clan of Greens, Kneelands, and Drapers, founded by the Boston printer Bartholomew Green Sr. in 1690, dominated the New England printing trade until the Revolution. Less extensive family or business dynasties could be found either in some of the same cities or in smaller colonial seaports.[17] Printing connections such as these, though they certainly provided for mutual encouragement and in some cases financial underwriting, did not bring about anything like a "chain" of newspapers. Publishing a newspaper was only one, though an important one, of many activities in which most printers engaged. If there developed a general uniformity in format and approach to gathering content, it was only as a result of training and imitation, resulting in the gradual adoption of accepted norms.

There was one other way in which associations of various kinds among printers worked, but not usually involving newspapers. Some printers of almanacs, such as Franklin, relied on fellow printers in other cities to distribute their products more broadly, and in 1774 Isaiah Thomas, then of Boston, assembled a network of sixteen other printers from Portsmouth to Charleston from whom his short-lived *Royal American Magazine* could be purchased.[18]

Aside from the structures that loosely linked many members of the trade, however, there was an inadvertent kind of organization of newspaper content throughout the colonies. It was standard practice among printers, apparently never challenged, to copy from other newspapers. With rare exceptions, all of the European news that dominated the content of most colonial newspapers until the Revolution was copied verbatim from the London newspapers to which the printers subscribed. The local and provincial items that each printer collected more or less haphazardly and printed in his newspaper were in turn copied, also verbatim, by newspapers elsewhere. Through a system of exchanges facilitated by the colonial postal service, American readers were thus becoming increasingly informed through the century about events in places other than their own. At the same time, there developed a kind of standardization, or printing conventions, in which news received from various sources was displayed.[19]

But to what end was this sort of organization in the colonial press? If one thinks as Justice Stewart did of the press as an unofficial but recognized fourth branch of government, the sort of "organized press" that comes to mind is something like a modern press corps, equipped with tools and accepted methodologies to carry on a systematic "scrutiny of government." The activity for which it is organized is *journalism,* which pre-Revolutionary printers practiced inexpertly and only incidentally to their printing trade. There were no "reporters" in any sense that approaches a modern understanding of the word. The "organized press," to the extent that it *was* organized before the Revolutionary era, was meant to facilitate the business and the craft of printing—meaning, it should be remembered, the printing not only of a printer's newspaper if he had one but also of books, pamphlets, almanacs, broadsides, blank forms, and anything else ordered up by his patrons—not the practice of journalism.

REVOLUTIONARY ORGANIZATION AND PARTISANSHIP

It was in the opposition to British colonial policy in the 1760s, most particularly the Stamp Act crisis, that the press took on yet another kind of organization, this one perhaps more relevant than the others to Stewart's understanding of the term. To a degree not seen before or since, the press, or most of it, became in effect a *political* organization. Since the Stamp Act of 1765 affected printers especially directly, their overwhelmingly negative response is hardly surprising, if only because of obvious economic interest. Beyond mere opposition, however, they reacted with noncompliance and dramatic protest, playing the most visible role in the surprisingly violent popular uprising against this first parliamentary attempt at a direct tax on the colonies. The Stamp Act was repealed after a few months, but other policies and actions offensive to an aroused public followed, producing a press that was very nearly unanimous in the opinions it expressed, and in its subservience to public opinion. The notion of a "free and open" press—the prevailing ideal of the provincial period—gave way quickly and entirely to an openly partisan press, a development that at first bewildered some of the older printers, such as David Hall and New Hampshire's Daniel Fowle, but which they found impossible to resist. In Robert Martin's terms, an "open press" became instead a "press of freedom."[20] As resistance ripened into rebellion, all the American printers—except James Rivington of New York, John Mein of Boston (who was driven out of town), and a small handful of others who took the Loyalist side—served as the printed voice of the Sons of Liberty and other manifestations of the organized Patriot movement. Neutrality was unacceptable. Political partisanship, though not by any means the virtual unanimity of Revolutionary times, thus became a characteristic of the American press well into the nineteenth century.

From one point of view, the press of the Revolutionary period was perhaps more closed and unautonomous than that of any other time in our history. Public opinion turned out to be the most efficient censor yet discovered. It is not without irony, therefore, that the closed and unautonomous press of this period, by raising awareness of obnoxious British policies and stimulating public discussion and resistance, was an instrument in the revival of the ideal perceptively analyzed by Richard D. Brown, that of the informed citizenry.[21] And it is precisely this role that, during the Confederation period and especially in the debates over the ratification of the Constitution, made the press indispensable to republican government as practiced in America. In 1787, to take the most dramatic example, little more than two weeks after the adjournment of the Constitutional Convention, the one hundred newspapers of the United States had the entire text of the proposed document in the hands of what was by and large a remarkably literate population. Providing the text in this way was undoubtedly more important in informing the state ratifying debates that followed than the various argumentative pieces in the largely Federalist newspapers of the day. (The *Federalist* essays may have been the exception, but they were not widely copied outside New York.)[22] James Madison, whose role both in framing the Constitution and advocating the Bill of Rights is well known, later recognized the significance of what the newspapers had done in that respect, and at the same time suggested something close to Stewart's notion of "autonomy." In 1799, reporting on the Virginia Resolutions against the Alien and Sedition Acts, he emphasized among other things both the key role that the newspapers had played in the ratification process and the importance of assurances during the ratification debates that the proposed new government would have no power to interfere with the press.[23]

Whether autonomous or not, the Revolutionary press certainly was organized, as was, though perhaps inadvertently, the hundred-member de facto press association of 1788 that carried the Constitution to a very extended American readership. The practice of mutual copying, highly developed by 1740, had led to a vague uniformity of content and essential unanimity on values. The community of printers thus shaped was in operation well before the Revolutionary crisis swept away both restraint and almost every printer's customary pose of neutrality.

THE QUESTION OF "EXPERT"

But if the eighteenth-century press was "organized" in a certain sense, was it also "expert"? Again, the evidence is mixed, and its meaning uncertain. If by "expert" we mean a professionalized objective journalism and especially investigative reporting, there was no such thing in 1790 or at any time before, and would not be for another several decades. The very term "journalism," in fact, had yet to be used in its modern sense.[24] The only training that most pre-Revolutionary producers of newspapers had undergone was the craft apprenticeship that had fitted them for their main occupation, which was printing. True, the things they printed could include contributions, usually anonymous, by commentators of some learning and occasionally with access to the decision-making elite. For the most part, however, these were polemical rather than expository. In fact, if there was one area in which the newspapers of the Revolution and very early republic might be said to be "expert," it was propaganda. As Thomas C. Leonard has shown, Revolutionary printers introduced the newspaper "exposé" in an attempt to disclose the villainy of the opposition.[25] The tradition continued with the partisan papers of the Washington and Adams era. As we shall see, however, that era was also bringing about other important changes in what we would call journalism, pointing in the direction of a kind of professionalism.

Pre-Revolutionary publishers made no pretense at being anything other than craftsmen, and in fact could protest that as "meer mechanics," or "leather apron men" as Benjamin Franklin put it, they simply kept their presses open to all sides of opinion.[26] They did not claim for the most part to be "expert" in anything other than the craft of printing. Eighteenth-century publishers, actually, were so far from the much later understanding of the special responsibility of the journalist to have a care for accuracy that they could make a plausible excuse for error simply by pleading that anyone could have made the same mistake. The most egregious example that has come to my notice, admittedly a very early one, is the case of John Campbell. In 1705 he was sufficiently taken in by the preposterous fictional tribulations of a young swindler passing through town to give him a huge sympathetic proportion of the precious space in his *Boston News-Letter.*

The next week, the trick having been discovered, he tried to hide his embarrassment by picking up the story again as if it were simply a continuation of the first installment. He finally admitted having fallen for the hoax but added, "perhaps there are a few Readers, but what have themselves now & then told a Story that needed a further *Elucidation*."[27]

For many decades after the pioneering and often faltering attempts of John Campbell to teach himself how to publish a newspaper, printers routinely compiled their weekly reports from three kinds of source. These were other newspapers, primarily English; unsolicited contributions, such as letters, essays of opinion, and occasional literary endeavors including poetry; and tidbits of information and gossip that found their random way into the printing office. Some publishers occasionally conducted interviews with recently arrived ship captains and others, and the short-lived literary newspaper the *New-England Weekly Journal* (1727–1741) claimed to have recruited correspondents throughout the region, probably ministers on the lookout for "Remarkable Judgments and Singular Mercies," as the paper put it. On rare occasions some printers, such as New York's William Bradford and Boston's John Boydell in one notable exchange in the 1730s, actually stepped out of their customary role and wrote opinion pieces themselves. In general, however, the collection of news was almost entirely passive and obviously unsystematic. The news content of every newspaper up to the Revolution, it should be added, was dominated overwhelmingly by European events copied from London.[28] During the Revolutionary era, as we have seen, the printers, often in collaboration with groups of political compatriots, took a more active role in determining, manipulating, and writing the content of their newspapers than had been the case previously, but in every case these efforts were unabashedly for partisan purposes.

While partisanship continued to be the most obvious and most remarked upon feature of the newspaper press through the Confederation period and beyond, there was also an emerging understanding of how newspapers might play their informational role more effectively while assuming a new centrality in the ecology of civic discourse. In 1783, for example, the *Boston Gazette*, which had been a fiery instrument of the Patriot cause, was giving its readers the full texts of the commercial treaty with the Netherlands and the peace treaty with Britain; the official record of the acts of the Massachusetts General Court; the proceedings of the disbanding Army at Newburgh, including the full text of Washington's speech and the officers' final toned-down address to Congress of March 15; and the full text of the proceedings of the Boston Town Meeting.[29] The actual reportorial techniques employed here were no different from those of the pre-Revolutionary period, since they involved little more than copying official records. On the other hand, the selection and timeliness of these documents show a far more acute sensitivity to the presumed immediate concerns of the readership than was evident in the much more random selection of materials in an earlier day.

By 1787, when the *Gazette* was printing the motto "A Free Press Maintains the Majesty of the People," either the young printer Benjamin Edes Jr. or a representative was taking a more active role in collecting the news. (The motto seems to suggest what Martin called "free"—that is, the watchdog role—rather than simply "open.") While the paper was still running official texts as before, its account of the action of the Massachusetts House to call a ratifying convention for the proposed federal Constitution was obviously the work of the newspaper's "reporter," or at least a primitive version thereof. That is obvious from the way in which the account summarizes not just the outcome of the proceedings but the debate, and especially in references in the account to "our readers."[30] The same kind of reporting is evident early in 1788 in the *Gazette*'s account of the proceedings of the ratifying convention, and finally the act of ratification and the ensuing celebration, obviously in the voice of the paper itself.[31] Even in the documents selected for copying, the *Gazette* was making significant gestures toward a kind of objectivity. In 1787 it printed not only a number of governmental texts but also a petition to the governor and General Court from the town of Leominster during Shays's Rebellion and the remarkable letter from Elbridge Gerry, a Massachusetts delegate to the Constitutional Convention in Philadelphia, in which he opposed adoption of the Constitution.[32]

The most remarked upon journalistic phenomenon during the early years of the federal government under the new Constitution is the vicious paper war between the Federalist *Gazette of the United States* and its Jeffersonian rival, the *National Gazette.* The two rivals undoubtedly deserve their notoriety as polemical partisans, encouraged if not actually sponsored by the competing factions in Washington's cabinet, but they nevertheless disclose a tendency in the direction of professionalism. Each of these papers was run not by its printer but by an editor, John Fenno and Philip Freneau, respectively. Not since Jeremiah Gridley had founded and briefly edited the Boston literary journal the *Weekly Rehearsal* in the 1730s had the mechanical and editorial functions of an American newspaper been in entirely separate hands. This development away from printers as publishers, recognized sixty years ago by Frank Luther Mott in a groundbreaking history of America newspapers,[33] would not take full shape for a decade or more to come. Country printers, moreover, could still be found compiling newspapers as an adjunct to their business through the nineteenth century and beyond. But the development of an entirely new calling that began in a small way in the 1780s, exemplified especially by the two conspicuous rivals edited by Fenno and Freneau and successors such as William Cobbett's *Porcupine's Gazette* and Benjamin Franklin Bache's *Philadelphia Aurora,* was a powerful inducement toward the professionalization of journalism.[34] "The press," in other words, was beginning to allude less to the mechanics of printing than to the works of writers and editors that were being printed. And as "the press" in this new sense became the province of what were usually called "able" editors, even expressions of their personalities,[35] it moved toward becoming, in a very limited sense, "expert." This is not to deny its vicious partisanship, or even its lack of true "autonomy." But consider the following:

Of the two rivals, the first on the scene, Fenno's *Gazette of the United States,* is the more relevant to ascertaining the state of "the press" at the time of the First Amendment, since Freneau's *National Gazette* would not appear until 1791. A look at the paper at the beginning of its career in 1789 discloses what appears to be a real attempt on the part of its editor to provide a useful and comprehensive report of the actions of government. Though the paper's editor is clearly sympathetic at this stage with the new Federal government and respectful of its leading officers, the venom associated with it and its rival paper would not come until the appearance on the scene of Freneau. Instead of controversy, we find elaborate reports of proceedings of the new Congress complete with debates, brief expository articles on the states of the Union and other fundamental topics, and useful essays of analysis and opinion signed, not with a pseudonym as had been common practice only recently, but either "John Fenno" or "The Editor." His original plan, as expressed in the first number, included making his "early and authentic accounts" of Congressional proceedings "connected so as to form a history of the transactions of the Federal Legislature." Another part of the plan was to include "Impartial sketches of the Debates of Congress."[36] This he seems to have done quite effectively, whether using the published *Journal* of the House and Senate or taking advantage of the open galleries, both of which were available to press and public from the beginning. He probably used both. His extensive use of verbatim documents does recall John Campbell's primitive attempts to construct a "thread of occurrences" from the use of such materials almost a century earlier. However, Fenno differed significantly from Campbell not only in that he actively sought out and selected the documents he needed to tell his story rather than passively copying what chanced to come to him, but also in that he supplemented the official record with summaries and commentaries of his own. When Freneau started up his *National Gazette* two and a half years later, he also prefaced the various essays of opinion, whether his own or those of his contributors, with the official documents.[37]

None of this negates the polemical purposes to which both editors and some of their contemporaries in other cities put their papers, a tendency that would be continued in even shriller tones by some of their immediate successors, such as the editors of *Porcupine's Gazette* and the *Aurora*. Both editors, however, were also working toward defining the nature of a professionally edited newspaper that would effectively serve and help create (as well as persuade) an informed citizenry. These editors and others like them obviously fell short of what "expert" journalism might mean in the future. They had nevertheless come a very long way from the John Campbell whose excuses for falling for a hoax eighty-five years earlier did not even pretend that his business of purveying the news carried with it any special obligation.

"THE PRESS" IN 1789

What, then, was the state of "the press" when the Bill of Rights was being considered? On June 8, 1789, James Madison proposed in Congress that the Constitution be amended to provide that "The people shall not be deprived or abridged of their right to speak, to write, or to publish their sentiments; and the freedom of the press, as one of the great bulwarks of liberty, shall be inviolable."[38] As the debate progressed until Congress reached agreement in September, this proposal in shortened form was folded into the more comprehensive article, ratified by the states in 1791, that became the First Amendment. Were the characteristics of this "great bulwark of liberty," if that's what it really was, those that Justice Potter Stewart enumerated in 1974? Was it an autonomous institution? Was it then, or did it have the obvious potential of, carrying out "organized, expert scrutiny of government"?

In none of these particulars did the scattered newspapers of the provincial period meet the test. Not until at least 1740 could more than a handful of these newspapers be considered in a real sense "autonomous," and even then there were ample checks and discouragements to inhibit the exercise of that limited autonomy. Not until about 1750, with a couple of exceptions, was there even an attempt to scrutinize government, and not only for fear of censorship or punishment, as has sometimes been argued. It was also because the purposes of most publishers and presumed interests of their readers were elsewhere, and because the printers lacked both example and the methods to carry out such scrutiny. They were, therefore, certainly not expert, at least in political journalism. It is doubtful that we can even properly think of this collection of provincial newspapers as an institution, certainly not an "organized" institution, called collectively "the press." At least their contemporaries did not perceive them that way.

The Revolution, however, as revolutions do, brought about change. Already partly politicized by the second generation of printers who took over from their fathers in mid-century, the newspapers of the 1760s, especially under the impetus of the Stamp Act, became more so. There also emerged a network of Patriot printers and newspapers that might be called "organized" in a sense beyond the familial and business relationships that embraced many printers, and one begins to encounter frequent references to "the press."

Partisanship, which one gathers from the debates in Congress and in some of the state ratifying conventions that the makers of the First Amendment took for granted, remained a feature of the post-Revolutionary press, but it was not the only feature. In fact, it would be a mistake to think of the primarily political journals at the center of government upon which I have been focusing as representative of the American press of the period at large. Though many of those in the outlying areas were indeed partisan, some showed greater interest in either more general news or literary content than in partisan politics.[39] The 1790s were also supplying a proliferation of monthly magazines, a genre that had been a long and rather slow time developing from the first attempts in 1741. While a few of these specialized in political discourse, most were aimed at specialized audiences with other interests.[40] The new breed of newspaper editor with which we have been mainly concerned, while admittedly and often flagrantly partisan and guilty of distortion, was becoming seriously engaged in political reporting and in presenting to his readership, the citizenry, a systematic account of government. It was still, however, an account depending more on official records than investigative reporting, and one could argue that, especially after the political wars heated up, it was a side of his operation that was subordinate to the presentation of opinion.

"The press," as it could now with confidence be called, had not yet developed an ideal of objectivity, nor had it achieved the techniques of investigative reporting and news analysis that were still a long way in the future. On the other hand, there had not yet developed in government itself the elaborate mechanisms for manipulating the news, which along with conglomerate ownership of the media results in our own remarkably uniform view of the world. The very presence of partisanship, which a modern journalist might decry as unprofessional, resulted in a greater diversity in emphasis and interpretation in those late eighteenth-century newspapers than we are likely to find in our own day.

This is the sort of "press" with which the makers of the First Amendment were most immediately familiar, and which they sought to protect from interference. It could easily by then, I would argue, have been considered a coherent institution. If it was autonomous, meaning the absence of direct government control (and even that is open to debate in the case of the *Gazette of the United States*), it was an autonomy that was largely negated by control and powerful influences of other kinds. It was not an autonomy conducive to dispassionate scrutiny. Whether it was "expert" depends upon how you define the word. In one sense, it was becoming so. Its expertness, however, was not in scrutinizing government with what we would recognize as the techniques of the professional journalist. It was in fighting the political wars of the day both as a combatant and as a provider, to paraphrase Teddy Roosevelt badly, of a bully platform. This function could be considered in some sense that of a watchdog. But the role that would have been most experienced and therefore most recognized by the founders was that of providing a forum for the intense, usually acrimonious discussion of the issues and personalities of this contentious time in the life of the new republic.

NOTES

1. Robert W. T. Martin, *The Free and Open Press: The Founding of American Democratic Press Liberty, 1640–1800* (New York: New York Univ. Press, 2001), 100–1. Timothy E. Cook preserves the same distinction in "Freeing the Presses: An Introductory Essay," above.

2. "An Account of the Supremest Court of Judicature in Pennsylvania, viz The Court of the Press," *Federal Gazette,* September 12, 1789. The essay is unsigned in the *Gazette,* but is attributed to Franklin by J. A. Leo Lemay, editor of *Benjamin Franklin: Writings* (New York: Library of America, 1987), 1150–4. Yale University Press's monumental *Papers of Benjamin Franklin* has so far reached only volume 37, ending in August 1782.

3. Pennsylvania Constitution, Article IX; see, e.g., Neil H. Cogan, ed., *The Complete Bill of Rights: The Drafts, Debates, Sources, and Origins* (New York: Oxford Univ. Press, 1997), 95. English common law had long criminalized published utterances tending toward an "ill opinion of government," in the words of one judgment in 1704, whether true or false. When a jury was involved in such a case, its role was limited to determining the facts of publication, not whether the law had been breached. As a practical matter, this offense had been prosecuted very rarely in the American colonies in the eighteenth century, and by the end of the century the application of the law was undergoing challenge and modification even in England. The 1790 Pennsylvania Constitution provided that in cases in which the libel had concerned official conduct or was otherwise "proper for public information," the truth of the utterance could be entered in its defense. It also granted the right to juries in such cases to determine the law as well as the facts, which had been done without precedent in New York's Zenger case in 1735 (see below). On seditious libel, see Fredrick Seaton Seibert, *Freedom of the Press in England, 1476–1776* (Urbana: Univ. of Illinois Press, 1965), 269–75, 380–92; Leonard W. Levy, *Emergence of a Free Press* (New York: Oxford Univ. Press, 1985), 1–61; and Richard D. Brown, "The Shifting Freedoms of the Press in the Eighteenth Century" in *The Colonial Book in the Atlantic World,* edited by Hugh

Amory and David D. Hall (Cambridge: Cambridge Univ. Press, 2000), 368–72.

4. *Pennsylvania Gazette,* March 2, November 26, 1756.

5. Ibid., November 7, 1765; May 22, June 12, 1766; March 31, 1768; March 23, 1769.

6. Ibid., March 8, 1770.

7. Ibid., June 15, 1774; June 28, 1775; January 24, March 13, 1776; May 26, 1779; October 2, 1782; January 8, 1783. The poem appeared September 26, 1774.

8. Potter Stewart, "Or of the Press," *Hastings Law Journal* 26 (1975): 631–7, reprinted in *Hastings Law Journal* 50 (April 1999): 705–10. For "the press" as an "organized" institution, see pages 705, 706, 707.

9. Article XVI of the "Declaration of Rights," Part I of the Massachusetts Constitution, and Article XXII of Part I of the New Hampshire Constitution. Cogan, ed., *Complete Bill of Rights,* 94. On "watchdog model," see Cook, "Freeing the Presses," above.

10. In 1753, the American postal service was reorganized with Benjamin Franklin and William Hunter as codeputy postmasters for the colonies. Thereafter, Franklin worked consciously to establish a postmaster-printer connection in every important town but Boston, where newspapers had been published by postmasters who were not printers since 1704. The last such publishing regime ended with the death of the *Boston Post-Boy* under Ellis Huske in 1754. See Charles E. Clark, *The Public Prints: The Newspaper in Anglo-American Culture, 1665–1740* (New York: Oxford Univ. Press, 1994), 188.

11. The one exception was the *Boston Post-Boy* mentioned in note 10. Its owner was not only an absentee publisher but an absentee postmaster as well.

12. Clyde A. Dunlway, *The Development of Freedom of the Press in Massachusetts* (Cambridge, Mass.: Harvard Univ. Press, 1906), 79–96; Brown, "Shifting Freedoms of the Press," 368.

13. Zenger was acquitted of seditious libel after his Philadelphia lawyer Andrew Hamilton persuaded the jury that it could rule on the law as well as the facts of the case. The ruling turned out not to be precedent-setting in a legal sense, as was once believed. The case did, however, as Richard D. Brown has put it, "underscore the limited ability of royal officials to protect themselves by using seditious libel proceedings, especially where popular issues were being decided by juries." Brown, "Shifting Freedoms of the Press," 370–1.

14. Jeffery A. Smith, *Printers and Press Freedom: The Ideology of Early American Journalism* (New York: Oxford Univ. Press, 1988), 126–9; Charles E. Clark, "Early American Journalism: News and Opinion in the Popular Press," in Amory and Hall, eds., *Colonial Book,* 359.

15. *Providence Gazette,* October 30, 1762.

16. Richard L. Bushman, *King and People in Provincial Massachusetts* (Chapel Hill: Univ. of North Carolina Press, 1985), 261.

17. Charles Wetherell, "Brokers of the Word: An Essay in the Social History of the Early American Press, 1639–1783" (Ph.D. diss., Univ. of New Hampshire, 1980), 66–118.

18. Ibid., 122.

19. Clark, *Public Prints,* passim, esp. 211–2.

20. Martin, *Free and Open Press,* 74–92, esp. 81. Martin's is the most recent of many extended treatments of this transition, but see also, e.g., Stephen Botein, "Printers and the American Revolution," 11–57, and Richard Buel Jr., "Freedom of the Press in Revolutionary America: The Evolution of Libertarianism, 1760–1820," 59–97, in *The Press and the American Revolution,* edited by Bernard Bailyn and

John B. Hench (Worcester, Mass.: American Antiquarian Society, 1980).

21. Richard D. Brown, *The Strength of a People: The Idea of an Informed Citizenry in America, 1650–1870* (Chapel Hill: Univ. of North Carolina Press, 1996).

22. Clark, "Early American Journalism," 365–6. See also Elaine F. Crane, "Publius in the Provinces: Where Was *The Federalist* Reprinted Outside New York City?" *William and Mary Quarterly*, 3rd ser., 21 (1964): 589–92.

23. William T. Mayton, "From a Legacy of Suppression to the 'Metaphor of the Fourth Estate,'" *Stanford Law Review* 39 (November 1986): 148. Mayton's actual point in citing these arguments was to support his own argument against Leonard W. Levy's assertion that the founders had not meant to abandon the common-law rule of seditious libel.

24. Clark, "Early American Journalism," 347.

25. Thomas C. Leonard, *The Power of the Press: The Birth of American Political Reporting* (New York: Oxford Univ. Press, 1986), 33–58.

26. See esp. Stephen Botein, "'Meer Mechanics' and an Open Press: The Business and Political Strategies of Colonial American Printers," *Perspectives in American History* 9 (1975): 127–225.

27. Clark, *Public Prints*, 91–2. The numbers of the *News-Letter* are those of November 5 and 12, 1705.

28. Ibid., passim, but esp. 146, 185–8, 193–214. On content, see also Charles E. Clark and Charles Wetherell, "The Measure of Maturity: The *Pennsylvania Gazette*, 1728–1765," *William and Mary Quarterly*, 3d ser., 46 (1989): 279–303.

29. *Boston Gazette*, February 24, March 3, March 31, April 21, April 28, May 26, 1783.

30. Ibid., October 29, 1787.

31. Ibid., January 21, January 28, February 11, 1788.

32. Ibid., April 2, 1787; November 5, 1788.

33. Frank Luther Mott, *American Journalism: A History of Newspapers in the United States through 250 Years, 1690 to 1940* (New York: Macmillan, 1941), 114.

34. On the *Aurora*, see esp. Richard N. Rosenfeld, *American Aurora: A Democratic-Republican Returns* (New York: St. Martin's Griffin, 1997).

35. Mott, *American Journalism*, 114.

36. *Gazette of the United States*, April 15, 1789, *et seq.*

37. Mary W. Bowden, *Philip Freneau* (Boston: Twayne Publishers, 1976), 90–1.

38. Cogan, ed., *Complete Bill of Rights*, 83.

39. One particularly conspicuous example was Joseph Dennie's *Farmer's Museum* of Walpole, New Hampshire, which, though unquestionably Federalist in sympathy, made itself widely known and appreciated primarily for its witty literary content and discussions of general subjects supplied by Dennie and his associates.

40. Charles E. Clark, "The Long Experiment: The Quest for a Successful American Magazine Formula" (paper presented at the American Association of Eighteenth-Century Studies, Colorado Springs, Colo., April 5, 2002).

ON THE RELATIONSHIP BETWEEN PRESS LAW AND PRESS CONTENT

FREDERICK SCHAUER

For most journalists, especially American ones, belief in the "chilling effect" is a central feature of their professional ideology. Concern over the deterrent effect of potential legal liability is an omnipresent feature of journalistic discourse, and the view is widespread that the press is better when it is more free, that it is more free when there is less law, and that when there is less law the press is more able to perform its functions in a democracy. Yet, however commonsensical this view is, it may be more complex than its adherents believe, and the relationship between press law and press content may not be as straightforward as the common picture imagines. More specifically, the experience in many countries reminds us that many factors other than the presence of potential legal liability have considerably greater influence on press content. As a consequence, the existence or nonexistence of press-restrictive laws and legal doctrines, especially the doctrines that allow for civil liability, may have less to do with press behavior and press content than it first seems, and than most journalists think. Or, to put it differently, the chilling effect may under some conditions not be nearly as cold as many journalists, editors, and media lawyers have believed and have traditionally argued.

Press freedom generally and the chilling effect specifically are issues relevant throughout the universe of potential legal liability for the media, including subjects as diverse as prior restraints in the name of national security,[1] taxation of the press,[2] civil or criminal liability for disclosing the content of ongoing legal proceedings,[3] publication of illegally obtained material,[4] and the licensing of journalists.[5] Yet, however much consideration of all of these and other topics is necessary to complete a full picture of the relationship between press law and press behavior, in the interest of analytical clarity I will focus on only one area, the law of libel. In part because the very idea of the chilling effect is so associated, both historically and currently, with defamation law, and in part because cross-national similarities in libel law among common-law countries make cross-national comparisons slightly more manageable than would be the case where the fundamentals of the legal doctrine vary more substantially, restricting the inquiry to libel will provide a degree of analytic precision that a wider examination would obscure.

THE BASIC DOCTRINE AND THE BASIC STORY

As is well known, modern American libel law starts with *New York Times v. Sullivan*,[6] the case in which the Supreme Court first held that the law of defamation, previously lying entirely outside the First Amendment,[7] was now to be encompassed and constrained by First Amendment principles. Moreover, the Court said, the vital importance of public information about the performance and qualifications of our elected and appointed officials mandated a rule that treated the error of erroneous publication of falsity as being far less grave than the error of erroneous nonpublication of truth.[8] In a world in which no legal rule can eliminate error, the Court implicitly presupposes, the task becomes one of identifying the more harmful error, and Justice Brennan and his colleagues had little difficulty in determining that the very existence of the First Amendment implied that nonpublication of truth was more harmful than publication of falsity.[9] From this analysis there emerged a concern with the chilling effect as the phenomenon by which the very existence of potential liability can stifle the publication of truth in a world of uncertainty. Risk-averse publishers will seek to avoid liability under conditions of uncertainty by refraining from publishing material that might produce such liability, even though some of that material will turn out in fact to be true. In order to minimize this chilling effect, the *Sullivan* Court imposed a collection of stringent constitutional limitations on the common-law libel, most of them directed at eliminating the allegedly publication-deterrent consequences of common-law strict liability. After *New York Times v. Sullivan*, public officials can recover libel damages[10] only upon a showing with "convincing clarity" (a burden of proof somewhat higher than the normal preponderance of the evidence standard applied in civil litigation[11] that factually false material had been published with actual knowledge or actual suspicion of its falsity[12] at the time of publication. Several years later the Supreme Court brought nonofficial public figures within the ambit of the *New York Times v. Sullivan* rule,[13] and American libel law has not been the same since.[14]

At the heart of Justice Brennan's opinion for the Court is his insistence that "debate on public issues should be uninhibited, robust and wide-open, and that it may well include vehement, caustic, and sometimes unpleasantly sharp attacks on government and public officials."[15] And in the ensuing pages of the opinion Justice Brennan made clear that this environment of "uninhibited, robust and wide-open" debate on public issues could exist only with a constitutional "rule that prohibits a public official from recovering damages for a defamatory falsehood relating to his official conduct unless he proves that the statement was made with 'actual malice'—that is, with knowledge that it was false or with reckless disregard of whether it was false or not."[16]

New York Times v. Sullivan thus posits a relationship between its constitutional rule for defamation—the independent variable, if you will—and the condition of robust public debate—the dependent variable. More specifically, the *Sullivan* outcome and rule hinge on the view that the actual malice rule is a necessary even if not a sufficient condition for genuinely uninhibited, robust, and wide-open public debate to flourish. Were such robust public debate possible without disabling public officials from the libel remedies to which they would otherwise have access under the common law of libel, the Court plainly believed, then there would have been no need to set aside several centuries of a developed common-law doctrine.[17] Only because doing so was necessary for the state of affairs that the Court found constitutionally obligatory was the common-law approach to libel set aside in the name of the First Amendment.

New York Times v. Sullivan therefore rests on an empirical proposition about the relationship of libel law to the character of public debate, a relationship in which the common-law exercises a substantial constraint on the potential partici-pants in a robust public debate, and thus significantly decreases the probability that such robust debate will occur and decreases the vigor and thus the value of such debate when it does occur. Indeed, the most accurate reading of the Court's opinion does not even put the empirical question in these probabilistic terms, and clearly suggests that the actual malice rule is a necessary condition in the strong sense of that term—without that rule there will not exist robust public debate about the qualifications and performance of public officials.

This particular empirical proposition had been no part of the trial below, and not even of any attempt at an empirical showing before the Supreme Court itself. Rather, the Court, as it does far more often than is ordinarily assumed by those who take the exercise of legal reasoning to be a substantially logical or de-ductive or even interpretive exercise, simply announced its empirical conclusion and that was that. But because the empirical link between the elimination of the common-law rule and the existence in fact of robust public debate on matters of public importance is so important, it seems long overdue to examine more closely the Court's crucial but scarcely elaborated conclusion about the relationship among libel law, press content, and an environment characterized by vigorous public debate.

TESTING THE *SULLIVAN* TEST

The empirical keystone of *New York Times v. Sullivan*'s arch is certainly a reasonable one, and its very reasonableness has arguably helped forestall serious attempts to examine its soundness.[18] We all know that potential legal liability is intended to, and often does, lessen the incidence of the behavior at which it is directed, and so we rarely worry about whether it is true that laws against murder reduce the incidence of murder, whether speed limits lower the speeds at which people drive on the highways, and whether penalties for tax evasion increase the incidence of income tax compliance. In similar fashion, therefore, the Supreme Court hardly paused before reaching the conclusion that laws penalizing some aspects of robust public debate would significantly reduce the incidence and robustness of that debate.

Yet, although the truth of this empirical proposition was accepted without hesitation by the Supreme Court, and although its truth is asserted with considerable frequency by American journalists, and increasingly by journalists throughout in the rest of the world, a look outside the United States suggests that the empirical link that forms the linchpin of *New York Times v. Sullivan* may not exist, or at least may be far more attenuated and far more contingent than the Supreme Court in *Sullivan* supposed.

Consider the example of Australia. Although the libel laws in both Australia and the United States emerged from the same English common-law roots, the two are now dramatically different from each other. Until recently, Australia, more than any other developed common-law country, adhered to the common law of libel in its most stringent version—strict liability with no requirement that the plaintiff in order to make out a cause of action show either negligence or malice; truth being an affirmative defense rather than falsity being a component of the plaintiff's burden of proof[19] (and truth itself is only an absolute defense in four states—Victoria, Western Australia, South Australia, and the Northern Territories—whereas in New South Wales, Queensland, Tasmania, and the Australian Capital Territory only truth combined with public benefit/interest is a defense); no absolute protection for opinion[20]; and no defense of fair comment unless on true facts.[21]

Australian libel law is not only stringent in fact, indeed slightly more stringent than the common-law rule that the Supreme Court overturned in *Sullivan,* but it is widely used. Although the frequency of libel suits against the media in Australia is not nearly as frequent as Australian journalists maintain,[22] libel litigation is still a prominent feature of the Australian media and legal landscape. Libel actions are common and widely publicized, recoveries are frequent (former prime minister Bob Hawke reportedly was fond of describing the rooms in his house by reference to the name of the newspaper whose libel judgment in Hawke's favor had paid for the cost of renovations), the technicalities of libel law are a common focus of legal commentary, and the plaintiffs are often not just aggrieved "cranks," but instead many of the nation's most prominent political and public figures.

In recent years the Australian High Court has made some moves in the direction of recognizing implied free speech and free press concepts in the Australian constitution, which on its face contains no bill of rights in general and no rights to free speech and free press in particular.[23] And for a time the same court appeared willing to use its newly recognized constitutional rights as the springboard for imposing substantial limitations on the common law of libel and slander as they had developed in the Australian context.[24] Yet the High Court has substantially, even if not completely, backed away from this approach,[25] and both the courts and law reform commissions at both federal and state levels have explicitly rejected taking Australia in a *Sullivan* direction. As a result, the Australian common law of defamation has moved slightly away from its pre-1994 stringency, but not much. At the beginning of the twenty-first century, Australian defamation doctrine is characterized far more by its differences from American constitutionalized libel law than by any small areas of similarity.[26]

Surprisingly, however, and despite the pervasiveness of a regime of frequently enforced and stringent defamation law, even the most cursory examination of the Australian media reveals press practice and public debate that appears by all accounts to be as uninhibited, robust, and wide-open as that in the United States, and as that to which Justice Brennan was aiming in *New York Times v. Sullivan*. It is important that we scrutinize this seeming counter-intuitive state of affairs, but in order to examine the degree of robustness and uninhibitedness more closely, it will be useful to disentangle robustness and uninhibitedness into three separate elements—first, investigative journalism about official and public institution misconduct; second, strong substantive critique of policymakers and official policy; and, third, harsh, intemperate, and inflammatory language and commentary about those in authority.

Looking first at investigative journalism, it is not implausible to conclude that the culture of investigative journalism is at least as strong in Australia as it is in the United States. It is true that, as in the United States, Australian journalists constantly bemoan the constraints of the law, and, also as in the United States, bemoan even more the financial pressures in general and an increasingly profit-driven journalism in particular that have led mainstream newspapers and broadcasters to allocate fewer resources to investigative journalism.[27] Nevertheless, extremely hard-hitting investigative reporting of official misconduct is a pervasive feature of the Australian media environment. The Australian Broadcasting

Corporation's *Four Corners* and *7:30 Report,* for example, are as aggressive, and probably more so, than *60 Minutes, 20/20, Dateline,* and local investigative reporting on local television. The investigative tactics of Chris Masters now, and Derryn Hinch in the past, both prominent Australian television investigative reporters, include ambush interviews of major political figures and policymakers, secret cameras, hidden microphones, insinuations about undocumented misconduct, and broad speculation on the basis of limited facts.[28] In numerous respects, the tactics of Masters, Hinch, and quite a few others go at least as far and probably beyond what CBS, NBC, ABC, CNN, and Fox would countenance. If American network investigative journalism strives to stay at least slightly above the level of the tabloids, such restraint appears less often to be exercised in Australia, even though the topics are more the topics of policy and policymakers than the escapades of entertainers.

The same degree of hard-edged flamboyance even in investigating the behavior of political and business leaders applies to print investigative reporting. The major Australian newspapers—the *Sydney Morning Herald,* the *Melbourne Age,* the *Australian,* the *Canberra Times* (on national political matters), and several others—all have full-time investigative reporters on their staffs, and all feature scandal-focused investigative reports on their front pages with some frequency, often with headlines that are distinctly tabloidesque. Of particular interest is the way in which the focus of these exposés is not limited to the petty graft and bureaucratic featherbedding that characterizes much of American print investigative journalism. Rather, a great deal of Australian investigative journalism is about corruption and malfeasance at the highest levels of state and national government, and there is plainly little reluctance to name names in the course of the reporting.[29]

If we turn from investigation to editorial critique, we see an Australian press that is similarly uninhibited. Official policy, including both the traditional sacred cows of national security and the performance of the judiciary, is fair game not only on the editorial pages of newspapers and magazines, but also, as is often the standard practice in much of the world outside of the United States, throughout the reporting parts of newspapers, magazines, and television news broadcasts. Few policies or policymakers are immune from criticism, and in recent years press criticism of public policy and of the particular individuals who make it have been particularly harsh with respect to Australian cooperation with the United States in Iraq, to immigration policy, to land policy in the context of aboriginal land claims based on "native title," to government contracting on large public works projects, and even to numerous dimensions of the seemingly highly successful 2000 Summer Olympic Games.

Yet however robust the Australian press is in terms of investigative journalism and criticism of officials and their policies, it is in their use of intemperate invective that the Australian press truly shines. Unlike the *New York Times,* for example, Australian mainstream newspapers will not censor even the gamiest language of political debate, and if a politician uses a four-letter word, he is likely to see his exact language in print. Personal attacks—"scumbag" is a common term of political abuse both inside and outside the halls of Parliament—are common and eagerly reported in the newspapers, in newsmagazines, on television, and of course on the Internet. Letters and commentary containing words like "shit" and "fuck" are common even in mainstream newspapers such as the *Sydney Morning Herald.* And even when editorializing in their own voice rather than reporting the words of others, Australian newspapers—and by no means only the tabloids—display a tendency toward the inflammatory and the ad hominem that goes considerably beyond the degree of intemperateness that one finds in the daily and weekly American mainstream press.

Although Australia may be among the most extreme, the same environment exists in most other common-law countries, all of which also have libel laws more stringent[30] and more frequently enforced than is the case in the United States.[31] The style of the English tabloids is of course well-known, but their counterparts exist in South Africa and India as well as in Canada and New Zealand. The Israeli media is every bit as rough-and-tumble as its parliamentary debate, where members of the Knesset display their rancor at each other with abandon. Charges of official corruption are common in the Hong Kong newspapers, and the appalling repression of the press in Zimbabwe came about because the press operated in a way that treated President Mugabe as fair game. Throughout the world, or at least throughout the common-law world, it seems the existence of libel laws considerably stricter than post–*New York Times v. Sullivan* American libel law has done little to restrain or stifle press tendencies to be investigative, questioning, challenging, nasty, and often personal.

@ @ @

As is well-known, comparative research into political and social phenomena is bedeviled by an excess of variables. Although Australia is moderately similar to the United States in a number of dimensions—distrust of government, frontier heritage, vast land area, and federal system, to name a few—it is quite different in many others. We can perhaps suspect on the Australian evidence that the American press would look like the American press even in the absence of *New York Times v. Sullivan* and that the Australian press would be as it is even with an Australian *Sullivan* equivalent, but of course we cannot be sure, and perhaps we cannot even be confident enough to satisfy the standards of justified empirical confidence.

In the face of the often insurmountable difficulties in doing rigorous comparative political research, I am now, with a colleague, testing what we might call the *Sullivan* hypothesis in a more systematic way, largely with the assistance of one of the great providers of natural experiments, the American federal system. *New York Times v. Sullivan,* as the Court itself observed, was not the first American judicial decision to reach *Sullivan*'s conclusion. Fifty-six years earlier, in *Coleman v. McClennan,*[32] the Supreme Court of Kansas had cast aside much of the common law of libel and adopted a rule of intentional defamation with respect to attacks on public officials that was remarkably similar to the rule the U.S. Supreme Court would set forth in *Sullivan.*

For research purposes, one of the most important features of *Coleman v. McClennan* is that none of Kansas's neighbors followed *Coleman*'s lead. While Kansas made public official libel litigation vastly more difficult, Nebraska, Missouri, Arkansas, Illinois, Minnesota, and Oklahoma continued, in most cases up until *Sullivan* itself, to adhere to much of the common law and thus to maintain a regime of defamation law that resembled that of contemporaneous England far more than it resembled the law in Kansas.

If the *Sullivan* hypothesis is sound, then we should expect to see, starting shortly after the 1908 date of *Coleman,* a divergence between Kansas media and that in otherwise similar states with respect to most of the major indicia of uninhibited, robust, and wide-open public debate and criticism. In order to test this, we will perform rigorous content analyses focusing on criticism of public officials and candidates for public office for Kansas, Arkansas, Illinois, Missouri, and Nebraska for at least two newspapers per state, and for the years 1898 to 1918, that being ten years before and ten years after *Coleman.* A preliminary glance at the relevant newspaper archives suggests that what we have seen in Australia may also be the case in the American states: the period from 1898 to 1918 saw few if any changes in the Kansas media's willingness to be intemperate and direct in personal attack, and harsh in criticism of public policy, that were not also present in roughly the same degree in all of the other states. If this impression is confirmed by more rigorous content analysis, the implications of the Australian case study—that an actual malice rule is not a necessary condition for an uninhibited, robust, wide-open, and intemperate public debate about politicians and policies, and that the *Sullivan* hypothesis may not be true—may not be unique to Australia, and may have wider-ranging application.

If this conclusion about the robustness of public debate and the aggressiveness of press behavior even in countries with stringent libel regimes is sound, and if the example of Australia—as well as experience in other countries with libel laws more stringent than those in the United States but with a press and public debate that appears as vigorous, wide-open, and robust—shows that *New York Times v. Sullivan* makes less of a difference than Justice Brennan thought in 1964 and most journalists think now, then what might explain this counter-intuitive conclusion? How could it be that frequent and expensive press liability for defamation makes so little difference to press content?

We know, of course, that few regimes of legal regulation are 100 percent effective. Speed limits do not guarantee that all drivers will drive no faster than the posted rate, just as we know that the tax laws do not eliminate tax evasion and that Supreme Court decisions about school prayer have not completely ended the practice of organized prayer in the public schools any more than Supreme Court decisions about the Fourth and Fifth Amendments have brought an end to police misconduct. Indeed, we know, and have known since revolutionary times, that the existence of libel laws, including the late eighteenth-century laws of seditious libel, do not totally eliminate the press behavior that those laws, sometimes wisely and sometimes unwisely, have attempted to prevent.

Yet despite the fact that libel laws are no more likely to be completely effective than are the laws against speeding, tax evasion, shoplifting, and insider trading, we also recognize that most regulatory laws do decrease the incidence of the behavior at which they are directed. Driving is slower with a posted speed limit than without, tax compliance is at a higher rate than would be the case were taxation a voluntary enterprise, and there is less insider trading since the enactment of the securities laws than there was before. Our question, then, is not whether Australia, for example, has a degree of noncompliance with its defamation law, for of course it does. But if, as appears to be the case, it is not just that Australia's defamation laws are no more perfectly effective than its traffic laws and tax laws, but instead that the stringency of those laws is largely to no effect at all on press content, then we genuinely have a phenomenon in need of explanation. And in trying to explain why stringent libel laws have far less effect than Justice Brennan and others have assumed, a related series of hypotheses are worth exploring.

Perhaps the most plausible explanation is that the *New York Times* was bluffing in *Sullivan,* and that the Supreme Court blinked. That is, although the *New York Times* claimed that it would refrain from publishing strong critiques of officials and official policy unless the Supreme Court modified the common-law rules for liability, and although perhaps the *Times* might have done so in the narrowly similar context of a paid advertisement in a state which had targeted the *Times* for intimidation, and in which the *Times* sold few copies and virtually no advertising, we cannot be sure how the *Times* would actually have behaved had the outcome in its case been different. Perhaps instead of cowering in the face of potential legal liability, the *Times* simply would have proceeded as they had before. Perhaps journalistic norms of when a story is worth reporting and when there is sufficient confidence in factual allegations of wrongdoing to report them are the primary determinants of journalistic behavior, and that most reporters and editors treat defamation liability for pursuing what they perceive to be good journalism as the publisher's problem and not theirs. And if it is also the case that publishers share these values to a sufficient extent that they are willing to absorb the costs, then it may turn out that the press operates under something that looks like the *Sullivan* rule even in the absence of *Sullivan*.

There is some evidence that this explanation is actually the case. Although reporters and editors are eager to claim that they have been chilled by the threat of legal liability,[33] and although refraining from engaging in legally risky behavior seems rational in this context,[34] a significant number of American journalists maintain that the existence of potential libel litigation has no effect on their news judgment.[35] Most Australian reporters' and editors' behavior concerning libel is similar to that of most American reporters and editors, and most Australian publishers do not tell their reporters and editors to do otherwise. It is true that this is a costly strategy, because libel judgments have to be paid and libel lawyers have to be hired, but most Australian publishers treat libel as a cost of doing business, setting aside a reserve for this purpose and not finding it necessary or even desirable to treat litigation minimization as a significant part of the responsibilities of their reporters and editors.[36] And when the norms and values of journalism reinforce or require risky behavior on the part of journalists, editors, and publishers, the chilling power of libel law will be much less. So, if—as is often the case—journalistic awards, opportunities for professional recognition, routes to professional esteem, and avenues for promotion, among many other motivational factors, are all a function of doing just the kind of journalism that increases the likelihood of a libel suit, it may turn out that strong professional norms will more than counteract the chilling effect of libel law. Unless and until journalists are rewarded for minimizing libel exposure, which is usually not the case, then we should not expect the potential for defamation liability to have a significant effect on journalistic behavior, no matter how much—within reason—it costs the publishers and the shareholders to support this environment. Indeed, even publishers who wish to treat minimizing libel exposure as an important goal may well discover that there is a significant principal-agent problem as reporters and editors pursue goals that are helpful to their own professional advancement and reputation even as the pursuit of those goals is detrimental to the publisher's bottom line.

This phenomenon of significant journalistic disregard of the potential for legal liability is exacerbated by the existence of what economists typically refer to as *moral hazard,* the way in which insured actors will engage in socially detrimental risky behavior because insurance or indemnification removes from the actors the consequences of their own actions. As is well known but rarely discussed by journalists anguishing about the chilling effect, libel insurance is widespread, and most libel defendants in the United States and, increasingly, elsewhere are protected by libel insurance, usually offered by one of the four companies—three in the United States and one in Bermuda—that specialize in libel coverage. Although the very largest of publishing conglomerates are self-insurers, in general the world of libel litigation exists, like the world of automobile accident and products liability litigation, in a milieu in which the role of insurance looms large.

The typical libel policy contains a moderately high deductible—commonly $50,000 but sometimes higher and occasionally as low as $10,000—and very high policy limits. Coverage to $5 million or even $10 million is not uncommon. So although it is often thought that the chilling effect comes from the occasional (but almost always reversed on appeal) very large judgment, the actual chilling is much more likely to come from the effect of the high deductible on smaller publications than it is to come from the remote possibility of a huge and uninsured verdict. Ironically, it is not the *New York Times,* for whom covering the first $50,000 would not be a problem, that needs to worry about the chilling effect, but those publications whose noninsurable exposure is a much greater percentage of their operating capital.

Although insurance rates obviously vary with litigation experience, the rise in rates that is likely to come from frequently being the target of a libel suit has less of an effect than we might suppose because even heavy litigation turns out to be a very small part of the financial picture of the typical media organization. When American Media, publisher of the *National Enquirer, Star,* and similar publications reported its legal expenses to the Securities and Exchange Commission a few years ago, for example, it turned out that legal expenses—insurance, litigation, settlements, judgments, and prepublication legal scrutiny—amounted to, on average, less than 1 percent of gross revenues and less than 10 percent of after-tax profits. This was a significant expenditure, to be sure, but nothing like the kind of legal expenses that one would see for the manufacturers of chain saws, the operators of ski areas, and the providers of health care. In the full spectrum of profit-seeking enterprises, therefore, legal costs, not only in the United States after *Sullivan,* but in the rest of the common-law world as well, turn out to constitute a relatively small sum of money. Indeed, libel insurance rates are not only low in absolute terms, but are declining as the amount of libel litigation decreases, and the likelihood of plaintiffs' success decreases as well.[37] A representative of one of the major insurance carriers predicted in 1998 a 25 percent reduction in libel insurance premiums over the ensuing five years.[38]

It turns out, therefore, that the behavior of journalists in the face of libel law is not that different from the behavior of any other moderately wealthy actor with strong preferences and highly variable potential costs that even at the higher ranges of the variation exist in the flatter part of the actor's marginal utility curve. Just as moderately wealthy people will pay a thousand dollars to see the Super Bowl or five hundred dollars for dinner at a three-star restaurant in Paris even though they would of course prefer to pay half those sums, so too will moderately wealthy news organizations operating in a milieu of strong journalistic norms (preferences) pay a reasonably high price (in libel costs) in order to report what *they* and not the courts deem worthy of publication. These news organizations would of course prefer to pay less, but every case of inelasticity of demand provides support for the proposition that the desire to minimize expenditures is often insufficient to deter actors from indulging preferences that they deem especially important.

The best support for this hypothesis about the limited effect of cost minimization upon journalistic norms comes from the way in which the elite press behaves, or at least claims to behave, in the face of threats of advertiser withdrawal. As is well-known, advertisers often threaten to withhold advertising dollars when print and broadcast outlets contain material inconsistent with the advertiser's interests. Yet although such threats are common, and although some advertisers actually carry them out, it remains an article of faith in the elite press that it is better to absorb the losses than to subject media content to such external pressures.[39] The very fact that a significant number of the "Darts" for unprofessional behavior "awarded" in the *Columbia Journalism Review* are aimed at newspapers or broadcasters who succumb to financial pressures from advertisers to modify press content reinforces the view that the norms of journalism require journalists and their employers to immunize their news judgment from the financial consequences of that judgment.

If this norm holds, however, then there is no reason to believe that it should not apply as much to the external pressure of libel judgments as to the external pressure of advertiser withdrawal. And thus when we see a press whose content is more uninhibited than the existence of potential defamation liability would suggest, we need to remind ourselves that the same press is more uninhibited than the existence of potential advertiser withdrawal would suggest, and what emerges is a picture of a press whose own norms are such that absorbing some costs in order to maintain those norms is a not uncommon occurrence.

The combination of strong journalistic norms, libel insurance, and legal costs that even at their worst are a relatively small proportion of net worth (or any other measure of a publication's wealth) thus serves to make press content far more impervious to libel law than the traditional picture assumes. There are, to be sure, factors operating in the opposite direction. The economics of information and the economics of newspapers, for example, combine to produce an environment in which the marginal cost of producing an additional legally risky news item is likely to be considerably greater than the marginal revenue derived from that item.[40] Except in the tabloids and in the "Read All About It!" scenes in 1930s movies, sales, especially in the newspaper industry, are only slightly a function of the desire of readers to read a particular story. So the incentives to nonpublication of legally risky items are, at the margin, stronger than they would be for the manufacturer of a legally risky product to decide to not bring out a new and even legally riskier product line. These and related factors are not insignificant, yet actual press content reveals that such considerations plainly play a relatively small role.

CONCLUSION: PRESS INCENTIVES AND PRESS CONTENT
The principal lesson of the foregoing is that *New York Times v. Sullivan* may have been less necessary to the environment of public debate than is commonly supposed. Although it was then and is still necessary for the First Amendment to be available to deal with just the kinds of potentially crippling attacks that the *Sullivan* scenario represented,[41] the Supreme Court's grandiose conclusions about the empirical underpinnings and empirical necessity of the actual malice rule are more debatable. In short, the examples from Australia and elsewhere suggest that the kind of aggressive press we now have may well have emerged even with a more modest legal outcome.

The consequence of the Supreme Court's approach in *Sullivan* was thus not only to adopt a more sweeping rule than may then have been necessary, but also to impose the costs of a regime of freedom of the press upon the victims of negligent but legally immune press behavior. When reporters behave as if the *Sullivan* rule were the law even if it is not, as is arguably the case in Australia, the cost of a free press is borne by the publishers rather than by the victims of press misconduct. Moreover, much of this cost is then passed along to newspaper buyers—the public—and to a lesser extent (the relationship between newspaper circulation and newsstand price is notoriously inelastic, but even small changes in circulation may affect much more elastic advertising rates) advertisers, both of which seem better candidates for paying the cost of a free press. Indeed, if we think that the people are the most suitable ones to bear the cost of a free press, then we might even imagine forms of publicly subsidized libel insurance, much like publicly subsidized flood insurance,[42] to better allocate the costs of a free press away from its victims and toward the public who are the ultimate beneficiaries.

These possibilities for change, however, may have been possibilities better considered in 1964 than they are now. Law is path-dependent, and what might have been a serious possibility then may not be a serious possibility now, especially as publishers, editors, and public figures have adapted to a regime that has now been in place for forty years. Moreover, just as the Supreme Court may have been mistaken in its speculations about the relationship between libel law and press content, so too may the common law have been mistaken about the relationship between libel remedies and public behavior. One of the chief justifications for libel law has always been that it is necessary to control press untruths in order to encourage people to hold public office, but again this may not be the case. It is impossible in this essay to deal with the empirical side of the value of libel remedies, but it may be that there as well the traditional assumptions are in need of reexamination. It may perhaps turn out that libel law itself is no more necessary, except at the extremes, than was the Supreme Court's attempt to control it. Just as the behavior of reporters, editors, and publishers may turn out to be more impervious to legal control than the Supreme Court thought, so too may the behavior of those in public life, or who are considering entering it, be less dependent on the availability of legal remedies for falsity than the common law has traditionally assumed. Without an examination of this alongside an examination of the relationship between libel law and press behavior, it would be impossible to tell whether changes in the current state of affairs would be desirable, even assuming it were now possible to roll back time and produce that state of affairs.

As noted above, libel is but one point of intersection between the law and press content, and a full analysis of the relationship between press law and press content would have to take account of the full array of press-restricting (or press-promoting) laws. This is especially important, because on occasion the hydraulics of regulation are such that lesser regulation in one area may produce greater regulation in another, and so too with laws that promote rather than restrict press independence. Indeed, there is an example from Australian libel law itself, in that both the law of parliamentary privilege and the use of that privilege by political figures and the press to immunize otherwise actionable statements from legal action has been widespread. Thus, the law of parliamentary privilege may have developed in the common law[43] as a response to many of the same instincts that were crystallized as a matter of constitutional law by the Supreme Court in *Sullivan*. This is only a small corner of the Australian law of defamation, but it does illustrate the way in which different components of the law may be more interrelated than is ordinarily assumed.

Nevertheless, looking at the actual content of the press provides a better way of evaluating the effect of law on press freedom than the ordinary approach of examining laws in the abstract. When we look at press content itself in looking at press law, we can begin to glimpse the relationship of press laws to numerous other economic, sociological, institutional, cultural, and psychological factors that may far more than the law determine press content. Although law is rarely irrelevant, neither is it as important as many, especially lawyers, often suppose. Libel law has an effect on press content, but its effect is not nearly as large as is often argued. Considerably larger are those economic factors and institutional pressures that may at times enable the press to transcend the formal limitations of libel and other press-controlling laws, but which may just as often impose even greater restrictions than the law could ever hope to achieve.[44]

NOTES

Earlier versions of this essay were presented at the Faculty Research Seminar of the John F. Kennedy School of Government, at the Media Law Center of the University of New South Wales, at the Australian National University, and at the National University of Singapore. I have benefited from numerous conversations with Michael Chesterman and Matthew Stephenson.

1. See especially *New York Times Co. v. United States* (Pentagon Papers Case), 403 U.S. 713 (1971). See also *Snepp v. United States*, 444 U.S. 507 (1980); *United States v. Progressive, Inc.*, 467 F. Supp. 990 (W.D. Wis. 1979), case dismissed voluntarily, 610 F.2d 819 (7th Cir. 1979); Harry Kalven Jr., "Even When a Nation Is at War," *Harvard Law Review* 85 (1971): 3; Symposium, "National Security and the First Amendment," *William and Mary Law Review* 26 (1985): 715.

2. See *Minneapolis v. Star* and *Tribune Co. v. Minnesota Commission of Revenue*, 460 U.S. 575 (1983); *Grosjean v. American Press Co.*, 297 U.S. 233 (1936).

3. See *Nebraska Press Ass'n v. Stuart*, 427 U.S. 539 (1976); *Sheppard v. Maxwell*, 384 U.S. 333 (1966).

4. See *Bartnicki v. Vopper*, 121 S. Ct. 1753 (2001); *Landmark Communications, Inc. v. Virginia*, 435 U.S. 829 (1978).

5. The licensing of journalists, so patently unconstitutional in the United States as never to have generated a Supreme Court (or lower court) opinion, is the subject of lively debate elsewhere. See Michael Perkins, "International Human Rights and the Collegiation of Journalists: The Case of Costa Rica," *Communications Law and Policy* 4 (1999): 59.

6. *New York Times v. Sullivan,* 376 U.S. 254 (1964). On the background of the case and its subsequent impact, see Anthony Lewis, *Make No Law: The Sullivan Case and the First Amendment* (New York: Vintage Books, 1991). The classic contemporaneous analysis is Harry Kalven Jr., "The *New York Times* Case: A Note on 'The Central Meaning of the First Amendment,'" *Supreme Court Review* 1964 (1964): 191.

7. *Beauharnais v. Illinois,* 343 U.S. 250 (1952).

8. See Frederick Schauer, "Fear, Risk, and the First Amendment: Unraveling the 'Chilling Effect,'" *Boston University Law Review* 58 (1978): 685.

9. In decision-theoretic terms, we can say that the Type I error (the false negative) is the nonpublication of truth, and the Type II (the false positive) error is the publication of falsity. The analytic precursors of seeing the First Amendment in this decision-theoretic way can be found in Justice Brennan's opinions in *Smith v. California,* 361 U.S. 147 (1959), and *Speiser v. Randall,* 357 U.S. 513 (1958). See also In re Winship, 387 U.S. 358 (1970).

10. Or, more rarely, spur the initiation of a criminal prosecution. *Garrison v. Louisiana,* 379 U.S. 64 (1964).

11. See Frederick Schauer and Richard Zeckhauser, "On the Degree of Confidence for Adverse Decisions," *Journal of Legal Studies* 25 (1996): 27.

12. *Sullivan* refers to "reckless disregard" as an alternative basis for liability to actual knowledge of falsity, but subsequently the Court made clear that "reckless disregard" was not to be equated with recklessness or gross negligence, but instead required proof that the defendant "in fact entertained serious doubts as to the truth of his publication." *St. Amant v. Thompson,* 390 U.S. 727 (1968).

13. *Curtis Publishing Co. v. Butts* and *Associated Press v. Walker,* 388 U.S. 130 (1967).

14. Although the Supreme Court in *Gertz v. Robert Welch, Inc.,* 418 U.S. 323 (1974), refused to extend the *Sullivan* actual malice rule to plaintiffs who were neither public officials nor public figures, the *Gertz* Court did hold that strict liability (as opposed to requiring proof of the publisher's negligence) was inconsistent with the mandates of the First Amendment even for such private figures, and in doing so extended First Amendment constraints on defamation law even further.

15. *New York Times v. Sullivan,* 376 U.S. 254 (1964), at 270.

16. *New York Times v. Sullivan,* 376 U.S. 254 (1964), at 279–80.

17. Nor, of course, any need to disable genuinely aggrieved plaintiffs from the remedies to which they would otherwise be entitled. This may not be apparent in cases like *Sullivan* itself, where the damage to Commissioner Sullivan is somewhat hard to fathom, but is easier to see in cases like *Ocala Star-Banner Co. v. Damron,* 221 So.2d 459 (Fla. Dist. Ct. App. 1969), *cause dismissed,* 231 So.2d 822 (Fla. 1970), *rev'd,* 401 U.S. 295 (1971), in which an editor's extreme negligence allowed the wrong person to be accused of a crime in the newspaper, and in which the negligently false attribution of criminal behavior produced both political and financial losses for the erroneously identified plaintiff. I discuss this case in Frederick Schauer, "Uncoupling Free Speech," *Columbia Law Review* 92 (1992): 1321, at 1326–38.

18. For an empirical study of the chilling effect in the libel context, using for its methodology a survey of newspaper editors, see Stephen M. Renas, Charles J. Hartman, and James L. Walker, "An Empirical Analysis of the Chilling Effect," in *The Cost of Libel: Economic and Policy Implications,* edited by Everette E. Dennis and Eli M. Noam (New York: Columbia Univ. Press, 1989), 41. Renas, Hartman, and Walker conclude that the standard of proof, the central issue in *Sullivan,* does make a difference in the willingness of editors to publish investigative material, but they also conclude that the degree of willingness takes place largely in the context of noncompetitive markets. Even if the study's methodology leads to confidence in its results, a debatable proposition in light of the ease with which survey respondents could see the survey as essentially a referendum by newspaper editors on the value of the *Sullivan* rule, its conclusions are not inconsistent with the view that in competitive markets numerous factors other than the rule of legal liability play a greater role in determining what will and will not be published.

19. Placing the burden of proof on the plaintiff to show falsity is implicit but not expressed in *Sullivan,* but the Supreme Court has subsequently made clear that, unlike at common law (and unlike in Australia), the plaintiff must prove falsity in all media defamation cases, and not just those involving public officials and public figures. See *Philadelphia Newspapers, Inc. v. Hepps,* 475 U.S. 767 (1986).

20. See *Peterson v. Advertiser Newspapers* (1995) S.A.S.R. 152.

21. See T. K. Tobin and M. G. Sexton, *Australian Defamation Law and Practice* (Sydney: Butterworths, 1991); Michael Tilbury, "Uniformity, the Constitution and Australian Defamation Law at the Turn of the Century," in *Torts Tomorrow: A Tribute to John Fleming,* edited by Nicholas J. Mullany and Allen M. Linden (Pyrmont, Australia: LBC Information Services, 1998), 244–70.

22. See *Defamation,* New South Wales Law Reform Commission Discussion Paper No. 32 (August 1993). See also Tilbury, "Uniformity," 253 n. 64.

23. *Australian Capital Television v. Commonwealth* and *Nationwide News v Wills* (1992) 177 CLR 106.

24. See especially *Theophanous v. The Herald and Weekly Times, Ltd.* (1994) 182 CLR 104; *Stephens v. West Australian Newspapers, Ltd.* (1994) 182 CLR 211.

25. See *Lange v Australian Broadcasting Corporation* (1997) 189 CLR 520.

26. See Richard Potter, "The Development of Freedom of Speech Defences to Defamation in Australia and Other Common Law Jurisdictions," *Media and Arts Law Review* 3 (1998): 82–92.

27. See Chris Masters, *Not for Publication* (Sydney: ABC Books, 2002); "The Death of Investigative Journalism," http://www.uws.edu.au/media/general/1999/july99/jurno.html, accessed February 2003; Australian Centre for Independent Journalism, http://acij.uts.edu.au/old_acij/ACIJ/acij.html, accessed February 2003.

28. See the descriptions of Australian journalistic practices in *Australian Broadcasting Corporation v. Lenah Game Meats* (2001) 185 ALR 1. See also Allens Arthur Robinson, "Journalism, Privacy, and the High Court," *Focus: Media* (April 2002).

29. More than one political figure, and at least one entire state government, has been brought down by aggressive print investigative reporting. See Alan Knight, "Truth, Politics, and the Limits of Investigative Journalism," *Central Queensland University Drawingboard,* www.econ.usyd.edu.au/drawingboard/digest/0205/knight.html, accessed February 2003.

30. Explicit rejection of *New York Times v. Sullivan* is a common feature of the legal terrain in much

of the Commonwealth. See, for example, *Lange v. Australian Broadcasting Corporation* (1997) 189 CLR 520; *Hill v. Church of Scientology* (1995) 126 DLR (4th 174) S.C.C. (Canada).

31. See Ian Loveland, ed., *Importing the First Amendment: Press Law in Great Britain, Canada, and Australia* (Oxford: Hart Publishing, 2001).

32. *Coleman v. McClennan,* 78 Kan. 711, 98 P. 281 (Kan. 1908).

33. See Renas, Hartman, and Noam, "An Empirical Analysis."

34. See Alain Sheer and Askhar Zardkoohi, "An Analysis of the Economic Efficiency of the Law of Defamation," *Northwestern University Law Review* 80 (1985): 364.

35. See David A. Anderson, "Libel and Press Self-Censorship," *Texas Law Review* 53 (1975): 422, quote at 434; David A. Hollander, "The Economics of Libel Litigation," in Dennis and Noam, eds., *The Cost of Libel,* note 26, p. 257–81, quote at 258 n. 3; Barry F. Smith, "The Rising Tide of Libel Litigation: Implications of the Gertz Negligence Rules," *Montana Law Review* 44 (1983): 71, quote at 87.

36. Interview by the author with Jack Waterford, editor, *Canberra Times,* Canberra, Australia, July 22, 1993.

37. In 1995–1996, according to the Libel Defense Resource Center, an exclusively media- and defense-centered organization, defendants prevailed on motions to dismiss and summary judgment in 82.3 percent of cases in 1995–1996, and prevailed at trial in 84.6 percent of cases. Even putting aside appeals, therefore, plaintiffs prevail in only 2.7 percent of all cases filed.

38. See David B. Martens, "Libel: Are You Covered?" *NAA Presstime,* www.naa.org/presstime/9812/libel.html, accessed February 2003.

39. See Norman E. Isaacs, *Untended Gates: The Mismanaged Press* (New York: Columbia Univ. Press, 1986), 164–65; Tom Wicker, *On Press* (New York: Berkeley Books, 1979), 181–2.

40. For an application of broader points about the economics of information to First Amendment theory, see Daniel A. Farber, "Free Speech without Romance: Public Choice and the First Amendment," *Harvard Law Review* 105 (1990): 554.

41. At the time of the case, there were other suits pending against the *Times* and the other defendants, and $500,000 verdicts, uninsured, represented real money, to say nothing of multiple verdicts of that order of magnitude. Still, Australia, Great Britain, and other countries deal with that issue by lowering unjustifiably high awards (as is routinely done in the United States in tort cases generally, especially in recent years—see *BMW of North America v. Gore,* 517 U.S. 559 [1996]), and it is not entirely clear that the pervasive revamping of libel law represented by *Sullivan* was the only remedy available for the type of abuse that the facts of the case represent.

42. I develop these ideas at greater length in Schauer, "Uncoupling Free Speech."

43. On the potential ability of the common law to deal as well (or better) with press freedom issues than constitutional adjudication, see Richard Epstein, "Was *New York Times v. Sullivan* Wrong?" *University of Chicago Law Review* 53 (1986): 782.

44. John Stuart Mill's warnings in *On Liberty* about the ways in which social intolerance can be more inhibiting than legal intolerance are valuable in the press context as well, with the additional qualification that the social pressures on the press can come not only from external political and economic factors, but also from the internal norms of press behavior themselves.

PART TWO:
AT PRESENT

INTRODUCTION

JACK M. WEISS

Lawyers who represent media organizations in the courts, including myself, have devoted many hours to discussing the development of First Amendment law as it applies to journalists. I confess that not many minutes of those hours were devoted to the empirical literature of journalism, or its implications for First Amendment law.

The two essays in this section, by Michael Schudson and Regina Lawrence, challenge us to consider the relationship between these bodies of thought. Both insightfully address a bedrock assumption of First Amendment thinking: that the autonomy the Amendment affords the institutional press in fact meaningfully affects the content of press "output." Both question the same constitutional assumptions and draw upon much the same body of empirical data. But they reach quite different conclusions.

Professor Schudson implies that the "hands-off-the-press" law we identify with the First Amendment is relevant because the speech of journalists does remain autonomous—and beneficially so. He grants that there are many limits on what the press has to say. Nevertheless, he suggests that journalists are liberated from these constraints by competing forces. He notes how recurrent wildcard news events produce unmanaged, novel, sometimes diverse coverage; how even mundane governmental activities launch conflict that is hard for politicians to manage; and how many journalists maintain a skeptical "outsider" attitude.

Professor Lawrence sees a press world where watchdog and marketplace of ideas functions are heavily compromised in practice by influences at many levels, and she tentatively endorses a different vision of the First Amendment. In her view, the press is neither government watchdog nor government lapdog. While she rejects the view that the First Amendment is no more than an excuse for protecting profitable media organizations from competition, she describes the content of the news as heavily determined by nonlegal influences—and perhaps not strongly nurtured by press law.

These essays inspire a question from this media lawyer: In deciding critical First Amendment issues, should the courts pay more attention to empirical studies of U.S. press performance?

Suppose that we could invent a device for perfectly measuring the overall performance of the press on a "scale" of "robustness" suggested by Justice Brennan's opinion in *New York Times v. Sullivan*. If the American press were scoring a B- or even a C on the Brennan scale month in and month out, would it follow that press law landmarks like *Sullivan* itself should be revisited? Here are a few reasons why not.

First, generalized data do not tell the full story. The *Sullivan* actual malice rule would be worth its constitutional weight in gold even if it made the difference in the decision to publish only one Watergate-like (or Monicagate-like) revelation per generation. The same would be true if there were just one metro daily for which the rule frequently was key in deciding what to publish (thus earning that paper a B+ or better on the Brennan scale) for every hundred media outlets that published "indexed," "budget-impaired" grist and scored a C.

Second, the empirical evidence is often the *content* of media speech: is it sufficiently vigorous, independent, diverse and substantive? Or is it frivolous, uniform, kowtowing, and profit-driven? But it would be intensely problematic if judges—who are, after all, government officials—were to determine the parameters of constitutional protection for the press based upon inherently subjective notions of press content and performance.

Finally, our Constitution is designed to achieve a "*more* perfect Union." The proper question is not whether the performance of the American press squares in daily practice with the Supreme Court's lofty ideals. More appropriate is whether it comes closer to those ideals than it would if our modern First Amendment framework were substantially revised.

I have my doubts, then, about whether these essays should compel us to revise established First Amendment law. At the same time, I do not for a moment question the need for those of us who represent the news media in the courts to become knowledgeable and current in the empirical literature—which is all too absent from media law and First Amendment teaching in the law schools. These essays have given me a lot to think about and a lot to learn.

WHY DEMOCRACIES NEED AN UNLOVABLE PRESS

MICHAEL SCHUDSON

Alexis de Tocqueville, widely cited for his view that the American press is a necessary and vital institution for American democracy, did not actually have much affection for it. He objected to its violence and vulgarity. He saw it as a virtue of the American system that newspapers were widely dispersed around the country rather than concentrated in a capital city—they could do less harm this way. He confessed, "I admit that I do not feel toward freedom of the press that complete and instantaneous love which one accords to things by their nature supremely good. I love it more from considering the evils it prevents than on account of the good it does."[1]

It may well be, taking a leaf from Tocqueville, that today's efforts to make journalism more serious, more responsible, and, generally speaking, nicer are misplaced. I want to propose that most critics of journalism, in and outside journalism itself, have attacked just those features of the press that, for all their defects, best protect robust public discussion and promote democracy. The focus of the news media on events, rather than trends and structures; the fixation of the press on conflict whenever and wherever it erupts; the cynicism of journalists with respect to politics and politicians; and the alienation of journalists from the communities they cover make the media hard for people to love but hard for democracies to do without. These are the features that most regularly enable the press to maintain a capacity for subverting established power.

This is not to suggest that there is anything wrong with in-depth reporting of the sort that Pulitzer juries and media critics applaud and I greatly admire. Nor do I mean to suggest that the dialogue of democracy should jettison editorial writers, op-ed columnists, investigative reporters, and expert analysts who can produce gems of explanatory journalism. That would be absurd. But I do mean to suggest that the power of the press to afflict the comfortable derives more often than not from the journalistic equivalent of ambulance chasing. Just as the ambulance-chasing trial lawyer sees another person's tragedy as a million-dollar opportunity, the newshound reporter sees it as an attention-grabbing, career-advancing, front-page sensation. I want to explore here the ways the most narrow and unlovable features of news may make the most vital of contributions to democracy.

THE PRESS AS AN ESTABLISHMENT INSTITUTION

The press is presumably the bastion of free expression in a democracy, but too often it has been one of the institutions that limits the range of expression, especially expression that is critical of leading centers of power in society. Almost all social scientific studies of the news reveal that journalists themselves, of their own volition, limit the range of opinion present in the news. There are at least three significant ways this happens. First, there is source-dependence. Reporters rely on and reproduce the views of their primary sources, and these tend to be high government officials. Second, reporters and editors operate according to a set of professional norms that are themselves constraints on expression. Third, journalists operate within conventional bounds of opinion, opinions common among a largely secular, college-educated, upper middle class. All of this has been abundantly documented, including in the work of contributors to this volume, notably Lance Bennett, Tim Cook, and Regina Lawrence. I will quickly review this literature, but only as a preface to arguing that this account of the compliant press has been overdrawn.

DEPENDENCE ON OFFICIAL SOURCES Media scholars have consistently found that official sources dominate the news. This is invariably presented as a criticism of the media. If the media were to fulfill their democratic role, they would offer a wide variety of opinions and perspectives and would encourage citizens to choose among them in considering public policies. If the media allow politicians to set the public agenda, they may unduly narrow public discussion and so diminish democracy. This is the argument made, for instance, by W. Lance Bennett in his account of the "indexing" function of the press. For Bennett, the media "tend to 'index' the range of voices and viewpoints in both news and editorials according to the range of views expressed in mainstream government debate about a given topic." Bennett argues that this helps perpetuate a "world in which governments are able to define their own publics and where 'democracy' becomes whatever the government ends up doing."[2]

Sociologist Herbert Gans makes an argument about official sources related to Bennett's. For him, the routines of daily journalism undermine democracy. If supporting democracy means encouraging citizens to be active, informed, and critical, then the standard operating procedures of mainstream journalism subvert their own best intentions. Since most news is "top down," relaying the views of high government officials over lower government officials, all government officials over unofficial groups and oppositional groups, and groups of any sort over unorganized citizens, it diminishes the standing and efficacy of individual citizens.[3]

Whether the normative implications of journalism's favoring high government officials are as dire as Gans fears may be doubted, but it is indisputable that news media coverage emphasizes the views and actions of leading politicians and other top government officials. It is likewise indisputable that this limits the range of opinion to which the general public is exposed.

THE CONSTRAINTS OF PROFESSIONAL CULTURE Journalists favor high government officials—but why? The answer is that they work within a professional culture or a set of professional values that holds that a journalist's obligation is to report government affairs to serve the informational functions that make democracy work. One might still ask why that general function should lead to such a strong emphasis on government officials. The answer seems to me that newspapers, once divorced from direct service to political parties (the leading nineteenth-century model) and once aspiring to neutral or objective professionalism, developed occupational routines and a professional culture that reinforce what media scholar Janet Steele calls an "operational bias" in news reporting. That is, in the work of political reporting, journalists emphasize "players, policies, and predictions of what will happen next."[4] So even when the press goes to outside experts rather than inside government officials, they seek people with experience in government, access to and knowledge of the chief players in government, and a ready willingness to speak in the terms of government officials, interpreting and predicting unfolding events. In television reporting and to a large degree in the print media, too, historians or area experts on the Middle East, for instance, are unlikely to be asked to comment on developments there to set contemporary events in a broader historical and cultural context. It is rare almost to the vanishing point for the press to seek out people even further from the policy community to comment on daily political affairs—for instance, religious leaders. The use of religious leaders to discuss key foreign policy matters is essentially nonexistent.[5] Why? No publisher dictates that religious opinion is irrelevant. There is no force anywhere dictating anything about this except the well-learned habits and patterns of journalists.

THE CONSTRAINTS OF CONVENTIONAL WISDOM Journalists swim in conventional wisdom. They are wrapped up in daily events, and it would be disconcerting for them and for their readers if they took a long view. It might also be disconcerting for them to take a comparative (non-American) view. It would certainly be disconcerting for them to spend too much time with academics or others removed from the daily fray of political life. It is in relation to the conventional wisdom that journalists know how to identify "a story." Individual journalists may take issue with convention. Some journalists who work for publications with nonconventional audiences may write with unconventional assumptions and unusual points of departure. But the mainstream journalist writing for a standard news institution is likely to be ignorant of, or, if informed, dismissive of opinions outside the fold.

In Washington, in state capitals, and even more in smaller countries, journalists pick up conventional wisdom through lives intertwined with the lives of politicians. In France, for instance, Thomas Ferenczi, associate editor of *Le Monde,* complains that journalists and politicians—and it does not matter if they are left-wing or right-wing—belong to the same "microcosm": "when they are young they go to the same schools, later they live in the same areas, go to the same holiday resorts, and so on." Ferenczi warns, "There is real danger for democracy here: namely, that, journalists and politicians, because they are so closely linked, have their own, narrow, idea of what the media should cover . . . and ignore the interests of the people."[6] This is less of a problem in the more pluralistic United States than it is in France. In the United States, there is a more widely dispersed journalistic elite—at least across two cities, New York and Washington, and with important pockets of opinion shapers in Los Angeles, Chicago, and Cambridge-Boston, rather than concentrated in one—and it is much more diverse in social and educational background. However, the same general phenomenon occurs.

Other factors also limit the range of opinion in the American media, vitally important factors, although they lie outside the news media as such. For instance, the American political system generally offers a narrower political spectrum, and one less accommodating of minorities, than most other democratic systems. Ralph Nader complained bitterly after the 2000 election that he had not been well covered in the press. Why, he asked, when he was raising real issues, did he get no coverage while Al Gore and George W. Bush, the Tweedle-dum and Tweedle-dee of American politics, were covered every time they blew their noses?[7] The answer seemed pretty straightforward: Ralph Nader was not going to be elected president of the United States in 2000. Either Al Gore or George W. Bush would. The press—as part of its conventional wisdom—believed its job was to follow what the American political system had tossed up for it. It was not the job of the press to offer the public a wide range of issues but to cover, analyze, and discuss the issues the two viable candidates were presenting. Imagine, however, if Ralph Nader had been running for president in Germany. Would the German press have shown greater interest in his ideas? Yes, but not because the German press is better or more democratic, but because Germany has a parliamentary political system. It is because if Ralph Nader received 5 percent of the vote in Germany, his party would receive 5 percent of the seats in Parliament and would be a force, potentially a decisive force, in forming a government. If Ralph Nader received 5 percent of the vote in the United States, he would get no seats in Congress.

So there are many reasons why media discourse in the United States fails to approximate an ideal of robust and wide-open discussion. Even so, journalism as it functions today is still a practice that offends powerful groups, speaks truth to power, and provides access for a diversity of opinion. How and why does this happen despite all that constrains it? The standard sociological analysis of news places it in so airless a box that exceptional journalistic forays are not readily explained. They are the exceptions that prove the rule. They are the ones that got away from the powers of constraint and cooptation and routine. But these "exceptions" happen every year, every week, at some level every day. How can we explain that?

STRATEGIC OPPORTUNITIES FOR FREE EXPRESSION

EVENTFULNESS There is a fundamental truth about journalism that all journalists recognize but almost all social scientists do not: things happen.[8] Not only do things happen, but, as the bumper sticker says, shit happens. That is what provides a supply of occurrences for journalists to work with. Shit even happens to the rich and powerful, and it makes for a great story when it does.

Because shit happens, journalists gain some freedom from official opinion, professional routines, and conventional wisdom. Journalism is an event-centered discourse, more responsive to accidents and explosions in the external world than to fashions in ideas among cultural elites. The journalists' sense of themselves as street-smart, nose-to-the-ground adventurers in places where people do not want them has an element of truth to it, and it is very much linked to event-centeredness.

News, like bread or sausage, is something people make. Scholars emphasize the manufacturing process. Journalists emphasize the raw material their work brings them to; they insist that their jobs recurrently place them before novel, unprecedented, and unanticipated events. While sociologists observe how this world of surprises is tamed, journalists typically emphasize that the effort at domestication falls short.[9]

The journalists have a point. Sometimes something happens that is not accounted for in any sociology or media studies. Take President Bill Clinton's efforts to create a system of national service. This was part of his 1992 campaign, and he mentioned it as one of the priorities of his administration the day after his election. He appointed a friend, Eli Segal, to run a new Office of National Service, and Segal set to work to get appropriate legislation through Congress. The administration's efforts led to passage of the National and Community Service Trust Act, which Clinton signed into law in September 1993. One year later, AmeriCorps would be officially launched. Segal took charge of orchestrating a major public relations event that would feature President Clinton swearing in nine thousand AmeriCorps volunteers at sixteen sites around the country by satellite hook-up. Every detail was checked, every contingency plan was rehearsed. Segal looked forward to a triumphant day on the South Lawn of the White House followed by extensive, favorable news coverage. At 4:30 A.M. on the morning of the ceremony, Segal's phone rang. The event as planned would have to be scrapped. Why? Because at that hour a deranged pilot crashed his Cessna aircraft into the back of the White House precisely on the spot where the ceremony was to be staged. The news media predictably went gaga over this bizarre and unprecedented event and could scarcely be bothered by the launching of AmeriCorps—no doubt more important than the plane crash, but infinitely more routine.[10]

Social scientists insist that most news is produced by Eli Segals, not deranged pilots. Quantitatively, they are right; the vast majority of daily news items on television or in print come from planned, intentional events, press releases, press conferences, and scheduled interviews. Even so, journalists find their joy and their identity in the adrenaline rush that comes only from deranged pilots, hurricanes, upset victories in baseball or politics, triumphs against all odds, tragedy or scandal in the lap of luxury, and other unplanned and unanticipated scandals, accidents, mishaps, gaffes, embarrassments, and wonders. The scholars delight in revealing how much of news is produced by the best laid plans of government officials who maneuver news to their own purposes; the journalists enjoy being first to the scene when the best laid plans go awry.

On September 13, 1994, the *New York Times'* lead story, and two related stories, covered the plane crash at the White House. Other news was swamped. The story on AmeriCorps ran on page seventeen. Even there it seemed to be folded into the big story of the day. The third paragraph read: "Some 850 were inducted as more than 2,000 dignitaries and supporters took part in the ceremony on the North Lawn of the White House. They were kept sweltering there for more than two hours, and an elaborately synchronized satellite television transmission was thrown awry because of the crash of a light plane early this morning on the South Lawn where the event was supposed to have taken place."

Journalists make their own stories, but not from materials they have personally selected. Materials are thrust upon them. It can even be argued, as Regina Lawrence has contended, that in recent years news has become more event-driven and less institution-driven. Moreover, the news media take events not as ends in themselves but as "jumping-off points for thematic exploration of social issues." Content analysis of news over the past one hundred years indicates that journalists pay increasing attention to context, to reporting events in detail especially when they serve as "invitations for the news media to grapple, however gracefully or clumsily, with political and social issues."[11] This preoccupation with unpredictable events keeps something uncontrollable at the forefront of journalism. The archetypal news story, the kind that makes a career, the sort every reporter longs for, is one that is unroutinized and unrehearsed. It gives journalism its recurrent anarchic potential. And it is built into the very bloodstream of news organizations, it is the circulatory system that keeps the enterprise oxygenated.

CONFLICT Almost all journalists relish conflict. Almost all media criticism attacks journalists for emphasizing conflict. But conflict, like events, provides a recurrent resource for embarrassing the powerful.

Consider a story by Randal C. Archibold that appeared in the *New York Times* on January 11, 2003, with the headline "Nuclear Plant Disaster Plan Is Inadequate, Report Says." To summarize, New York governor George Pataki had commissioned a report on safety at the Indian Point nuclear power plant just thirty-five miles away from midtown Manhattan. The report was produced by a consulting group the governor hired, Witt Associates. James Lee Witt, its chief executive, was formerly the director of the Federal Emergency Management Agency. So journalists knew the report was being written, knew its chief author was a high-ranking former federal official, and knew roughly when it would appear. This sounds like the kind of government-centered "official" news story critics complain about.

But was it? Why did Governor Pataki commission the report? Clearly, he commissioned it after the September 11 terrorist attack made more urgent the concerns that citizens and citizens' groups had already expressed about the safety of the Indian Point nuclear reactor. The plant's safety became a major local political issue in 2000 when a small leak forced the plant to shut down for nearly a year. So an event—a leak at the plant—spawned political mobilization; lively political mobilization plus September 11, another event, made it necessary for the governor to at least make a show of doing something. September 11 further mobilized opposition to the plant, particularly because one of the hijacked jets flew very close to the plant en route to the World Trade Center. Governor Pataki finally commissioned the report in August 2002 "in response to the rising outcry over safety at the plant." The Witt report, whose conclusion could not have been fully anticipated by the governor or anyone else if it was to have legitimacy, declared that the disaster preparedness plan was inadequate for protecting people from unacceptable levels of radiation in case of a release at the plant. The elected executive of Westchester County, Andrew J. Spano, commented, "the bottom line is the plant shouldn't be here." The reporter made it clear that Witt Associates did not remark on whether the plant should be shut down but, at the same time, noted that the report's view of the emergency plans for the plant "largely reflected complaints voiced for years by opponents of Indian Point."

The Witt report became news not because the governor's office generated it, but because the governor acted in the face of raging controversy. The continuing controversy made the story news and made the news story interesting. In the end, the report obviously gave support to the environmentalists and others who have urged that Indian Point be shut down. The news story helped keep opponents of government policy alert, encouraged, and legitimated.

CYNICISM Political reporters in the past generation have increasingly made it a point not only to report the statements and actions of leading public officials but to report on the motives behind the actions as best as they can. They report not only the show and the dazzle that the politician wants foregrounded, but the efforts that go into the show and the calculations behind them. They may not intend to undercut the politicians, but they do intend not to be manipulated. The result is a portrait of politicians as self-interested, cynically manipulative, and contemptuous of the general public.

Take, for instance, the *New York Times'* April 16, 2003, front-page story on the proposed Bush tax cut, "In a Concession, Bush Lowers Goal of Tax Cut Plan." The story began by curtly observing that President Bush lowered his target for a tax cut in a tacit admission that his original package was "dead." Then reporter Elisabeth Bumiller cited White House advisers who said "that they were now on a war footing with Capitol Hill" to pass the biggest tax cut they could. They, along with other Republican strategists, said "it was imperative for Mr. Bush to be seen as fighting hard for the economy to avoid the fate of his father, who lost the White House after his victory in the 1991 Persian Gulf war in large part because voters viewed him as disengaged from domestic concerns." The orientation of the story was to the timing and style of the president's speech on the economy, not to its substance. The background—strategy and image—is the foreground. This kind of a story, once exceptional, has become standard.[12]

At the end of September 2003, Laura Bush went to Paris as part of the ceremonies signaling the American reentry to UNESCO after a boycott of nearly two decades. The First Lady's trip was, of course, a well-planned public relations gesture. Would anyone have suspected otherwise? But Elaine Sciolino, the *Times'* veteran foreign correspondent and chief Paris correspondent, made a point of it, noting that Mrs. Bush did not face the American flag as the American national anthem was sung. "Instead, she stood perpendicular to it, enabling photographers to capture her in profile, with the flag and the Eiffel Tower behind. The scene was carefully planned for days by a White House advance team, much to the amusement of longtime UNESCO employees."[13]

Reporting of this sort—showing the president or in this case his wife as performers putting on their makeup—is a sign of a free press. A particularly dramatic example was the decision of *Time* magazine to run as its October 6, 2003, cover the carefully staged and widely celebrated photograph of President Bush, attired in a flight jacket and standing on the deck of an aircraft carrier in early May. Behind the president was the much discussed banner that boldly proclaimed, "Mission Accomplished." But now the magazine provided its own emphatic headline: MISSION NOT ACCOMPLISHED.

This kind of reporting may not be a sign of a press that motivates or mobilizes or turns people into good citizens. It may do more to reinforce political apathy than to refurbish political will. But it may be just what democracy requires of the press.

OUTSIDER NEWS   Why is Trent Lott no longer majority leader of the U.S. Senate? The answer is that on December 5, 2002, he made remarks at Senator Strom Thurmond's one hundredth birthday party that suggested we would all be better off if Senator Thurmond, running on a segregationist platform for the presidency in 1948, had won the election. The room apparently was full of politicians and journalists, none of whom immediately caught the significance of the remark. It was all part of the general celebration of the extraordinary event of a one hundredth birthday party for the man who had served in the Senate longer than any other person in American history. No one objected to the over-the-top encomium that could at best have been interpreted as thoughtless but, if it was judged to have any real content at all, would have to have been viewed as racist.

But if no one at the party recognized Lott's remarks as a story, how did it become news and force Lott's resignation from his leadership post?

The first part of the answer is that several practitioners of the still novel "blogs," or personal Web sites of a kind of highly individualized public diary, took note of Lott's remarks, including several prominent and widely read bloggers. These included Joshua Marshall (at talkingpointsmemo.com), Timothy Noah (at slate.com), and Andrew Sullivan (at AndrewSullivan.com)—all three of them journalists. Noah and Sullivan were once employed by (and in Sullivan's case served as editor of) *The New Republic*. Marshall had worked for *The American Prospect*. Although mainstream press outlets, both print and broadcast, noted the remarks (and C-SPAN had aired them), the bloggers pressed the fact that Thurmond ran as a segregationist and that Lott had taken many conservative stands through the years, including speaking before white supremacist groups and voting against the Civil Rights Act of 1990. Matt Drudge, in his online report, even found that Senator Lott had made an almost identical statement in praise of Thurmond in 1980.

Thanks to the "blogosphere," the party that Senator Lott and nearly everyone else present regarded as an insider event was available for outsider news. Moreover, as Heather Gorgura argues, the bloggers succeeded in getting the "dump Lott" bandwagon moving not simply by pointing out an indiscreet remark, but, in documenting Senator Lott's long and consistent history of association with organizations and policies offensive to African Americans, by persuading mainstream journalists that Lott's remarks were not casual and thoughtless but representative of a racism Lott had repeatedly expressed and acted upon.[14]

The bloggers do not yet have an economic base. Those with apparently the greatest influence are those who either are, or were recently, journalists for standard news publications. In 2003, the California gubernatorial recall race attracted national blogospherean controversy when Dan Weintraub, a political opinion columnist for the *Sacramento Bee*, roused the ire of Latinos at his paper and beyond for remarks on his own Weblog critical of Lieutenant Governor Cruz Bustamante. His newspaper decided that blogs of its reporters should be submitted to editing—but many journalists and other free speech advocates around the country were horrified by that policy.[15]

The cyber-pamphleteers today can attract broad attention, including the attention of the old media. They do so, I might point out, by name-calling sensationalism. The most prominent and most consequential cases are that of Matt Drudge breaking the Monica Lewinsky story—"The president is an adulterer"—and the bloggers who cried, "The senator is a racist." An unlovable press, indeed, but perhaps just what democracy requires.

Outsiders are always troublemakers. The news media are supposed to be institutionalized outsiders even though they have in fact become institutionalized insiders. There is much more that might be done to keep journalists at arm's length from their sources. This is something that journalism education could orient itself to more conscientiously—for instance, insisting that journalism students take a course in comparative politics or a course on the politics and culture of some society besides the United States. A serious U.S. history course would also help. The idea would be to disorient rather than orient the prospective journalist. Disorientation—and ultimately alienation of journalists—helps the press to be free.

Social scientists regularly observe how much reporters have become insiders, socializing with their sources, flattered by their intimacy with the rich and powerful, dependent on intimacy for the leaks and leads officialdom can provide. All of this is true, but it is all the more reason to observe carefully and nurture those ways in which journalists remain outsiders. Bloggers in the Trent Lott case, although journalists, took up outposts on journalism's frontier. But even standard issue journalists are outsiders to the conventional opinions of government officials in several respects. For one, they advance the journalistic agenda of finding something novel that will set tongues a-flutter across a million living rooms, breakfast tables, bars, lunchrooms, and lines at Starbucks. Second, journalists have access to and professional interest in nonofficial sources of news. Most important of these nonofficial sources is public opinion as measured by polls or by informal journalistic "taking of the pulse" of public opinion. The American press in particular has a populist streak that inclines it toward a sampling of civilian views. A front-page story in the April 24, 2003, *Chicago Tribune,* for instance, by Jill Zuckman, the *Tribune's* chief congressional correspondent, and datelined Northfield, Wisconsin, was based on both national opinion polls and local interviewing of people who objected to the USA Patriot Act. The story piggybacked on the frequent informal sessions Wisconsin senator Russ Feingold held with his constituents. Feingold, not incidentally, was the only senator to vote against the Patriot Act on October 26, 2001.

Zuckman wanted, as she says, "to take the pulse of the voters," especially on the war in Iraq, and she thought that she would be able to sample the widest range of opinions if she traveled with a Democratic senator during the spring recess. She ended up with Senator Feingold when she learned that he holds town meetings almost every recess and weekend in fulfillment of a campaign pledge to visit every county in the state. As it happened, the Iraq war was declared to be over before the town meetings began, and people had little to say about the war—but they had a surprising amount to say about their fears for domestic civil liberties. So the topic Zuckman wrote about was not what she intended to cover, but her populist instinct made it possible to report on a phenomenon that elites did not anticipate and that the administration could not have found comforting.[16]

CONCLUSION

Journalists are not free agents. They are constrained by a set of complex institutional relations that lead them to reproduce day after day the opinions and views of establishment figures, especially high government officials. They are constrained by broad conventional wisdom that they are not particularly well located nor well enough educated to buck and they are powerfully constrained by the conventions and routines of their own professionalism. At the same time, they are not without some resources for expanding the range of expression in the news. What structures do or could preserve their capacity to speak freely and to expand the range of voices and views they represent in their reporting? What journalistic predispositions do or could enable them to take advantage of their limited but real autonomy to fulfill the potential of a free press for vigorous, robust discussion of public issues? I am defending, somewhat to my surprise, what is usually attacked as the worst features of the American press—a preoccupation with events, a morbid sports-minded fascination with gladiatorial combat, a deep, anti-political cynicism, and a strong alienation of journalists from the communities they cover.

I hasten to add that the journalists I most admire get behind and beneath events, illuminate trends and structures and moods and not just conflicts, believe in the virtues and values of political life and the hopes it inspires, and feel connected and committed to their communities—global, national, or local. The journalists of greatest imagination discover the nonevents that conceal their drama so well. They recognize the story in conflicts that never arose because of strong leadership or a stroke of luck, or the conflict that was resolved peacefully over a painstakingly long time without sparking a front-page "event." But I propose, nonetheless, that some of the greatest service the media provide for democracy lies in characteristics that few people regard as very nice or ennobling about the press. These features of journalism—and perhaps these features more than others—make news a valuable force in a democratic society, and this means that—if all goes well—we are saddled with a necessary institution we are not likely ever to love.

NOTES

1. Alexis de Tocqueville, *Democracy in America,* edited by J. P. Mayer (Garden City, N.Y.: Doubleday, 1969), 180.

2. W. Lance Bennett, "Toward a Theory of Press-State Relations in the United States," *Journal of Communication* 40 (spring 1990): 103–25, quotes at 106, 125.

3. Herbert Gans, *Democracy and the News* (New York: Oxford Univ. Press, 2003). Gans and Bennett, like many other contemporary theorists, both presume that the press at its best should not only report the doings of government but that it should do so in a way to encourage and provide for the participation of ordinary citizens, informing them in advance of governmental decisions so that they can make their voices heard. This is by no means an undisputed assumption. As John Zaller has argued, the job of the press in a mass democracy may be to help people evaluate leaders, not policies. The press should try to make it possible for the public to evaluate leaders after they have acted, not policies before they have been put in place. See John Zaller, "Elite Leadership of Mass Opinion: New Evidence from the Gulf War," in *Taken by Storm: The Media, Public Opinion, and U.S. Foreign Policy in the Gulf War,* edited by W. Lance Bennett and David Paletz (Chicago: Univ. of Chicago Press, 1994), 201–2.

4. Janet Steele, "Experts and the Operational Bias of Television News: The Case of the Persian Gulf War," *Journalism and Mass Communication Quarterly* 72 (1995): 799–812, quote at 799.

5. Daniel Hallin, Robert Manoff, and Judy Weddle, "Sourcing Patterns of National Security Reporters," *Journalism and Mass Communication Quarterly* 70 (1993): 753–66.

6. Thomas Ferenczi, "The Media and Democracy," *CSD Bulletin* 8, no. 1 (winter 2000–2001): 1–2.

7. Ralph Nader, "My Untold Story," *Brill's Content* (February 2001), 100–3, 153–4.

8. The most notable exceptions among scholars are Harvey Molotch and Marilyn Lester, "Accidents, Scandals, and Routines: Resources for Insurgent Methodology," *Insurgent Sociologist* 3 (1973): 1–11; Regina Lawrence, *The Politics of Force* (Berkeley: Univ. of California Press, 2000); and Steven Livingston and W. Lance Bennett, "Gatekeeping, Indexing, and Live-Event News: Is Technology Altering the Construction of News?" *Political Communication* 20 (2003): 363–80. And I would like to add, however belatedly, me—see *The Sociology of News* (New York: Norton, 2003), 1–8, from which I borrow in this paper.

9. Scholars have not ignored the question of journalistic autonomy. They have provided important explanations for this autonomy. Daniel Hallin sees autonomy provided structurally by divisions among elites. See Daniel C. Hallin, *"The Uncensored War": The Media and Vietnam* (New York: Oxford Univ. Press, 1986). Laws that make it tough to sue for libel also enhance autonomy. These explanations direct attention to structural opportunities for aggressive reporting, but they do not provide journalists with a motive to pursue challenge and critique.

10. Steven Waldman, *The Bill* (New York: Viking, 1995), 240.

11. Lawrence, *The Politics of Force,* 188.

12. This is not to mention background stories that are exclusively focused on stagecraft. See, for instance, Elisabeth Bumiller, "Keepers of Bush Image Lift Stagecraft to New Heights," *New York Times,* May 16, 2003, p. 1.

13. *New York Times,* September 30, 2003, A 4.

14. Heather E. Gorgura, "Lott Gets a Blogging: Did the Amateur Journalists of the Blogosphere Bring Down Trent Lott?" (unpublished paper, University of Washington, March 2003). This student paper is extremely thoughtful and well documented.

15. See Mickey Kaus, "Kausfiles," September 22, 2003, at http://slate.msn.com and www.laobserved.com, September 23, 2003, and September 24, 2003.

16. Email to the author from Jill Zuckman, September 20, 2003.

DAILY NEWS AND FIRST AMENDMENT IDEALS

REGINA G. LAWRENCE

When I teach a course on the politics of the news media, I begin the class by surveying my students. I ask them to complete two sentences: First, "The biggest problem with the media today is . . . ," and second, "The role of the media in a democracy should be. . . ." The results have varied in interesting ways over the years. In the aftermath of the Clinton impeachment scandal, for example, students were much more inclined to say that the greatest problem with the media was excessive sensationalism and intrusiveness into politicians' private lives, whereas in the aftermath of September 11, 2001, students voiced more concern over their inability to gain a comprehensive understanding of world events through mainstream news. But some answers never vary much, particularly the predominance of three images of the role of the media in democracy: the "neutral transmitter" that conveys information without bias; the "watchdog" that critically scrutinizes government; and the "marketplace of ideas" that provides a forum for debate among diverse perspectives on public issues.

My students do not differ much in this regard from legal theorists or Supreme Court justices, especially in their attachment to the latter two ideals. The watchdog metaphor has been crucial to the thinking of jurists such as William Brennan and Potter Stewart, as when Stewart argued in 1974 that, to the framers, "the free press meant organized, expert scrutiny of government."[1] The marketplace image has been crucial in legal and regulatory thinking as well. One study found that "in the classic texts [on the First Amendment], the metaphor of the market is a dominant presence," appearing in over one thousand law review articles by 1995[2]; another found that ideal repeatedly invoked in Federal Communications Commission documents as well.[3]

These normative expectations of media performance are shared not just by legal theorists, but by the general public as well. A survey conducted by the Pew Research Center in late 2001, on the heels of the September 11 terrorist attacks, found that even in that highly charged context the public expressed support for these ideals, at least in the abstract. As the Center reported, "The survey finds a solid majority in favor of war coverage that is neutral rather than pro-American. An even larger percentage (73%) favors coverage that portrays all points of view, including those of countries unfriendly to the United States, over pro-American news. And by 52%–40%, respondents say that when covering the war, news organizations should dig hard for information rather than trusting government and military officials who refuse to officially release information."[4]

These prevailing ideals of the media's role in democracy are not fully compatible. In fact, the "neutral transmitter" ideal almost necessarily conflicts with the other two. News that critically scrutinizes government will strike some citizens as necessary and appropriate and others as inappropriate or motivated by partisanship. A more recent Pew Center survey discovered that people's evaluations of news coverage of the Bush administration and the military varied with their partisan attachments, with Republicans less likely to approve of the media critically scrutinizing these institutions.[5] The public's expectation of media "neutrality" when it comes to diverse perspectives typically extends only as far as the bounds of patriotism and politically acceptable debate, leading the public to hold sometimes paradoxical expectations. Indeed, the later Pew survey found that "seven-in-ten Americans see it as a good thing when news organizations take a 'strong pro-American point of view.' However, when asked specifically if it is better for coverage of the war on terrorism to be neutral or pro-American, fully 64% favor neutral coverage."[6]

Despite these tensions and contradictions, the watchdog and marketplace metaphors in particular offer powerful ideals that have shaped public expectations of the media, the development of legal reasoning, and the making of public policy.[7] In this essay, I will argue that these idealized images are problematic not because of the expectations they evoke, but because they shed an imperfect light on the real nature of news. Both the watchdog and the marketplace of ideas images share a presumption that the news media must enjoy considerable independence from government and other powerful sources. Indeed, both models exist largely as rationales for media independence: In the watchdog model, the media must be free to scrutinize government on behalf of the people, and in the marketplace of ideas model, the media must be free to offer a variety of viewpoints to the public and encourage real debate. But neither image takes into account the simple fact that news organizations are enormously reliant upon government officials and institutions in order to produce that product we call "news."

The U.S. media (by "media" I mean both print and broadcast news organizations) are of course formally autonomous from government. The White House does not maintain an office within the *New York Times* or the NBC newsrooms, so in that sense there is a formal, structural separation between government and media. But all the major news organizations do assign reporters day in and day out to the White House, reflecting an equally important *dependence* of news organizations upon powerful news sources. Powerful norms among journalists offset this structural dependence to some degree, particularly the informal prohibition against appearing "soft" on the politicians and other officials one covers. Indeed, the First Amendment ideal of an independent press is woven into the fabric of contemporary journalism in a variety of subtle ways. But this ideal of independence is offset by another powerful journalistic norm that ensures that government officials and other powerful elites virtually always get to tell their side of the story. Other voices come in and out of the news more sporadically.

So, despite the formal structural autonomy of the media from government, "content autonomy" is not always evident. The structure and norms of news gathering encourage not just the independence championed by the watchdog and marketplace ideals, but also a dependence upon those in power for the raw materials of news. This dependence upon government does not necessarily represent a serious deviation from First Amendment ideals. It makes sense for news organizations to pay close attention to what government is doing—indeed, they must if they are to fulfill the watchdog role—and to do so requires a certain degree of interconnection between the media and governmental institutions. The beat system, through which reporters are stationed at government listening posts to report what happens there as "news," is probably necessary if news is to be gathered efficiently by reporters with (ideally) some expertise in their subject. But the watchdog metaphor in particular connotes a kind of constant and freestanding scrutiny of government that does not square with what scholarly research on the news has repeatedly shown: news coverage often, though certainly not always, defers to politicians and other officials to set the agenda and frame the issues.

Thus, the real question for social scientists is, *under what conditions* do news organizations produce hard-hitting investigative reports, substantive critiques of government officials and policies, and robust editorial-page dialogue about important issues? Why do news organizations sometimes decide that hard-hitting news and wide-open debate are newsworthy, while at other times forgoing such coverage? Scholars have been tracking the clues for decades, and several patterns have emerged. The upshot of this research is that, first, despite the formal autonomy enjoyed by the U.S. media, most daily news is deeply entwined with daily governing; second, the degree of critique (the watchdog ideal) and the breadth of debate (the marketplace ideal) that can be found in the news depend on the current political context, which is usually defined largely by what government officials are saying and doing; and third, much critique and debate found in the news is not spurred by deliberate, planned "scrutiny of government" so much as by accident and circumstance.

All this suggests that the formal law embodied in the First Amendment, and the watchdog and marketplace metaphors symbolically attached to it, matter less to the daily production of news than other factors. The divide between legal philosophy and empirical reality is, as Timothy Cook argues in his opening essay, wide indeed. One reason for this disjuncture is, as Frederick Schauer argues in his chapter, that while the First Amendment acts as a shield to protect the media against outside censorship, it cannot provide the *incentives* for news organizations to produce critical coverage or robust debate. The other significant reason, which I will focus on in this chapter, is that First Amendment protections have little effect on the primary *constraints* on daily news production. The First Amendment is primarily a shield against outright attempts at censorship, but it says nothing about the routine daily interchange among reporters and officials that creates much of the news.

PREVAILING IDEALS OF PRESS PERFORMANCE AND THE REALITY OF DAILY NEWS

In the watchdog ideal, the press serves as a crucial counterweight to governmental power. Justice Stewart stated this expectation in formal terms when he argued that the First Amendment's free press clause was intended "to create a fourth institution outside the Government as an additional check on the three official branches."[8] The more informal and perhaps more widely accepted aspect of this ideal is simply the notion that it is the job of the press to critically scrutinize government on behalf of the public.

The marketplace of ideas metaphor has two incarnations: as an economic ideal, in which an unregulated media marketplace presumably delivers to consumers the "goods" they want most efficiently; and as a democratic ideal of free expression in the service of democracy and truth.[9] It is the latter ideal to which I will primarily refer throughout this chapter, though I will revisit the economic incarnation of the marketplace ideal toward the end of the essay. Free expression is valued because it honors individual rationality while contributing to the ongoing societal search for truth and accommodation of competing interests.[10] According to this ideal, robust mass-mediated debate that includes a wide variety of perspectives is the necessary mechanism for the "best" or "truest" ideas to emerge and for societal consensus to take shape.

In the watchdog model, the press acts on behalf of the public (as the public's "eyes and ears") with an explicitly skeptical and adversarial stance vis-à-vis government; the prime relationship envisioned is that between the press and government. In the marketplace of ideas model, the primary relationship is between the media and the public: the press makes available to the public a variety of viewpoints from which to choose, with the "best" ideas presumably rising to the top. In the first model, the press should hound the government to enforce accountability and counteract unacceptable uses of power, whereas in the second model, the press should provide a range of perspectives on public issues, thus enabling rational democratic choice among competing values and policy options.

The watchdog and marketplace metaphors are distinct. Note that Justice Brennan embraced both ideals, while Justice Stewart rejected the marketplace of ideas role as too "neutral." Brennan's opinion in *New York Times v. Sullivan* evoked both ideals, most notably in the terms he borrowed from Judge Learned Hand, citing "a profound national commitment to the principle that debate on public issues should be uninhibited, robust and wide-open"—the marketplace of ideas ideal—"and that it may well include vehement, caustic, and sometimes unpleasantly sharp attacks on government and public officials"—the watchdog ideal. In Justice Stewart's view, however, the Constitution did not protect the press merely "to insure that a newspaper will serve as a neutral forum for debate . . . a kind of Hyde Park corner for the community."¹¹ Stewart seemingly wanted the "expert scrutiny" of a watchdog press without the input of the multiple and possibly nonexpert voices implied by the marketplace ideal.¹²

Despite their distinctions, both metaphors share an attachment to the ideal of autonomy that has powerfully shaped the evolution of legal thought and public expectations of the news media. Yet, the idealized watchdog relationship between the press and the government looks quite unlike the symbiotic relationship of the institutional press and the institutions of government that is well established by empirical research. Nor does the marketplace model fit well with patterns of real-world news production, which often filter out diverse perspectives on issues.

KEY CONSTRAINTS ON DAILY NEWS

First Amendment ideals are fundamentally concerned with *ideas*: Is a significant range of ideas available in the media arena, including ideas that are critical of government officials and actions? Understanding how well the media live up to First Amendment ideals thus requires us to analyze which sources are quoted and which perspectives are expressed in the news.

What follows is a brief discussion of some key constraints on the daily production of the news. The first constraint stems from the fact that, in contrast to the media autonomy envisioned by many First Amendment theorists, the production of daily news is in a variety of ways *embedded,* not autonomous. And I do use that term consciously: Similar to the embedding of U.S. reporters with troops invading Iraq, U.S. news organizations are embedded in political and professional relationships within a specific economic and cultural context. This media embeddedness shapes the bulk of daily news content just as significantly, or perhaps more significantly, than the media's formal autonomy. A second constraint flows from journalistic norms that encourage journalists to be professional by not unduly rocking the ship of state. News organizations prove quite willing to criticize government and open the news gates to a wider, more critical range of views, but only given the right set of cues that license this behavior. This leads to a final point: the content of the news varies over time and across issues as the political context varies. The critical coverage and robust debate championed by the watchdog and marketplace ideals does occur, though it is often spontaneous and circumstantial rather than constant and deliberate.

The news is influenced by a variety of factors, and a complete theoretical model is beyond the scope of this chapter. Were we to examine all the major influences on news production in America, we would have to include the economic structure of the news industry and the political culture of the United States, for the news is deeply embedded in these as well. The general effect of economic and cultural forces on the news is to filter the voices and views present in society to a narrower range, and particularly to filter out content that is deemed unmarketable and culturally unpalatable. But for our present purposes, I will zoom in on factors lying closer to the surface of daily political news: the professional norms and news-gathering routines that guide how news organizations respond to politicians' news management strategies, the norms that encourage journalistic deference to officials on the substance of the news, and the occasional intrusion of major news events.

PROFESSIONAL NORMS, ORGANIZATIONAL ROUTINES, AND OFFICIAL COMMUNICATIONS STRATEGIES

The production of daily news is organized by news gathering routines and shaped by journalistic norms. The "embedding" of reporters within government institutions, from the White House to the local police station, helps news organizations produce the news efficiently. Not only does it place reporters on the scene of where important things are likely to happen, but it guarantees a steady flow of newsworthy events to news organizations that somehow must produce a news product of roughly the same size and style of content at the same time every day—or every hour.[13]

Not surprisingly, given this news gathering structure, two of the clearest findings of scholarly research have been that officials are nearly always the predominant voice in news coverage of politics and public policy, and that news content tends to reflect the range of views and the degree of debate among relevant officials. Official voices and views predominate in political news coverage—both directly, through journalists' reliance on officials for the events, soundbites, and frames that structure most news stories, and indirectly, through indexing content to the range of debate among key political elites. Official predominance in the news is made even more likely by the pressures of pack reporting, which intensify politicians' control over the news. As groups of reporters from different news organizations are assigned to cover beats such as the White House or a candidate's presidential campaign, the competition among them becomes competition for access to the same key spokespeople.[14]

Journalistic reliance on officials stems not only from routines of news gathering but from norms shared by mainstream journalists. Certainly, many—though not all—American reporters share the watchdog ideal as one normative expectation of their profession.[15] But there are competing norms as well. The expectation of professionalism includes the notion that journalists should transmit *legitimate* information to the public. In practice, this most often means information that has been officially verified. Moreover, professionalism requires that news organizations do not actively or intentionally set the public agenda or unduly amplify social or political conflict—a norm, in other words, of deference to duly elected officials by relying on official cues and official sources for most news stories.[16] Closely bound up in notions of professionalism is the disputed but still powerful norm of objectivity, fairness, and balance. "The norms of [the journalistic] profession include a commitment to the balanced treatment of the two political parties, a code that is enforced by the layer of editors who oversee the work of reporters."[17] Yet the difficulties associated with producing unbiased news ironically create news that is often dominated by official voices and views. As one reporter recently described it, this norm "exacerbates our tendency to rely on official sources, which is the easiest, quickest way to get both the 'he said' and the 'she said,' and thus, 'balance.'"[18] Finally, meeting the requirements of storytelling usually leads journalists to narrow the focus of the news onto views that "matter," which generally means those that count politically. Reporters gravitate to those sources well-positioned to be "in the know" and "move the story along."[19]

Consequently, the range of views available in the news tends to roughly reflect the range of views being advanced by politically powerful news sources. For example, Lance Bennett demonstrated that *New York Times* coverage of American policy toward Nicaragua in the 1980s took its cues from Congress, varying as congressional critics of that policy stepped forward and then were silenced by their opponents in the White House.[20] Thus, when congressional debate shut down, so did the *Times*' critical coverage. This "indexing" has since been tested in a variety of news contexts. While the specific findings have varied (for example, which officials are the most powerful cue-givers in which contexts), the general finding that the range of views in the news expands as official debate expands has not been seriously challenged. As a former official in the Clinton administration has observed more anecdotally, the news is not influenced as much by ideology as by "stenography," so that the news is by and large "what political officials say and do."[21]

The upshot of this research is that the watchdog and marketplace ideals are more likely to be realized when powerful officials are engaged in conflict with one another in a way that is likely to affect their political fortunes. The news is less likely to offer critical scrutiny or robust debate when key officials are in agreement or when their squabbles do not threaten serious political consequences. Official consensus can create a "frame dominance" in the news,[22] keeping the news gates closed against opposing views. Or, debate among powerful elites can swing the gates open to allow a wider range of perspectives to enter the news. So these times of greater scrutiny and debate are variable and are generally triggered by what officials do.

As the discussion thus far suggests, governmental news management techniques are part and parcel of daily news production. Indeed, officials in a very real sense "govern *with* the news."[23] Official news management techniques often succeed for the simple reason that political reporters are generally careful to get the official side (or sides) of the story, while only sporadically allowing interest groups, grassroots organizations, and academic experts to speak through the media microphone. Thus, in general, government affects the news less by silencing the press than by speaking through it. First Amendment ideals fit imperfectly with the reality of daily news because news censorship is far less prevalent than governmental news management.

This does not mean that the relationship between reporters and officials is cozy, or that journalists uncritically accept everything government feeds them. The competing journalistic norm of objectivity can encourage reporters to be tough on officials and to unmask their efforts to manage the news. Conscientious reporters generally consider it unprofessional and a violation of objectivity to jump on any bandwagon, and journalists may criticize other journalists for failing to exhibit a sufficiently independent stance from their sources. As television reporter Brit Hume once observed, to be thought soft on the officials one covers is "the kiss of death" among Washington reporters.[24] Thus, given the commercial incentives that can attend a high-profile scandal, we see the occasional "feeding frenzy" during which a particular politician comes under intense scrutiny for hypocrisy or malfeasance. This norm of "toughness" is also one reason for the well-documented "game framing" of political news so prominent today, news that diligently deconstructs politicians' political strategies (but often does little to illuminate the substance of their policy proposals).[25]

Finally, a norm of writing "good stories" also enhances media independence. As Cook explains, "official sources may instigate the news and direct the attention of the reporters toward particular events and issues, without controlling the ultimate story" because journalists "need to provide stories that maximize production values of vividness and clarity alongside journalistic norms of balance and neutrality."[26] While the norm of professionalism subtly encourages reporters to defer to officials' "right" to set the agenda, the competing norm of writing narratively (and commercially) appealing stories can interfere with officials' efforts to control news content.

In short, the relationship between the media and the government is complex and full of tension and even contradiction. The media do not consistently produce critical coverage of government or a wide range of debate. Yet, when the stars align, the news looks much like the idealized watchdog and/or marketplace of ideas. The critical news coverage of the Vietnam and Watergate eras that Justice Stewart was responding to in his 1974 address reflected such a convergence of favorable factors. But while the elite press obviously played a key role in prying open those stories, they also followed the cue of congressional critics, particularly in the case of Vietnam.[27]

The stars can also align in the opposite direction, producing news that is deferential even when critical media scrutiny and robust mass-mediated debate might be most required. A recent case in point is in news coverage of the U.S.-led war on Iraq, in which "an extraordinary convergence of factors . . . produced near perfect journalistic participation in government propaganda operations."[28] These factors included the masterful communication strategies of Karl Rove, through which "even the president's deer-in-the-headlights media presence was countered with the relentless spin that he in fact has a natural 'swagger,'"[29] and extended to outright intimidation of journalists and sources who challenged the official story coming out of the White House.[30] Meanwhile, few political leaders on the Democratic side of the aisle chose to publicly challenge the Bush administration's war plans or its rationale, leaving journalists without the all-important official cue to open the news gates and turn up their scrutiny of the administration. And on the war front itself, the essential dependency of the news media on the government was clear: "The price for more intimate . . . access to the frontlines for the press was steep: agreement to a long list of ground rules, submission to unit commanders' authority over their reports, and practical neutralization of independent reporting. In addition, journalists were wholly dependent on the military for basic necessities, transportation and protection, not to mention the news itself."[31] Together, these factors provided powerful—though not unusual—constraints on the news.

UNEXPECTED EVENTS AND CRITICAL NEWS

But there is another source of variation in the content of the news. Interrupting the general pattern of officially cued, even officially managed news is the occasional dramatic, unexpected news event. Such events can jar open the news gates temporarily to create a range of perspectives usually not present in the news.[32] As tied as they may be by their beat systems to government institutions and the routine events they produce, the news media are also irresistibly drawn to the next "big story" (and ever more so in an era of pitched competition for market share). When a dramatic, unexpected event occurs, news organizations converge on the event and interpret it for their audiences whether or not officials are ready to drive the coverage. In the wake of a big event, they troll for sources who are able to move the story forward or provide a provocative new story angle, which can create opportunities for voices normally marginalized to enter the news. This pattern has been documented following a range of news events: the beating of motorist Rodney King, which brought formerly marginalized perspectives on racism and policing into the mainstream[33]; the ill-fated voyage of the garbage barge *Mobro* and the grounding of the Exxon *Valdez,* both of which allowed environmentalist perspectives into the news more prominently than before[34]; and the shootings at Columbine High School in 1999, which increased the range and volume of debate in the news about an array of contemporary problems.[35] Dramatic, unexpected events can thereby enhance journalistic autonomy by shifting the story off the institutional beat and suggesting a more critical take on government policies (police management in the Rodney King coverage; oil dependence in the Exxon *Valdez* coverage; and the prevalence of firearms and the power of the gun lobby in the aftermath of Columbine).

Such "event-driven news" has important limitations. Moments when the news gates swing open to a broader range of perspectives are not common and may not last long. Journalists still tend to follow the lead provided by officials, once officials have figured out how to "get on top of" the event-driven story. For example, for a short time after the shooting at Columbine High School in 1999, the news became a remarkably diverse forum of ideas about the problems in American life which that event represented and how they should be dealt with. Yet the universe of news themes narrowed significantly over time. Not surprisingly, the two most persistent news stories to come out of that event—the congressional debate over gun control and the allegedly malign influence of popular culture on youth—were the themes championed by leading Democrats and Republicans in Congress and the White House.[36] In this respect, the news about unexpected events that arise off the standard newsbeats may not differ from news about more predictable, routine events. Marjorie Hershey has demonstrated, for example, how the range of news interpretations of a presidential election outcome narrows over time.[37] The news media are centrally in the business of defining events, whether those events are routine or nonroutine. Defining events means winnowing possible interpretations down to a few dominant themes.

Nor do all unexpected events result in the critical coverage envisioned by the watchdog ideal, even when they do provide an opportunity for new voices to enter the news. After the bombing of the Murrah Federal Building in 1995, for example, the news media constructed a public problem of dangerous domestic militia groups. The news drew prominently from sources such as the Southern Anti-Poverty Law Center and the Anti-Defamation League, whose claims that militia groups represented a serious threat to public safety fit neatly, if unintentionally, with the efforts of law enforcement agencies to use the event to legitimize their authority and secure additional funding from Congress.[38]

No better example exists of the limits of event-driven news to engender critical media discourse than the terrorist attacks of September 11, 2001. In the aftermath of that tragedy, the elite press contained very little critical commentary about subjects such as the possible roots of terrorist rage in America's foreign policies, even though that potential explanation for the events of 9/11 resonated widely around the world.[39] Marginalized views on U.S. foreign policy remained marginalized, despite the suddenly intense media attention to terrorism and, presumably, the strong desire among citizens for news that would help make sense of what had just occurred. That environment was conducive to the Bush administration's considerable efforts to shape news coverage and, in particular, to silence leaks and dissent.[40]

Despite these limitations, dramatic, unexpected news events offer one of the few regular vehicles through which the contemporary media fulfill either the watchdog or the marketplace of ideas roles. Much as Harvey Molotch and Marilyn Lester first observed years ago, such events can throw officials off message and raise issues that might otherwise never be heard over the daily hum of routine news.[41] Moreover, unexpected, unplanned events have the considerable advantage of being just that: unplanned. News organizations uncomfortable with their own ability to set the political agenda can sense a new license to raise critical issues when faced with a gaping news hole created by a dramatic news event. Such events create incentives that can move news organizations beyond reliance on official sources and officially provided news stories. The range of debate widens as more voices and perspectives are ushered in, and the news can present a fairly robust marketplace of ideas. When the event suggests official malfeasance or a serious and unresolved public problem, the media can indeed set the agenda, put officials on the defensive, and create pressures for political reform or policy change. Given the "right" event, in other words, the media do realize the watchdog and marketplace ideals.

RETHINKING THE FIRST AMENDMENT

The simple story told here is that the range of voices and views available in the news varies across issues and across time. The autonomy of news content from government sources and news management strategies is variable. In much routine daily news, officials enjoy privileged access to the media microphone. During intense elite debate or after some dramatic news events, the news gate often widens and officials enjoy a less privileged place in the news than usual, though some major events can actually increase official control of the news. While the formal structural autonomy of the media endures, the content of the news is constrained by the dependence of news production upon official sources and by journalistic norms that encourage that reliance.

The scholarly research reviewed here suggests that the legal protection enjoyed by the news media is not a prime determinant of daily news coverage. Perhaps the focus of much scholarly research on the news has overlooked the First Amendment's impact by focusing attention on the social processes of daily news production rather than the legal realm.

Nevertheless, the fact remains that prevailing legal thinking about the First Amendment fails to address important questions about the *motivations* of news organizations to emulate either the watchdog or the marketplace of ideas model. As deployed by Justices Brennan and Stewart, these images seem to assume that the incentives and motivations for realizing those ideals are in place, a given of the political environment, and all that is required for effective scrutiny of government and robust mass-mediated debate is that government must not censor the press. The Amendment is undoubtedly a powerful shield for news organizations inclined to critically scrutinize government. But substantive criticism and truly robust debate are not prevalent in the news unless the political conditions for it are ripe.

This empirical record should encourage us to rethink the meaning and effectiveness of the First Amendment as it has been interpreted by courts and policymakers—and to think more carefully about the popular ideals of the watchdog and the marketplace of ideas. While we do this, it is important to be clear about a few points.

First, the mainstream media's informal reliance upon government is probably inevitable to some degree and may not in itself be a serious problem for democracy. If daily news about government is to be produced efficiently by reporters with adequate expertise and connections to sources of information, the beat system probably must exist. Thus, the top-down news flow from government to the media will probably always exist to some degree, as will the problem of journalists who do not want to antagonize those official sources. First Amendment protections do not provide the incentives for individual reporters or the news organizations they work for to overcome the constraints on daily news production outlined here.

Second, while the public occasionally gets from the media "organized, expert scrutiny of government," they more commonly get scattershot scrutiny that is less by design than by coincidence. Prevailing images of the First Amendment miss the largely *accidental* nature of much critical news coverage (the occasional excellent piece of investigative journalism notwithstanding). Again, the fact that critical news is usually driven by official debate is not necessarily bad. It is simply different than the images the watchdog and marketplace metaphors often evoke. As Lance Bennett argued in his research on "indexing," news that follows and responds to official debate is not objectionable unless stable patterns of informed public opinion run counter to what elected officials do. In a well-functioning representative democracy, it would make sense for news media to regularly follow the lead of officials in defining key issues for debate. (Of course, this argument hinges on the very large assumption that the United States is currently a well-functioning representative democracy.)

Nor is event-driven critical news necessarily a bad thing. As Thomas Patterson has recently argued, event-driven news may be the best we can reasonably expect from the news business: "The media are adept at covering events. They are, in fact, organized to carry out this task."[42] And the heat that accompanies major news events brings some light as well, allowing marginalized voices and views to come to center stage. Were it not for the beating of Rodney King, would members of minority and other grassroots groups have gained access to the national microphone to protest patterns of racial bias in policing?

Finally, just because the daily business of news-making is not as autonomous from government as the watchdog and marketplace ideals imagine, those ideals are not meaningless. The power of normative ideals rarely rests upon their being fully realized. It is doubtful that Justices Brennan and Stewart and others who have employed these metaphors were attempting to describe or even prescribe actual media behavior. But in stressing a legal framework to guarantee meaningful *legal* freedom for the news media, the ideals obscure how the American news media are significantly constrained by other factors.

RETHINKING THE ECONOMIC FIRST AMENDMENT

Despite this serious limitation on First Amendment ideals, there seems little reason to challenge or change basic First Amendment protections against censorship. But there is good reason to rethink the *economic* uses to which the Amendment has been put, because they are actually undermining the very ideals the Amendment is presumably designed to help realize.

The First Amendment—or rather, the prevailing interpretation of it—does matter powerfully to the daily production of news by shaping the policies that govern the economic structure of the news business. Thanks in part to Timothy Cook's *Governing with the News* and Robert McChesney's *Rich Media, Poor Democracy,* it is clear that U.S. media policy in the past three decades has been strongly influenced by the belief that government may do virtually nothing with regard to the media except deregulate it. McChesney argues that the First Amendment serves as an ideological wall erected around the private, for-profit media system, doing little to protect meaningful free expression but instead protecting a hypercommercialized media system that carpet bombs American life with its ever-steamier, ever-more obnoxious "entertainments."[43] In sharp contrast to its image in the civil liberties context, the First Amendment here plays the role of handmaiden to economic imperatives that increasingly constrict budgets and weaken backbones of news organizations that are embedded in these entertainment media empires.

This use of the First Amendment does not stem from the plain language of the Amendment itself. It is as if policy-makers read "Congress shall make no law" but stop reading before the crucial phrase "*abridging* the freedom of the press."[44] Just as the assumption that government may not censor the news holds strong, so does the assumption that government may not aggressively regulate the media industry, even in the interest of realizing watchdog-style media scrutiny and substantive, robust public debate. For example, at the Senate hearings in the spring of 2003 on corporate conglomeration in the radio industry, the reigning presumption seemed to be that government would only be able to intervene if illegal business practices were uncovered in the industry (for example, coercing artists who want play on a parent company's stations to contract with its concert production company), not simply on the basis that the recent dramatic conglomeration of radio station ownership is not in the public interest. The subsequent congressional vote to roll back FCC rules that would have increased ownership limits for television networks from 35 percent of the national audience to 45 percent reflects, it seems, splits in the broadcasters' lobbies more than a rethinking of the reigning economic interpretation of the First Amendment.

But even with regard to the economic uses of the First Amendment, empirical research on news content urges us to think carefully. Those like McChesney who see the Amendment primarily as a wall around the privatized media structure often assume that the corporate parents of news organizations will not critically scrutinize those on whom they rely for continuation of the favorable regulations that make corporate media profits so considerable.[45] This view assumes a media that can only be a lapdog, not a watchdog. But the record suggests that news organizations are neither incapable nor unwilling to expose government corruption, lying, and abuse of power. Rather, they do so only when conditions are favorable.

Nor can we assume that a different economic structure would automatically improve news content. Some relationship between the current economic structure of the mass media and the quality of news Americans receive surely exists. Quality news can only be produced with adequate resources, and the resources available to reporters at virtually every news organization are in decline today, largely because of business decisions that privilege the bottom line over serious journalism. By the same token, quality news seems in danger of being crowded out entirely by its more profitable "infotainment" competitors. But even if we changed the media's economic incentives by creating more not-for-profit or publicly financed news outlets, would that change the other influences on the news outlined here?

The norms that guide journalists' decisions about news might remain even without the intense market pressures felt by most commercial news organizations today. If journalists were still influenced by the pressures of the pack, by official news management techniques, and by the allure of big events, the news might not look very different. Timothy Crouse, author of the 1973 classic *The Boys on the Bus*, unearthed the absurdities of the pack system for covering elections when commercial pressures were not nearly as strong as they have become today. News programming decisions at PBS are strongly influenced by journalistic norms of professionalism and following the official lead even without market pressures. Nor does PBS's news programming necessarily reflect more diversity of people or perspectives than that on commercial television.[46] Put another way, does the journalistic "pack" exist because the market demands that kind of news, or because journalists think it is necessary and appropriate to cover politics that way?

Focusing on these questions is important not only to redeem the watchdog ideal, as Justice Stewart advocated, but to redeem the ideal of the marketplace of ideas as well. Tim Cook has argued elsewhere that "[s]o much of the history of the First Amendment has focused on whether government can regulate or restrict the press that we tend to forget that it is eminently constitutional for government to shape the news by providing subsidies or otherwise encouraging a diversity of points of view."[47] In the context of the immediate post-Watergate era, Stewart was essentially arguing against the proposition that government should have more power to *curb* the press. Today's context is quite different. Deregulation has unleashed the profit motive while releasing the media from virtually all public interest obligations, and techniques of governmental news management have simultaneously evolved. Meanwhile, journalistic reliance on government for daily news remains virtually unchanged. Were Stewart addressing us today, he would be forced to consider a different question. In 1974, Stewart could argue that "the elimination of a strong and independent press is [not] the way to eliminate abusiveness, untruth, arrogance, or hypocrisy from government."[48] That truism still resonates, of course, but whether we should consider "eliminating" a strong and independent press hardly seems the question. The question of our day is how to invigorate the critical scrutiny and robust debate for which the media have ideally been prized.

NOTES

1. Potter Stewart, "Or of the Press," *Hastings Law Journal* 26 (1975): 634.

2. David F. Prindle, "The Idea of a Marketplace of Ideas" (paper presented at the annual meeting of the Western Political Science Association, March 15–8, 1995, Portland, Oreg.), 5.

3. Philip M. Napoli, "The Marketplace of Ideas Metaphor in Communications Regulation," *Journal of Communication* 49 (1995): 151–69.

4. Pew Research Center, "Terror Coverage Boost News Media's Images," http://people-press.org/reports/display.php3?ReportID=143 (November 28, 2001), accessed September 25, 2003.

5. Pew Research Center, "Strong Opposition to Media Cross-Ownership Emerges; Public Wants Neutrality *and* Pro-American Point of View," http://people-press.org/reports/display. php3? ReportID=188 (July 13, 2003), accessed September 15, 2003.

6. Ibid.

7. I will not focus further here on the "neutral transmitter" ideal because it is less crucial to the development of legal thought and media regulation. Indeed, the crux of the strong First Amendment protections established in American law has been, as Frederick Schauer explains in his essay, the notion that the occasional publication of "false" ideas is the price to be paid for robust media criticism and debate. The problem of media bias, ranging from inaccuracies to outright lies, presumably falls within the established legal bounds of protected speech limited by laws against libel. A lack of media neutrality, in other words, is a professional not a legal problem. As important as it is to the public and to journalists themselves, media neutrality does not emerge in legal thinking as a motivating ideal.

8. Stewart, "Or of the Press," 634.

9. Napoli, "The Marketplace of Ideas Metaphor."

10. Thomas Emerson, *The System of Freedom of Expression* (New York: Vintage, 1970).

11. Stewart, "Or of the Press," 634.

12. It is worth noting that Justice Stewart's interpretation of the marketplace of ideas metaphor focuses on whether individual news organizations should somehow be made to carry a range of views—a proposition unlikely to carry much constitutional weight, given the general direction of Supreme Court decisions on press freedom that he reviews. The more important question of media policy is whether the mass media *overall* should be structured with an eye to maximizing diversity of perspectives.

13. Gaye Tuchman, *Making News* (New York: Free Press, 1978).

14. W. Lance Bennett, *News: The Politics of Illusion*, 5th ed. (New York: Longman, 2002).

15. David H. Weaver and G. Cleveland Wilhoit, *The American Journalist: A Portrait of U.S. News People and Their Work*, 2d ed. (Bloomington: Indiana Univ. Press, 1996).

16. W. Lance Bennett, "Toward a Theory of Press-State Relations," *Journal of Communication* 40 (1990): 103–25; Timothy E. Cook, *Governing with the News* (Chicago: Univ. of Chicago Press, 1998); Harvey Molotch, "Media and Movements," in *The Dynamics of Social Movements*, edited by Mayer N. Zald and John D. McCarthy (Cambridge, Mass.: Winthrop, 1979), 71–93; Herbert J. Gans, *Deciding What's News* (New York: Vintage Books, 1979).

17. Thomas E. Patterson, "Bad News, Bad Governance," *Annals of the American Academy of Political and Social Science* 546 (July 1996): 99.

18. Brent Cunningham, "Rethinking Objectivity," *Columbia Journalism Review* (July/August 2003): 23–32.

19. Timothy E. Cook, "Political Values and Production Values," *Political Communication* 13 (1996): 469–81.

20. Bennett, "Toward a Theory of Press-State Relations."

21. Matthew Miller, "The Two-Percent Solution," public address at the Joan Shorenstein Center on the Press, Politics, and Public Policy at the John F. Kennedy School of Government, Harvard University, Cambridge, Mass., October 2, 2003.

22. Gadi Wolfsfeld, *Media and Political Conflict* (Cambridge: Cambridge Univ. Press, 1996); Regina G. Lawrence, *The Politics of Force* (Berkeley: Univ. of California Press, 2000); Robert M. Entman, *Projections of Power: Framing News, Public Opinion, and U.S. Foreign Policy* (Chicago: Univ. of Chicago Press, 2004).

23. Cook, *Governing with the News.*

24. Quoted in Hedrick Smith, *The Power Game: The Unelected, the Media and Lobbyists,* PBS.

25. Thomas E. Patterson, *Out of Order* (New York: Vintage Books, 1994); Joseph N. Cappella and Kathleen Hall Jamieson, *Spiral of Cynicism* (New York: Oxford Univ. Press, 1997); James Fallows, *Breaking the News: How the Media Undermine American Democracy* (New York: Vintage, 1997); Regina G. Lawrence, "Game-Framing the Issues: Tracking the Strategy Frame in Public Policy News," *Political Communication* 17 (2000): 93–114.

26. Cook, *Governing with the News,* 105.

27. James Boylan, "Declarations of Independence," *Columbia Journalism Review* (November/December 1986): 30–45; Daniel C. Hallin, *The "Uncensored War": The Media and Vietnam* (New York: Oxford University Press, 1986); Michael Schudson, *Discovering the News* (New York: Basic Books, 1978).

28. W. Lance Bennett, "Operation Perfect Storm: The Press and the Iraq War," *Political Communication Report* 13 (summer 2003): 1; on media "patriotism" after September 11, see also Kathleen Hall Jamieson and Paul Waldman, *The Press Effect* (New York: Oxford Univ. Press, 2002).

29. Bennett, "Operation Perfect Storm," 3.

30. Bennett, *News: The Politics of Illusion*; see also Ted Gup, "Working in a Wartime Capital," *Columbia Journalism Review* (September/October 2002): 21–7.

31. Paul McMasters, "Blurring the Line between Journalist and Publicist," *Nieman Reports* (summer 2003): 70.

32. Harvey Molotch and Marilyn Lester, "News as Purposive Behavior: On the Strategic Use of Routine Events, Accidents, and Scandals," *American Sociological Review* 39 (1974): 101–12; Lawrence, *The Politics of Force.*

33. Lawrence, *The Politics of Force.*

34. W. Lance Bennett and Regina G. Lawrence, "News Icons and the Mainstreaming of Social Change," *Journal of Communication* 45 (1995): 20–39; Regina G. Lawrence and Thomas A. Birkland, "The Exxon *Valdez* and Event-Driven Policy Discourse" (paper presented at the annual meeting of the International Communication Association, San Francisco, Calif., May 27–31, 1999).

35. Regina G. Lawrence, "Defining Events: Problem Definition in the Media Arena," in *Politics, Discourse, and American Society,* edited by Roderick P. Hart and Bartholomew H. Sparrow (Lanham, Md.: Rowman and Littlefield, 2001).

36. Regina G. Lawrence and Thomas A. Birkland, "Guns, Hollywood, and School Safety: Defining the School Shootings Problem across Different Arenas," *Social Science Quarterly,* forthcoming.

37. Marjorie Randon Hershey, "The Constructed Explanation: Interpreting Election Results in the 1984 Presidential Race," *Journal of Politics* 54 (November 1992): 943–76.

38. Stephen M. Chermak, *Searching for a Demon: The Media Construction of the Militia Movements* (Boston: Northeastern Univ. Press, 2002).

39. Regina G. Lawrence and Thomas A. Birkland, "Defining the Times: Patterns in News Coverage of September 11th" (paper presented at the annual meeting of the American Political Science Association, August 29–September 1, 2002, Boston, Mass.); Michael Traugott and Ted Brader, "Patterns in the American News Coverage of the September 11th Attacks and Their Consequences" (paper presented at The Restless Searchlight: Terrorism, the Media, and Public Life, Joan Shorenstein Center on the Press, Politics, and Public Policy at the John F. Kennedy School of Government, Harvard University,

Cambridge, Mass., August 28, 2002).

40. Bennett, *News: The Politics of Illusion,* 22; Gup, "Working in a Wartime Capital," 26.

41. Molotch and Lester, "News as Purposive Behavior."

42. Thomas E. Patterson, "The Search for a Standard: Markets and Media," *Political Communication* 20 (2003): 142–3.

43. Robert McChesney, *Rich Media, Poor Democracy* (Urbana: Univ. of Illinois Press, 1999).

44. Cook, *Governing with the News,* 182.

45. "Bill Moyers Talks with John Nichols and Robert McChesney," *Now,* www.pbs.org/now/transcript/transcript_nicholsmcchesney.html (February 23, 2003).

46. William Hoynes, *Public Television for Sale* (Boulder, Colo.: Westview Press, 1994); see also James Day, *The Vanishing Vision* (Berkeley: Univ. of California Press, 1995).

47. Cook, *Governing with the News,* 182.

48. Stewart, "Or of the Press," 636.

PART THREE:
TOWARD THE FUTURE

INTRODUCTION

RALPH IZARD

The technological revolution of the late twentieth century was not the first such period in our history to change the face of the communication process and open questions about the society in which we live, about First-Amendment freedoms, and about the role of both the individual and government. These are issues highlighted in essays prepared for this section by Lance Bennett of the University of Washington and Diana Owen of Georgetown University.

Bennett's and Owen's discussions underscore the fact that, as overwhelming as technological forces seem to be today, there is nothing historically unusual about their impact, except perhaps the rapidity. Gutenberg's printing press made it possible to communicate to larger numbers of people. Development of the telegraph—and, indeed, the railway—reduced restrictions of space and time as factors in communication. Certainly, the telephone, radio, and television expanded the reach of the human voice and image. In the early to mid-twentieth century—the period of yellow journalism, radio, and then television—communication was making a transition to the concept of mass: of undifferentiated mass communication in a society dominated, for example, by mass education and mass production.

But then occurred evidence that American society was redefining itself. Increasing pluralism grew from the ashes of mass society, fed by such political activist movements as those for African American civil rights and against the Vietnam War, and by continuous protests by feminists, seniors, gays, and others seeking personal equality. At the supposed height of mass communication, we witnessed many reminders of news outlets serving smaller, sometimes subversive audiences, from the long-established black press to dissident movement rags. These social changes foreshadowed, and provided context for, what happened when the computer and all of its subsequent developments stimulated the transition from mass media to increased roles in communication for individuals and their various smaller communities.

Technology, then, has provided a catalyst for a potential redefinition of the fundamental requirements of democracy, as new technological networks placed individuals—not huge media corporations—at the center of a communication process that was personal, often activist, and far-reaching. These trends raise questions of freedom that are different from what they were fifty years ago. Bennett suggests that political information is now easily available to the average citizen quite outside of the formats of traditional journalism, which have shrunk and downgraded political communication. And indeed, there are many indications of an actual increase in citizens' direct involvement in political action, many of them drawing upon the new resources provided by new media. As Bennett says, "Personal digital networks are *freeing the presses,* but in quite novel ways."

In this way, freedom therefore is accorded to the individual in a manner somewhat reminiscent of the time of the writing of the U.S. Constitution, when citizens were granted certain rights with the constant challenge—individually and through the press of the time—of monitoring their government.

Modern questions of freedom are dominated by at least two important factors: the way computers may be used to circumvent external restraint, especially by government and the political system, and how their increasing availability and almost ubiquitous training, especially among the young, facilitate political participation and activism. They provide the springboard for perhaps history's best example of satisfaction of the Hutchins Commission's 1947 requirement that "it is the whole point of a free press that ideas deserving a public hearing shall get a public hearing and that the decision of what ideas deserve that hearing shall rest in part with the public, not solely with the particular biases of editors and owners."

From 1947, let's fast-forward to Diana Owen's listing of developments by 2003 of new media that facilitate such democratizing potential: The new media (1) connect average citizens, political leaders, and journalists in less hierarchical communication networks that downplay disparities in social status, (2) facilitate citizen oversight of government action, (3) give citizens the prerogative to set policy agendas, and (4) stimulate a new era of civic activism.

However true these factors may be, many questions remain. It is not clear, for example, that what has been haphazard development of technological impact will continue. Both short- and long-range questions remain about how the traditional media will respond, what the impact of commercial and social forces on the use of new media will be, whether individual empowerment will continue, and what the role of government (especially the courts) will be.

These essays by Bennett and Owen, however, provide a substantial beginning toward understanding what has happened and, perhaps, what the future holds.

THE TWILIGHT OF MASS MEDIA NEWS
MARKETS, CITIZENSHIP, TECHNOLOGY, AND THE FUTURE OF JOURNALISM
W. LANCE BENNETT

This is a tale of two communication systems, one in decline and one in ascent. The system in decline was once commonly known as the mass media, a system defined by sending one-way content to large audiences who faced the task of drawing personal uses and gratifications from centrally produced, common inputs. The ascendant media system is digital and personal, including what may be termed *micro media* (for example, email, lists, and personal Weblogs, or blogs) and *middle media* (for example, Webzines, community blogs, and advocacy organization sites).[1] Many of these personalized digital media channels blur the distinction between producers and consumers of information, easily accommodating individual preferences with diverse content. Interactive digital communication technologies send content through pagers, cell phones, personal computers, and other devices that enable multipath, interactive (one-to-one and many-to-many) communication. A central question about each media system is how the flow of news and other political content measures up against freedom of information standards regarded as essential to the independence and effectiveness of citizens in democracies.

In thinking about contemporary mass media journalism, Potter Stewart's distinction between freedom of speech and separate safeguards for freedom of the press remains an important precept. Journalists must be protected in their investigations if citizens are to receive political information that is not controlled by government. However, investigative journalism is seldom the first order of business in today's corporate media that all too often hide behind their press protections to defend the right to air low-quality mayhem, chaos, and sensationalism in place of more responsible public interest news fare. Michael Schudson's contribution to this volume suggests that there is still room to defend contemporary journalism quality. However, the chorus of criticism from citizens, scholars, and journalists suggests that the hallowed role of the free press in American democracy is entering a period of contentious redefinition. If Stewart's press standard is becoming confused in the sphere of traditional journalism, it is nearly impossible to apply it to the political discourses flowing across free-wheeling personalized digital information networks. These inventive communication forms integrate journalism and personal speech through a variety of open publishing Web venues, from blogs to citizen action sites. At the same time, these interactive information networks raise other important questions about democratic information standards, such as trust and verification of communication content in the absence of traditional standards of journalism and separate roles for citizens and press.

The digital communication age enables citizen journalism reminiscent of when printers published citizen broadsides at the time of the American Revolution—but on a far larger scale. Today, anyone with a computer or a mobile phone is a potential reporter and publisher. A more enduring democratic ideal for this era of rapidly changing communication practices may be Justice Brennan's freeing notion of "uninhibited, robust and wide-open debate." It is ironic that commercial mass media news in recent decades has all but abandoned this ideal, substituting sensational punditry for serious debate, and avoiding robust, critical questions about state and economy until public officialdom has cued the press about the admissible bounds of policy debate.[2] At the same time, growing numbers of interactive digital media channels offer lively debate, often supported by policy research from grassroots advocacy networks.

An important focus of this essay is to evaluate the prospects for making these new and fragile communication arenas more robust and protected in the future. More generally, the first half of this essay explores some of the press abuses that have flowed from the special protections granted to commercial media, while the second half explores new forms of citizen-driven communication that may end up transforming the very ways in which we think about the press, journalism, and democratic information standards.

CHANGING MEDIA SYSTEMS, CHANGING CITIZENSHIP

In a provocative article titled *The End of Mass Communication?* Steven Chaffee and Miriam Metzger suggest that the convergence of different media systems—along with the erosion of the defining properties of mass media—requires rethinking the most fundamental categories of mediated communication research.[3] They even invite us to consider shifting standard media effects measures from such categories as the number of murders a child sees by age eighteen, to the number of murders a child commits (virtually) by age eighteen.[4] It is equally provocative to imagine political communication environments in which transmission is not one-way and time-specific, but interactive and at personal convenience.

Evolving personal media systems are reshaping what we know as news, and, more generally, public information. The convergence between one-way (mass) media systems and interactive (personal) digital networks is hardly a seamless process. For example, many of the emerging political information forums on the Web display highly personal narratives freed of standard journalistic constraints by open publishing, collective editing, and other democratizing software created for Weblogs, protest and issue campaign sites, and citizen news sites such as Indymedia.org. Many political issues (health, environment, human rights, labor standards, world trade, and development) now have prominent Web networks that carry rich flows of information on demand—in contrast to the sporadic and often diminishing attention that those issues receive from conventional media.

Even when conventional news organizations make gestures toward digital interactive formats, the content formulas pumped through them tend to reflect mass media political economies. Due in part to profit and marketing constraints, conventional news content has undergone a period of profound change in the last twenty years, and not for the better in the view of many scholars and journalists.[5] From the standpoint of large media organizations, the downsizing and reformatting of political news content reflects the machinations of corporate behemoths trying to assemble mass audiences in an ever-fragmenting communication environment. In this corporate context, news is just another product line, subject to production formulas, profit imperatives, and branding opportunities. The results are predictably mixed: loss of depth and diversity, combined with notable adherence to still-recognizable story, source, and journalistic styles.

Most media corporations could deploy digital information technologies that put audiences more in control of content, even making them as much information producers as consumers. Yet conventional media organizations persist in controlling and standardizing their content, either to assure profits or to maintain professional production standards, or both. Thus, with few exceptions—most notably, the public service BBC *iCan* initiative[6]—media giants have not moved very far in the direction of Web-driven interactive news that might redefine the role of the audience in content construction, or incorporate citizen engagement opportunities into news formats.

The irony is that most of these organizations have also learned that it is difficult to standardize, control, or profit from the information products that they have introduced into cyberspace. For example, giant music companies have generally failed to develop viable online business plans even as they watched their profits and products consumed by hard-to-defeat file sharing systems. Despite the proliferation of online news sites, few news organizations have been able to make them profitable, and even fewer have used interactive features (beyond chats, click polls, searches, and hyperlinked content) to change the core of news itself.

In short, this is not a tale of harmonious media convergence in which news organizations interact neatly with their audiences to create richer, deeper, more personally meaningful information flows. It is more a story of the disjointed evolution of different systems in which there are some points of concerted integration, some points of accidental integration, and many points of divergence. For example, some concerted attempts at convergence have failed dramatically (think AOL-Time Warner), while others still hold promise for well integrated one-way and interactive information systems (think BBC digital media initiatives).

At a less concerted level, the sheer proliferation of links connecting different media levels—micro, middle, and mass—open new paths for information to flow from individuals to larger audiences.[7] For example, competition among cable channels with needs for 24/7 content delivery may tempt journalists to dip into the middle media for story ideas, and to go with stories that are poorly researched, driven by the awareness that the competition may report them if they do not (think Matt Drudge and Monica Lewinsky). In some cases, this flow even facilitates radical political messages entering mass media channels.[8]

In other cases, information does not flow readily across media levels because content is so far beyond the penumbra of conventional production standards—although it is clear that such standards are subject to renegotiation. For example, an important barrier to the easy flow of information across media levels is that Internet activist networks often merge information and action in ways that challenge the citizen-spectator model implicit in much conventional political reporting. Diverse information formats (e.g., news, action alerts, policy reports) and interfaces (blogs, chats, open publishing forums, collectively edited sites, self-organizing protest networks, and more) reflect the capacity of digital information systems to integrate information and political action in personalized ways that conventional information media generally handle awkwardly.

Running parallel to these tales of uneven convergence in media systems are stories of changing conceptions of society, citizenship, and political participation styles in many northern industrial democracies. Societies like the United States are experiencing boomerang effects of globalization coming back home. Transformations of economy and communication associated with economic globalization have undermined common social and political experiences, from introducing new career and family models to freeing individuals from group, party, and in some cases government and national identifications. These shifts in personal lifestyles and identities, in turn, are changing the ways in which people receive and share political information. I have described elsewhere the gradual disconnection of citizens from collective political projects vested in parties, ideologies, or governments, offset by the increasing importance of personal symbolic connections between issues, actions, and lifestyles.[9] In his history of citizenship in America, Schudson talks about the relatively recent shift from an informed citizen model to a rights-oriented, more personal style of citizenship.[10] Whatever we choose to call this evolving citizenship style, it is likely that these personal-level changes will have a range of different effects on the production and consumption of news and political information across conventional, middle, and micro media systems. Consider, first, the state of mass media journalism.

MASS MEDIA NEWS AT A CROSSROAD

An ironic finding emerged from a study of journalists in five nations: Italy, Britain, Sweden, Germany, and the United States. Journalists in the United States reported fewer limits and restrictions on their reporting than did their colleagues in any of the other nations. Yet, when asked how they would approach different hypothetical news stories, the U.S. journalists proposed interviewing a narrower range of sources and considered a smaller number of possible storylines than did their counterparts in the other four nations.[11] This narrowing of the news in what is often regarded as the world's most competitive, deregulated, speech protected media system can be explained by several factors. One must, of course, acknowledge the centrist political culture of the United States and the strong professional journalism norm of "objectivity" that tends to produce stunning levels of content uniformity across competing news organizations. However, other changes, such as shrinking the political news space and the movement toward infotainment, mayhem, and lifestyle formulas, have occurred while journalistic norms of objectivity have remained stable. These transformations of news content cannot be explained easily by consumer demand, as news executives often claim. To the contrary, the media, and their news products in particular, have fallen in public esteem to the lowest levels recorded in the modern era of polling.[12] The failure of easy explanations to account for changes in public information content points to a different and less culture-bound explanation that is useful for thinking about the future of democratic media systems in the United States and other nations.

During the twenty-year period from 1980 to 2000, the media markets in the United States experienced an unprecedented historical explosion of mergers and corporate growth. This economic revolution has reduced government regulation and lowered the public service obligations of media organizations as the swing toward a free market ideology has ironically created near monopoly business practices. True, there is fierce competition among media outlets for audiences. However, profit calculations require many of the products (from news to entertainment formulas) to be standardized by sharing common sources of production, and recycling the content through multiple outlets in the same corporate chain. Moreover, product innovation and consumer demand are generally satisfied only after profit-maximizing considerations have been factored into production formulas.[13]

During this grand period of merger and deregulation, the editorial content of newspapers, television, and magazines transformed strikingly in the direction of more dramatized, entertainment-oriented, and personality-centered images of society and politics. Was there simply less significant news to report during the end of the twentieth century? Consider the international arena, which prior to September 11, 2001, suffered the greatest shrinkage of corporate attention, and after September 11 seldom reported stories that deviated much from the press handouts offered by government. Beyond a few megastories (the fall of the Soviet Empire, genocidal regimes in the Balkans and Rwanda, and tensions in the Middle East), world affairs occupied an ever-diminishing news space after the end of the 1970s. These episodic occurrences of wars and crises tend to be scripted largely by government officials, often with disappointing journalistic results, as in the case of the Iraq War of 2003. As Regina Lawrence notes in this volume, event-driven news may occasionally free the press to report independent views, but news organizations more often stick to government scripts until the spin proves impossible to reconcile with reality.

Beyond the crises, much of enduring importance seems to be occurring in the world these days. Surely, for example, there is reason to look beyond episodes of event-driven crises to provide sustained, investigative coverage of the sweeping process of globalization that has resulted in dislocating the lives and careers of a majority of workers in America and elsewhere. This new human experience ranges from the relatively trivial McDonaldization of the planet to the important world digital communications revolution upon which trade regimes and new corporate structures depend. This global restructuring emanated at least in part from the United States. More importantly, the forces of globalization, once unleashed and given the blessings of multinational leaders, left and right, came back home in forms that changed lives, lifestyles, and the basic institutional structures in which those lives played out.[14] As we shall note later, coverage of globalization in recent years has been framed in polar stereotypical terms of economic success or political protest. While global social justice activists have created their own information channels, largely through digital networks, general media audiences might easily conclude that the protesters are neo-Luddites who are against economic progress, rather than favoring the creation of social justice accountability mechanisms in global economic policies.

There was, of course, a great deal of optimistic business coverage of global economic trends aimed at investors and consumers. And there was also coverage of the personal stories of the age of globalization: the victims of corporate downsizing, the mid-careers lost, the traditional family blown apart, the epidemics of emotional disturbances, and the invention of miracle cures, such as Prozac—all set against a media backdrop featuring the lifestyles of the rich and the famous. But the big picture of world economic and political affairs that might make sense of these personal stories was squeezed out of the news by editorial choices to feature, instead, a world of chaos, disaster, famine, flood, and other biblical epics. In the calmer moments between fires and floods, the precious news space was given to social scares, such as an over-dramatized twenty-year crime wave, the serial disorders of the tragic Princess Di, or the endless year that was devoted to the unappealing sexual appetites of Bill Clinton. As Anuradha Vittachi remarked about the British press at the dawn of the millennium, the story of the year that somehow missed the papers was the possibility of ending world poverty by redirecting the money squandered through corruption each year from the World Bank and other so-called development programs. Instead, news consumers in the United Kingdom were treated to front-page coverage of the earth-shattering revelation that footballer David Beckham enjoyed wearing wife Posh Spice's knickers.[15]

As demonstrated later in this analysis, this so-called tabloid trend in media content has replaced coverage of power, policy, institutions, social change, and other topics that might help individuals grasp the personal impact of global changes that swept society at the end of the millennium. This does not imply that the public information system of the United States was a model of democratic virtue prior to 1980—such nostalgia would not serve us well. However, the potential to use an ever more technologically sophisticated media to communicate more useful (or even more accurate) images of society and global affairs is being wasted.

DOES MARKET-DRIVEN INFORMATION REFLECT PUBLIC DEMAND?

The bottom line in this analysis is that open media markets and the accompanying relaxation of corporate social responsibility norms promote business decisions above public service and public interest information considerations. This explanation is far better supported by data than is the ideological proposition that free markets perfectly reflect and respond to consumer demands.[16] Understanding information content in terms of profit constraints suggests that the balance between profit and social responsibility can be used to trace changes in media representations of politics and society through different societies and through different media sectors within those societies. For example, as American broadcast and cable outlets compete aggressively for the attention of increasingly fragmented audiences, print media feel pressures to change their formats as well. Even as they change their formats and marketing strategies, embattled print organizations are swallowed by conglomerates with holdings in broadcast, film, cable, and Internet.

The efficiencies of these empires include free (internal) advertising, shared marketing, recycling product across different outlets, and the convergence of technologies for distributing content to consumers. In the area of news, for example, the goals of business efficiency in these media empires are most easily achieved by using the same (often diminished) reporting resources to feed all the outlets in the chain. Those outlets, in turn, select what to report according to the marketing studies that shape the most cost-effective content for audiences. These common information streams and industrial formulas can then be styled and formatted using different packaging and marketing to draw those niche audiences to the various brands in the corporate product line. Consider some content trends in various American media sectors that reflect this market logic:

· A national study of local news by the Center for Media and Public Affairs found that crime dominated most programs, and that after removing the combination of crime, weather, accidents, disasters, other "soft" news, and sports, only 5 minutes and 40 seconds remained out of the 24 minutes and 20 seconds of noncommercial news time for coverage of government, health, foreign affairs, education, science, and the environment. This means that "hard" news gets no more time than commercials.[17]

· The increased violent crime news cannot be explained as reflections of actual rates of crime in society; nor are these profitable news formulas just limited to local programs. To the contrary, the trends in crime news have been going up as actual crime has declined. In the period from 1990 through 1998, for example, the number of crime stories broadcast annually on the NBC, CBS, and ABC evening news programs rose from 542 to 1,392, during a time in which the actual levels of most violent crimes dropped significantly in society.[18] If we look just at news about murder on the national networks, the number of murder stories increased by 700 percent between 1993 and 1996, a period in which the murder rate in society actually declined by 20 percent.[19]

· According to a national survey, two-thirds of the people get most of their views about crime from television, compared to just 20 percent from newspapers, 7 percent from radio, and less than 10 percent from friends, neighbors, coworkers, or personal experience.[20]

· Network television newscasts between 1990 and 1998 more than doubled the time devoted to entertainment, disasters, accidents, and crime, while reducing the coverage of the environment, government activities, and international affairs to make the room.[21]

· International news on network television declined from 45 percent of stories in the 1970s to 13.5 percent of stories in 1995.[22]

· Newspapers reduced international news coverage from over 10 percent of nonadvertising space in the early 1970s, to 6 percent in the early 1980s, to less than 3 percent in the 1990s.[23]

· Among the national news weeklies, between 1985 and 1995, international news declined from 24 to 14 percent in *Time*, from 22 to 12 percent in *Newsweek*, and from 20 to 14 percent in *U.S. News and World Report*. Entertainment, celebrity stories, recreation, lifestyle, and sports filled up the editorial space.[24]

· In 1987, *Time* ran eleven covers that put the focus on international news. Only one cover in 1997 was about an international story.[25]

· Overall, the network news, the cover stories of news magazines, and the front pages of major newspapers witnessed an increase from 15 percent to 43 percent between 1977 and 1997 in celebrity, scandal, gossip, and other human interest stories.[26]

· A national sample of over five thousand news stories (from two television networks, two weekly magazines, three leading newspapers, and twenty six local daily papers) between 1980 and 1999 found that stories with no public policy content (soft news) comprised 35 percent of all stories in 1980 and nearly 50 percent in 1999. In this study, sensationalism increased from 25 percent to 40 percent of news. Human interest stories increased from 11 percent to 26 percent of news content. And the journalistic tone of the news during this time became more negative and cynical, with journalists introducing their own voices more into stories, often at the expense of direct quotes from the political sources they cover. In broadcast coverage of the 2000 U.S. election, for example, journalists spoke six minutes for each one minute allocated to the candidates.[27]

· Despite (or because of) these efforts to attract (cost-effective) audiences with sensationalism and soft news, the news audience in the United States has declined dramatically in the period from 1990 to 2000.[28]

· Of those who now pay less attention to news than they did before, 93 percent say the news is negative (by comparison, 77 percent of the general population say the news is negative).[29]

The point here is that these news images of American society and public problems have changed notably during the recent period of media market deregulation and increased competition among media outlets for profitable audience niches. Does any of this matter? It turns out that it does. For example, people who watch more news, and more "reality programs" in general (i.e., programs like *America's Most Wanted* and *Cops*), are significantly more likely to misjudge the seriousness of the crime problem and to misjudge their own chances of being victims. These trends are less pronounced in nations that still attempt to regulate the content of such programs to better reflect social realities.[30] In the United States, fewer people felt safe in their neighborhoods (29 percent) in the late 1990s than in the early 1980s (44 percent), even though objective crime conditions warranted just the opposite feelings.[31] In this and many other policy areas, perceptions of public problems and their solutions are shaped by images of society that are to varying degrees constructed in or out of the news by short-circuiting serious reporting and replacing it with topics and treatments based on cost calculations and audience marketing studies.

The marketing formulas through which news is now produced have undermined the overall amount of public issue coverage on which sound public policy-making depends. In addition, the quality of the remaining political information that makes it through the media profit filters is more politically suspect as well. The logic of cost-conscious news organizations is a politically unfortunate one from the standpoint of the citizen. The shrinking space for serious political news combines with diminishing organizational resources to make the news vulnerable to more public relations, political spin, the promotion of parent corporation celebrity and entertainment products, and professionally staged events. Serious journalism does not need to be dull; it merely needs to be engaging. By nearly any measure of engagement, the commercial sensationalism passing for journalism today does not engage; it discourages. As with the trends introduced earlier in the argument, these patterns vary from nation to nation, and system to system, but they are the evident to varying degrees throughout the advanced democracies.

BEYOND BAD NEWS: DECLINING CONFIDENCE IN JOURNALISTS AND LEADERS

Commercialized media systems are particularly vulnerable to the corps of communication professionals who supply much of our public information content. These publicity agents run election and issue campaigns, place stories about political allies and enemies, spin the day's events, and generally represent the first line of contact for journalists working on stories. The decline of reporting resources in commercialized media systems means that news organizations rely on materials produced directly by public relations firms, along with the information and staged performances produced by the professional communications consultants hired by parties, government agencies, politicians, and election campaigns. In the United States, many of the scandals, dramas, and other "big stories" of recent years have come directly out of strategic communication campaigns aimed at using the news to elevate an issue, a leader, or a cause—often while damaging the images and causes of opponents.[32] Once these media dramas get going, news organizations keep them going, whether or not the issues involved are important, or the waves of allegations and rumors are even accurate. On the other side of the equation, since politicians are faced with shrinking space for serious news coverage of their issues, they must rely on professional public relations and news management to get their messages into precious news space.[33]

Perhaps the most ironic result of journalism that maximizes profit over robust, free-wheeling debate is that it undermines the confidence of people in the information they receive, along with regard for the journalists who produce it. This result is anything but a sign of the perfect harmony between profitable production and satisfying consumption that is often the alleged result of the hidden hand of the market. Not surprisingly, journalists have grown more cynical and dissatisfied with their jobs over this recent period. The result in the United States has been a spiral of cynicism about politics and public life.[34]

COMING TO EUROPE? MEDIA MARKETS, POLITICAL CONTENT, AND AUDIENCE TRENDS

In the not so distant past, most European polities featured fairly diverse, non-commercial media systems, with party papers, public service broadcasting, and various state information subsidies being more common than commercial outlets and deregulated markets. Yet recent trends toward more commercial media outlets, market deregulation, and monopoly ownership have begun to change these systems. While the public service sector generally remains far stronger throughout Europe than in the United States, the shifting balance between commercial and public broadcasting has produced notable effects on program content, particularly in public service outlets. Consider several patterns here:

· The consolidation of newspaper ownership in Eastern Europe has placed much of the press in Poland, Hungary, Bulgaria, and Romania under the control of the German conglomerates Springer, Bertelsman, and Westdeutsche Allgemeine Zeitung.[35]

· In television, the shift from public to commercial ownership and program formats has been dramatic. For example, in 1980, a survey of seventeen European nations revealed that 87 percent of broadcast channels were public and 13 percent were private. By 1997, 45 percent were public and 55 percent were private.[36]

· A survey of program content of European public service broadcasters found that the percentage of news and public affairs programming over this period of increased commercial competition dropped considerably. Pippa Norris reports dramatic declines in the percentage of all program content devoted to public information (news and public affairs) programs on public service broadcast channels in most European countries between 1971 and 1996. Examples of this diminishing public information programming trend include (public information content as a percentage of all programming): Austria, -4 percent; Belgium, -11 percent; Czech Republic, -23 percent; Denmark, -11 percent; Finland, -11 percent; France, -22 percent; Ireland, -12 percent; Norway, -24 percent; Sweden, -26 percent. While these percentage decreases have generally occurred in the context of overall increases in programming time, they do suggest a relative deemphasis on information aimed at citizens, and an increased emphasis on entertainment and lifestyle features, paralleling the trends in the more advanced U.S. case.[37]

· There are signs that the tone of European news coverage may have grown more negative and sensational as well. Norris reports a study of European newspaper coverage of the European Union between 1995 and 1997. Of the twenty-five topics measured for tone, only four had a generally positive tone, and the rest were negative.[38]

· Similar to the case of crime coverage in the United States, alarming and negative European news treatments also seem to have effects on public perceptions of the political and social environment around them. For example, the tone of press coverage of the European monetary unit (Euro) correlates significantly with support for membership in the European Union in the sample of nations reported by Norris.[39]

These European patterns also seem associated with the deregulation of media markets and the rise of economic pressures and competition for audiences in both private and public service outlets. Viewed only from the standpoint of conventional media, it would seem that European trends also reflect erosion in the quality of public information that enhances democratic life and social cohesion. Yet, we must remember that this conclusion is based on just part of our story. People increasingly have access to political information beyond the conventional media. In both Europe and the United States, the current era is one of considerable political vibrancy both in activism and information flows, particularly if we look beyond the conventional media and the conventional politics of parties and elections. Recent years have witnessed the occurrence of vast, coordinated, transnational political demonstrations and social justice campaigns—perhaps the largest such coordinated political actions in the history of the world. For example, the BBC estimated that between 6 and 10 million people demonstrated in sixty nations over the weekend of February 15–16, 2003.[40] This may stand as the largest coordinated citizen political action in history. Viewed from this perspective, we may sense that many citizens are somehow getting and using information effectively, even if from a combination of conventional, middle, and micro media sources.

THE FUTURE OF PUBLIC INFORMATION: PERSONAL DIGITAL NETWORKS

In sharp contrast to the above news trends in conventional media are the networks of citizen activists and nongovernmental organizations now utilizing the low production and transmission costs of the Internet to communicate in information-rich terms about a host of pressing human issues. For examples of these direct citizen-to-citizen information channels, see the *Issue Campaigns* and *Democracy and Internet Technology* sections of the Center for Communication and Civic Engagement (www.engagedcitizen.org) and the Global Citizen Project (www.globalcitizenproject.org).

At first inspection, this digital public sphere may appear to be badly organized, often unreliable, limited in its audience reach, and excluded from governmental policy debates that continue to frame issues and set political agendas through more conventional news media. Some observers are concerned that the degree of fragmentation in conventional media is nothing compared to the splintering of digital media. As a result, decentered digital communication systems may appear in need of governmental policy initiatives that address digital divide issues and facilitate citizen-government deliberation. For example, Blumler and Coleman call for a "civic commons in cyberspace."[41]

Although greater public policy attention may ultimately be required to make cyberspace a viable communication environment for all citizens, there are signs that digital media networks are already providing important political channels for growing numbers of users. Far from requiring central portals or gatekeepers, many personal digital channels are self-networking and self-organizing in ways that enable both content and technological innovation to travel across diverse networks.

THE LOGIC OF PERSONAL INFORMATION NETWORKS

In order to grasp the significance of digital political communication, it helps to stop thinking in terms of mass audiences and group-based societies. Instead, let us think of audience and society as increasingly constituted by interactive communication networks.[42] These networks carry personal communications across digital links, or nodes, that structure (expandable and interconnectable) affinity and lifestyle networks. The potential weakness of each personal connection is balanced by the redundancy and interconnectedness of the other nodes around each link. Put in formal terms: "The number of potential connections between nodes grows more quickly than the number of nodes. If you have two nodes, each with a value of one unit, the value of joining them is four units. . . . When value increases exponentially more quickly than the number of nodes, the mathematical consequence translates into economic leverage: Connecting two networks creates far more value than the sum of their values as independent networks."[43]

This expansion power of personal networks helps explain how messages can leave the desktop and travel virally throughout the world, landing in hundreds, thousands, millions of in-boxes, and at the same time cross media levels, from email, to Weblogs, to Webzines, to newspaper columns, to television and radio programs. The distributed digital network model also explains how patterns of Web links to various news reports on a given topic can affect which of the stories float to the top in personal searches for news about the topic. Thus, frequent Web links to alternative news coverage of an issue or event can elevate marginal media outlets to the highest level results in Google news searches.[44]

The capacity of individuals at each link of the transmission process to personalize, shape, and direct the course of their communications explains how digital media both suit the age of personal politics and enable information and action to become integrated in the same communication context. Unlike most newspapers or television news programs, many political information sites on the Web enable people to personalize their information requests, return new information to the source, and consider various political responses to the issue under consideration.

Thus, the digital paradigm not only suits the era of personalized politics, but it also breaks down the old citizenship paradigm of the informed citizen by making the citizen both the producer and consumer of information, while presenting action options as part of the information bargain. Moreover, the resulting politics in this networked world easily spill across the conventional bounds and barriers of locality and nation, and into global arenas.

All of these personalized, interactive, networked communication features mean that the most important emerging formats for citizen information do not look very much like what we know as news. Various analyses suggest that these evolving formats for political information are better suited to the lifestyle politics and personalized citizenship styles of contemporary late modern societies than are the crudely personalized and commercialized efforts of news organizations to cope with fragmenting news markets and changing citizen information styles. In the space that remains, I can only sketch several of these interactive information characteristics.

PERSONALIZING POLITICAL INFORMATION

Schudson characterizes the model of citizenship that endured for much of the twentieth century as an informed or "monitorial" citizen model involving relatively detached learning about politics and public policy choices which are delivered through objective news reports that stress the dominant established views on an issue.[45] By contrast, the emerging rights-oriented or lifestyle citizen of the early twenty-first century may find the Web of politics more conducive to her information needs. While conventional news has evolved personalized and dramatized infotainment formats, they are often crude, sensationalized, and hard to personalize in terms of practical information. Digital sources more often enable individuals to define their own information requirements.

Many political sites on the Web offer individuals opportunities to personalize their issue definitions, information sources, and political responses. People can engage or not according to their levels of interest, their sense of where in the world political pressure is best applied (from local governments, to corporations, to transnational organizations), and whether they want to contribute to the information stream based on their own experiences. For example, the Stop the War Coalition site (www.stopwar.org.uk) was the central hub in an information network that produced the largest demonstrations in the history of London—variously estimated at between 750,000 and 2 million—on February 15, 2003.[46] The Stop the War site adopted the "no leader, any ideology" format of much of the new digital information order, letting individuals and groups find each other on their own terms. This personalized information matching capability is possible because of self-organizing software that enabled antiwar groups to join freely online, and to identify themselves with various "meta tags," such as age, work or union affiliation, culture or religion, political affiliation, region, and locality, and add a description of their political style and aims. Meanwhile, citizens looking for information about groups with which to affiliate could personalize their search terms in similar ways and thus simplify browsing through a roster of hundreds of organizations in search of ones best suited to personal considerations. In addition to matching individuals and organizations, the Stop the War site also provided a portal to activist news organizations, comedy sites, posters, buttons, street art, and animation clips that could be downloaded and sent or linked through email.

Another example of personalized information sharing through interactive digital media is the explosion of Weblogs that enable individuals to set their own information priorities, find news reports and other information from conventional or middle media sources, frame and share that information with others, and exchange comments and editorial ratings with those who are interested in a story. Blogs have become so pervasive and so linked to conventional news organization sites that their link patterns can influence the results of news searches, as noted above.

Further defining the direction of the personal digital information revolution is the shift in narrative voice from the impersonal third person that continues to define news writing, to the often emphatic first person. Although early network studies suggested that this personalization capacity may promote social and content homogeneity in networks, this conclusion may reflect the types of networks studied in early research—primarily business, professional, and work.[47] The openness of many global social justice networks, by contrast, invites inclusiveness and diversity by making personal expression a central virtue of communication. True, these activists are joined by a common commitment to social justice, but the discourse of diversity and inclusiveness in many issue networks—along with the fact that many networks cross traditional issue boundaries—suggests that ideological homogeneity is not a defining property of network politics. Indeed, the creation of software to identify and organize communication among friends and foes (see www.slashdot.com) suggests that even problems such as "flaming" are being worked out technologically.

THE INTEGRATION OF INFORMATION AND CITIZEN ACTION
Not only do networks put the individuals in them at the center of a multidirec-

tional information flow (rather than at the end of a one-way flow), but they often enable a personalized matching of information and political action. For example, Howard Rheingold credits the exchange of text messages via cell phones with organizing and directing the successful demonstrations and other protest activities that resulted in the popular overthrow of President Estrada in the Philippines in 2001.[48]

One of the biggest obstacles to the harmonious convergence of conventional mass media and interactive digital information networks is that, in the digital world, the barriers between citizen information and the action options associated with that information are dissolving. Whereas the informed citizen in the mass media audience was left to her own devices to connect news information to personal action, digital political information networks often package information, interpersonal judgments, and action options together, filtered by the preferences of the individual user. One can see examples of this in the various issue campaigns currently running on U.S. sites such as Netaction (www.netaction.org), Move On (www.moveon.org), and Global Exchange (www.globalexchange.org), and on European sites such as Clean Clothes (www.cleanclothes.org) and ATTAC (www.attac.org). Beyond interactive issue and campaign sites, thousands of issue advocacy groups produce information and action lists keeping members and interested bystanders informed about public problems, government responses, and action opportunities.

ISSUE CONTINUITY

Many issue networks support information bases and focus issue attention in ways that the news simply cannot. Even as issues rise and fall in conventional news attention cycles, they often remain vibrant in digital networks. Researchers at the Center for Communication and Civic Engagement (www.engagedcitizen.org) have tracked various issue networks over extended periods and found remarkable levels of activity. What is more surprising is that these issue networks often persist in the absence of much centralized coordination, and they may even persist when important hub organizations move on or shift attention to other issues.[49]

NEW SENSE OF PLACE: NEWS FROM EVERYWHERE

Digital networks can place individuals at the center of an imagined community that may be a vast global network or a locality. Groups and individuals can join action networks with an ease that belies conventional organization and coalition theories. For example, the British *Stop the War* site offered personalized shopping among hundreds of diverse anti-Iraq war groups in the United Kingdom, along with links to coalition sites in other nations and a rich array of information resources.

Some middle media sites now contain high-quality streamed video reports from information producers around the world (see, for example, OneWorld TV: http://tv.oneworld.net). Such reports equal the production values of television news, while offering material for interpersonal political networking. The capacity to organize these info-casts by topic, by the personal narratives of their producers, and/or by interests of the audience creates personal contexts for distant places that generally appear in conventional newscasts only when they are under siege. The capacity of audience members to publish their own digital reports from their own locations gives a new meaning to eyewitness news.

TRUST, COMMUNITY, AND RELIABILITY

What about trust, social solidarity, and community in this networked world? What about reliability of information? I am tempted to offer the flip reply that these things are not faring all that well in the crumbling worlds of mass media news and governmental systems that define the core of the modern polity. The prospects for reliable information and confident personal association in the relatively anonymous world of cyberspace are enhanced by the development of software for assessing and remembering the quality of various network transactions (think eBay). Rheingold predicts a scale change in the extent of cooperative online political relationships when an environment of "ad hoc networks, wearable computers, pervasive media, online reputation systems" meet the stabilizing technologies of "mutual monitoring, graduated sanctions, widespread dissemination of both positive and negative reputation information, ease of locating and verifying other potential cooperators, and global social networks that cluster people by affinity."[50] Indeed, a majority of Internet users regard most of the information on the Internet as reliable, and a strong 90 percent regard half or more as reliable.[51] All of these developments suggest important changes for information gatekeeping with important implications for conventional news.

CHANGING GATEKEEPING AND JOURNALISM NORMS

The proliferation of digital channels that combine speed with content depth present one set of challenges to conventional news. The preference of netizens to collectively evaluate the content they produce and use presents another kind of challenge. First, as noted above, the rise of stories from micro to middle media sites mixes greater source diversity and less source control, signaling a shift from a journalism in which editors decide in leisurely fashion what matters politically to a speed journalism that pushes information about which the audience must decide.[52] These source changes interact poorly with internal economic pressures to sensationalize the news that result in selection of stories that audiences may regard as less relevant, more negative, and less accurate than information that people find for themselves on the Internet.

The second gatekeeping challenge from below may be far more revolutionary for how we think of news. The audience participation in gatekeeping that is now common on some Internet sites suggests a radically different construction process for news content. Both libertarian nerds and social justice activists have embraced the principle that individuals should be empowered to report on their lives, and, equally important, to be judged by those who read their reports. Digital media offer these gatekeeping values a rapid forum for development. The features of Web sites and other communication technologies display what Andrew Feenberg describes as a technical code, revealing the social values of those who organize and design the media for their purposes.[53] Andrew Flanagan, Wendy Jo Manard Farinola, and Miriam Metzger generalize that "the spirit of the Internet is inclusive, rather than exclusive, and that information is designed to be accessible rather than proprietary."[54] Many sites are pushing these open and inclusive principles toward a new journalism in which audiences are the producers as well as the editors and transmitters of information. Thus, open publishing software enables any individual with Web access to answer Indymedia's (www.indymedia.org) call to "Be the Media." As noted earlier, OneWorld TV enables people to watch high-quality video reports from around the world and to submit their own reports with just a small investment in tools of the sort that many households already possess (http://tv.oneworld.net/help/).

The Weblog Slashdot (a.k.a. News for Nerds: www.slashdot.com) pioneered open publishing and collective editing systems in which rated material (1 = trash, 5 = really spiffy) enables other readers to choose their level of quality before entering a topic. Readers can become moderators by posting highly rated material. Readers can also moderate the moderators, to judge if the ratings seem fair. Those who display enough interest in the ratings become raters by receiving five rating tokens that must be used in a fixed time frame (and may be renewed based on continued displays of interest in quality and fairness). Users are given more credit if they post from a registered account than if they submit anonymously (with the admonition that they are an "anonymous coward"). Also, content that rates high is archived, while other material is dumped periodically. People can also form networks of fans and foes, and organize their interactions accordingly. In addition, regular users receive Karma points, which establish their reputations based on how their history of postings has been received (moderated) by other users. This system results in an organized, self-reported, collectively edited, high-quality information exchange.

Variations on open publishing, collective editing, reputation ratings, and other "new media" gatekeeping values are now employed across the Web. Developers of these technologies typically offer free open source downloads to others who wish to create their own sites based on these social information values (see the technology and democracy section of www.engagedcitizen.org). As these innovations come to define network cultures of personalized communication, the gatekeeping systems developed by mass media news are likely to become regarded as quaint artifacts of an historically bounded social moment.

AND NOW, THE OBLIGATORY CONCERN ABOUT THE DIGITAL DIVIDE

Internet access continues to vary widely across nations. It is also difficult to estimate the number of people who are moving online for various kinds of information and political engagement. Trends in access and political information seem impressive in places like the United States, and dismal in places like Bangladesh. In America, for example, roughly 50 percent of adults report some Internet use,[55] and the number rises to over 70 percent if we include users as young as twelve years of age.[56] The UCLA Internet Report of 2003 found that users log in an average of eleven hours per week, and their top uses are: email and messaging (87.9 percent), surfing and browsing (76 percent), news (51.9 percent), entertainment information (46.4 percent), and shopping (44.5 percent). Fully 90 percent of users regard the Internet as a moderate to extremely important information source, and experienced users (with at least six years of use) regard the Internet as their most important information source.

It is hard to find data on the connection between conventional news and personal empowerment, but it is unlikely that this connection among conventional news consumers approaches anything close to the 24.5 percent who regard the Internet as a tool to gain more political power.[57] In more specific terms, Bruce Bimber finds that among those who have used the Internet for political purposes, 41 percent investigated "what government or an official is doing," 14 percent contacted an official, 20 percent expressed views about government or politics, 37 percent learned about political issues, 34 percent browsed for political information, and 55 percent engaged in at least one of the above activities.[58]

The sheer number of users and political uses may matter less than how digital political information networks enable personal political actions and multiply the collective impact of those actions. As I write these words, I am thinking about the capacity of small numbers of netizens to organize simultaneous Iraq war demonstrations in sixty nations—events that surely stand as the largest coordinated protest demonstrations in human history. The last time anything approaching such massive demonstrations occurred was during the Vietnam era, a time associated with the height of the mass media. While the size of some Vietnam demonstrations approached the size of those against the Iraq war, there are important differences. For example, the Vietnam demonstrations reflected years of careful movement organizing in the context of intense, if generally unfavorable, mass media coverage of the protests.[59] Moreover, by the time that Vietnam protests became large, the war was already in full swing, there was a draft in the United States, and after 1968, news reports from the battlefields were in sharp conflict with the propaganda from the government.[60] By contrast, the massive Iraq war protests occurred in the context of no war, no draft, and little in the way of large, formal movement organizations.

The Iraq protests also erupted despite comparatively little prior media coverage of an antiwar movement. Indeed, the demonstrations emerged more rapidly than conventional media could comfortably write them into news scripts, in part because journalists had little sense of who the protesters were, and in part because journalists had trouble writing a domestic opposition narrative when the politics in Washington involved the Democratic opposition taking political cover. (A few weeks before the February demonstrations I did an interview with *Newsweek* that began with the reporter noting her sense that a large antiwar movement was out there, but wondering if I could explain why the media were not covering it, which I cheerfully did.)

While conventional American news media tried and failed to find a sustainable narrative on the antiwar network, news traveled across personal digital channels in thousands of ways, from emails among friends, to existing political lists that carried antiwar news, to relatively anonymous coalition sites that enabled individuals to find their comfort networks close to home. Typical of the sustaining power of digitally linked networks, the network infrastructure remained in place ready for the next wave of mobilization. Indeed, the week following the global demonstrations, the organization Move On (www.moveon.org) staged a virtual march on Washington and mobilized thousands of phone calls to Congress, posting the callers' own talking points online.

Simply put, the conventional-news-to-digital-information comparison is this: Conventional news reaches far more people who absorb relatively little of it and must surmount considerable barriers to collective action. Digital information flows may be initiated by relatively small numbers of people, who more easily achieve the capacity for large-scale collective action. Call the latter effect *"The incredible lightness of being networked."*

CONCLUSION: NEW INFORMATION AND PERSONAL POLITICS

There are two interrelated stories in this analysis. One is about how mass media news organizations are trying to remain relevant in the face of rapidly changing societies and individual information habits. The other story is about how individuals are creating new communication media and information formats to suit their needs. If this were just a story about the conventional news media, we would be hard pressed to find solutions for the problem of eroding citizen engagement with conventional news—in part because the personal information needs of many citizens today seem ill suited to the mass media news model forged in a different social and civic context. Yet, rapidly developing digital information networks reveal intriguing models for the citizen information future. What does the future of information look like in these two tales?

At best, news reformers are searching for something of a policy patch for news in the vanishing mass mediated society. In these reform efforts, the key question becomes how to balance the profit forces of increasingly deregulated information markets with the responsibility of journalists and democratic governments to provide citizen-audiences with commonly available and useful perspectives on their lives, societies, and governments. Since recommending that news organizations be more tightly regulated or separated from commercial corporate pressures is impractical in today's free market climate, we need to search for other solutions. One possibility is simply to find ways that make reporting important stories interesting and marketable.

Consider, for example, how to report what is arguably the biggest story in the world today—globalization—on terms that might compete with the daily run of sex, scandal, celebrity, and disaster. The hard question is how to tie the complexities of world economic and political change together in interesting, easy-to-digest news accounts. One place to begin is to rethink the common journalistic practice of relying on the packaged pronouncements of party and government leaders, business corporations, and world trade and development organizations. These pronouncements result in fragmentary understandings that convey the unrealistic impression that prosperity awaits those who leave complex economic development decisions in the hands of those party leaders, business corporations, and trade and development organizations. This story does not fit the realities of failure and corruption in less developed societies, or the painful experiences of economic restructuring and personal job insecurity in the more developed ones.

More importantly, most government and publicity-driven accounts of globaliza-tion leave out the stories of many citizens who are working actively to make a globalized world a more democratically accountable and humanly scaled place to live.

Perhaps the way to bring lost news audiences back to politics—particularly young people, who express the greatest cynicism about what they see in the news—is to put ordinary citizens into the news frame. This is surely not a new suggestion.[61] But the challenge for conventional journalism is how to introduce ordinary citizens more systematically into accounts of important public issues, such as globalization. One possibility is for journalists to gain enough distance from official sources to tell the story of globalization in terms of the historic struggles of citizens, workers, and consumers to gain democratic accountability and social responsibility from corporations and trade regimes. This story does not fit standard press-government routines or business-driven news formulas as neatly as the more typical news account of battles between chanting, lawless anarchists and the polite trade representatives in suits trying to hold their meet-ings. However, it might be a story that is more interesting to news audiences searching for understandings of their world—particularly young audiences who are abandoning news in all media except the Internet.

Few news organizations or journalists seem able to imagine, much less de-velop, a technical code for serious news told from the personal political stand-points of citizens. Meanwhile, digital media are already incorporating such in-formation formats, both as imagined by information producers and as written into the technical codes that make digital communication work. Citizen-activists have turned to digital channels to create information and action networks that dissolve boundaries between objective information and partisan application, as well as between journalist and citizen. The result is that political information is finding new formats quite apart from conventional journalism. In these many ways, personal digital networks are *freeing the presses*, but in quite novel ways.

The new freedom of information reflects an underlying shift in citizen iden-tity and action. It is worth noting that at a time in which many social scientists and public figures bemoan a civic engagement crisis, indicators of citizen involve-ment in direct action are up, from supporting policy advocacy organizations to participating in protest activities. Indeed, if one excludes voting and government contact, the American profile of civic and political engagement, even for younger generations, appears quite robust.[62] People are taking personal responsibility for many problems that they see affecting their lives. And many of the information and action resources encouraging and reflecting these trends are available on the Internet. While it seems alarmist to say that the proliferation of information sources on the Internet will reduce traditional journalism and news organizations to nostalgic "information boutiques," as claimed by one observer,[63] it seems safe to say that without greater innovation in both the technical codes and journalism practices of conventional media, the initiative for defining the future of political information in democracy will shift to the Internet and other personal digital media. The important question for democracy is how to protect uninhibited, robust, and wide-open debate in these newly emerging media.

NOTES

1. For an elaboration of the distinctions among mass, micro, and middle media, see Jonah Peretti, "Culture Jamming, Memes, Social Networks and the Emerging Media Ecology," http://depts.washington.edu/ccce/polcommcampaigns/peretti.html (2003), accessed October 16, 2004.

2. See W. Lance Bennett, "Toward a Theory of Press-State Relations in the U. S.," *Journal of Communication* 40 (1990): 123–40.

3. Steven Chaffee and Miriam Metzger, "The End of Mass Communication?" *Mass Communication and Society* 4 (2001): 365–79.

4. Ibid., 373.

5. For a review, see W. Lance Bennett, *News: The Politics of Illusion,* 5th ed. (New York: Addison Wesley Longman, 2003).

6. Leander Kahney, "Web Antidote for Political Apathy," *Wired News,* www.wired.com/news/politics/0,1283,58715,00.html (May 5, 2003), accessed October 16, 2004.

7. W. Lance Bennett, "Communicating Global Activism," *Information, Communication and Society* 6 (2003): 143–68.

8. See Peretti, "Cultural Jamming."

9. W. Lance Bennett, "The UnCivic Culture: Communication, Identity, and the Rise of Lifestyle Politics," *PS: Political Science and Politics* 31 (December 1998): 741–61.

10. Michael Schudson, *The Good Citizen: A History of American Civic Life* (New York: Free Press, 1998).

11. Thomas E. Patterson, "The Irony of a Free Press: Professional Journalism and News Diversity" (paper presented at the 1992 meeting of the American Political Science Association, Chicago, Ill., September 3–6, 1992).

12. Timothy E. Cook and Paul Gronke, "Disdaining the Media in the Post-9/11 World" (paper presented at the 2002 annual meeting of the American Political Science Association, Boston, Mass., August 29–September 1, 2002).

13. Ben Bagdikian, *The Media Monopoly,* 5th ed. (Boston: Beacon Press, 1997); Robert McChesney, *Rich Media, Poor Democracy* (Urbana, Ill.: Univ. of Illinois Press, 1999).

14. Bennett, "The UnCivic Culture."

15. Anuradha Vittachi, "From Information to Globalization," address to Salzburg Seminar Session 383, *Mass Media in the Age of Globalization,* October 12, 2000.

16. See, for example, Tom Rosenstiel, Carl Gottlieb, and Lee Ann Brady, "Time of Peril for TV News: Quality Sells, but Commitment—and Viewership—Continue to fade." *Columbia Journalism Review* (November/December 2002): 84–92.

17. Lawrence K. Grossman, "Does Local TV News Need a Nanny?" *Columbia Journalism Review* (May/June 1998): 33.

18. "Ticker," *Brill's Content* (July/August 1999): 143.

19. Richard Morin, "An Airwave of Crime: While TV News Coverage of Murders Has Soared—Feeding Public Fears—Crime Is Actually Down." *Washington Post National Weekly Edition,* August 18, 1997, p. 34.

20. Ibid.

21. Center for Media and Public Affairs. Study reported at: http://www.cmpa.com/factoid/prevyrs. htm (2001), accessed June 15, 2001.

22. James F. Hoge, "Foreign News: Who Gives a Damn?" *Columbia Journalism Review* (November/December 1997): 49.

23. Ibid.

24. Neil Hickey, "Money Lust: How Pressure for Profit Is Perverting Journalism," *Columbia Journalism Review* (July/August 1998): 32–3.

25. Ibid.

26. Ibid.

27. Thomas E. Patterson, "Doing Well and Doing Good: How Soft News and Critical Journalism Are Shrinking the News Audience and Weakening Democracy—And What News Outlets Can Do About It" (Joan Shorenstein Center on the Press, Politics, and Public Policy, Kennedy School of Government, Harvard University, Cambridge, Mass., 2000).

28. Ibid.

29. Ibid.

30. Mark Fishman and Grey Cavender, eds., *Entertaining Crime: Television Reality Programs.* (New York: Aldine de Gruyter, 1998).

31. Morin, "An Airwave of Crime."

32. W. Lance Bennett and Jarol B. Manheim, "The Big Spin," in *Mediated Politics: Communication in the Future of Democracy,* edited by W. Lance Bennett and Robert M. Entman (New York: Cambridge Univ. Press, 2001).

33. Timothy E. Cook, *Governing with the News* (Chicago: Univ. of Chicago Press, 1998).

34. Joseph Cappella and Kathleen Hall Jamieson, *Spiral of Cynicism: The Press and the Public Good* (New York: Oxford Univ. Press, 1997).

35. Sabine Lang, "Local Political Communication: Media and Local Politics in the Age of Globalization," in *Comparing Political Communication,* edited by Frank Esser and Barbara Pfetsch (New York: Cambridge Univ. Press, 2004), 151–83.

36. Pippa Norris, *A Virtuous Circle: Political Communication in Postindustrial Societies* (New York: Cambridge Univ. Press, 2000), 107–8.

37. Ibid., 197.

38. Ibid., 201.

39. Ibid., 201–3.

40. BBC News, "Millions Join Global Anti-War Protests," http://news.bbc.co.uk/2/low/europe/2765215.stm#text (February 17, 2003), accessed February 21, 2003.

41. Jay Blumler and Stephen Coleman, "Toward a Civic Commons in Cyberspace," unpublished manuscript, 2000.

42. Manuel Castells, *The Power of Identity* (Oxford, U.K.: Blackwell, 1997).

43. Howard Rheingold, *Smart Mobs: The Next Social Revolution* (Cambridge, Mass.: Perseus, 2002), 59.

44. John Hiler, "Google Loves Weblogs: How Weblogs Influence a Billion Google Searches a Week," www.microcontentnews.com/articles/googleblogs.htm (February 26, 2003), accessed March 15, 2003.

45. Schudson, *The Good Citizen*.

46. BBC News, "Millions Join Global Anti-War Protests," http://news.bbc.co.uk/2/low/europe/2765215.stm#text (February 17, 2003).

47. Barry Wellman, Janet Salaff, Dimittria Dimitrova, Laura Garton, Milena Gulia, and Caroline Haythornthwaite, "Computer Networks as Social Networks," *Annual Review of Sociology* 22 (1996): 213–38.

48. Rheingold, *Smart Mobs,* xvii.

49. Bennett, "Communicating Global Activism."

50. Rheingold, *Smart Mobs,* 132.

51. Jeffrey Cole et al., "The UCLA Internet Report: Surveying the Digital Future, Year Three," http://www.ccp.ucla.edu/pdf/UCLA-Internet-Report-Year-Three.pdf (2003), accessed October 16, 2004, p. 39.

52. Bill Kovach and Tom Rosenstiel, *Warp Speed: America in the Age of Mixed Media* (New York: Century Foundation Press, 1999).

53. Andrew Feenberg, *Alternative Modernity: The Technical Turn in Philosophy and Social Theory* (Berkeley, Calif.: Univ. of California Press, 1995).

54. Andrew J. Flanagin, Wendy Jo Manard Farinola and Miriam J. Metzger, "The Technical Code of the Internet/World Wide Web," *Critical Studies in Media Communication* 17 (2000): 416.

55. Bruce Bimber, "Data on Internet Users and on Political Use of the Internet," www.polsci.ucsb.edu/faculty/bimber/research/demos.html (2000), accessed October 2001.

56. Jeffrey Cole, "The UCLA Internet Report: Surveying the Digital Future."

57. Ibid.

58. Bimber, "Data on Internet Users."

59. Todd Gitlin, *The Whole World Is Watching: The Mass Media in the Making and Unmaking of the New Left* (Berkeley: Univ. of California Press, 1980).

60. Daniel C. Hallin, *The "Uncensored War": The Media and Vietnam* (New York: Oxford Univ. Press, 1986).

61. See, for example: Robert M. Entman, *Democracy without Citizens: Media and the Decay of American Politics* (New York: Oxford Univ. Press, 1989); and William A. Gamson, *Talking Politics* (New York: Cambridge Univ. Press, 1992).

62. Scott Keeter, Cliff Zukin, Molly Andolina, and Krista Jenkins, "The Civic and Political Health of the Nation: A Generational Portrait," CIRCLE—The Center for Information and Research on Civic

Learning and Engagement, University of Maryland, http://www.pauf.umd.edu/CIRCLE/research/products/Civic_and_Political_Health.pdf (2002), accessed January 2004.

63. George Krimsky, "The Role of Traditional Journalism in the Internet Age," address to Salzburg Seminar Session 383, *Mass Media in the Age of Globalization.* October 12, 2000.

"NEW MEDIA" AND CONTEMPORARY INTERPRETATIONS OF FREEDOM OF THE PRESS

DIANA OWEN

The late 1980s witnessed the genesis of a new era in American political media. Existing communication formats, such as talk radio and television talk shows, television news magazines, print and television tabloids, and music television acquired novel political roles. Technological innovations, such as online computer networks and, more recently, personal digital assistants (PDAs), created new outlets and delivery systems for reprocessing old communications content and hosting new forms, such as Internet chat rooms. These nontraditional formats for disseminating political information were labeled "new media." They were distinguished from the traditional institutional news media, such as newspapers and network evening news programs, by the promise of offering greater openness and accessibility to those outside the political and media establishments, as well as by their tendency to defiantly shun textbook journalistic norms in favor of entertainment values. Journalists working in the new media were buoyed by a regulatory environment that deemphasized the public service imperative for communications organizations, a shift in popular tastes toward more fast paced, engaging, less serious media fare, and an ability to meet the dynamic lifestyle and scheduling needs of an increasingly diverse public.[1]

Conflicting views about new media's significance for democratic politics abounded in the early years of their evolution.[2] Candidates' use of new media during the 1992 presidential election sparked a surge in political interest and participation, as Ross Perot declared his candidacy on *Larry King Live* and Bill Clinton donned shades and played his sax on *The Arsenio Hall Show*.[3] Some observers celebrated the new media's democratizing potential. Candidates were expanding their outreach to voters through entertainment programming. Media platforms, such as talk radio and televised town meetings, were credited with initiating a new "media populism" by providing outlets for those outside the political and traditional media power structure to express themselves. MTV became a political player, as young people encouraged their peers to register and vote, interviewed candidates, and expressed their views through creative videos.[4]

The potential of the new media seemed vast. New media could connect average citizens, political leaders, and journalists in less hierarchical communications networks that downplayed disparities in social status. They could facilitate citizen oversight of government action in realms where the traditional press is either reluctant or unable to tread. They could give citizens the prerogative to set policy agendas. Further, the new media were envisioned as stimulating a new era of civic activism by empowering those who lacked the resources and position to seriously engage the political process via conventional means.

During the initial period of development, skeptics, including myself, believed that this populist promise of new media was overrated at best. Evidence that they were living up to their potential as leaders of a new democratic movement was exaggerated, episodic, and anecdotal. The democratic possibilities new media offered were unintentional byproducts of a system whose primary imperative was profit-making.

By the 1996 presidential contest, public enthusiasm about new media had waned, as the novelty wore off and their less impressive characteristics became evident. Despite outward appearances to the contrary, the new media largely engaged those who already were politically empowered. Talk radio and Internet news audiences were skewed heavily toward white, educated, middle- to upper-middle-class males.[5] Access to the airwaves was still in the hands of powerful gatekeepers. Talk radio hosts routinely blocked particular types of callers from expressing themselves on the air: notably, females, older people, and those who disagreed with them. Some formats were even more exclusive in their reach and accessibility than traditional media. Talk radio was not only a bastion of conservatism,[6] but female hosts and callers were few and far between.[7] Technologies themselves also acted as gatekeepers. A substantial number of talk radio callers were cell phone owners who had the advantage of being able to connect while commuting, outdialing those who relied solely on landlines.[8] The Internet's democratizing imperative was inhibited by a "digital divide" between those who had the technology and the ability to use it and those who did not. This disparity was especially pronounced for political applications.[9] Finally, the free-for-all atmosphere in which new media actors operated without established codes of ethics or standards promoted a discourse that did little to promote meaningful consideration of issues or calls for citizen action. Much new media content consisted of vitriolic rants and misinformation that compromised the image and integrity of the genre. Such an atmosphere did little to foster consistent, serious, sustained attention from political leaders.[10]

The new media are now middle aged, having been a factor in the American media landscape for approximately fifteen years.[11] Further, as Lance Bennett's essay argues, the American media system is in the midst of a major transition marked by the twilight of old-style mass media and the rise of a new system of communications enhanced by personal digital devices. These technologies are conducive to the style and function of new media in that they enable individuals to establish communications networks outside of the institutional mainstream. Thus, it is time to reevaluate new media's democratic potential and limitations.

One of the most significant trends in favor of the new media's democratizing possibilities is the rise of *citizen news producers* facilitated by the proliferation of available communications outlets. In theory, virtually anyone with access to communications technologies can produce and publish information. Citizen news producers, in contrast to press professionals, often lack formal training in journalism and, for the most part, do not work for established media institutions. They are individuals who have acquired knowledge about how technologies work, and developed the particularized skill sets necessary to take part, such as setting up a Web site, administering a chat room, maintaining a Weblog, and hosting a local cable television or low power FM radio program. They have learned the rules governing information dissemination, which are often highly informal, and can negotiate comfortably within the new media communications environment. Younger people tend to be at the forefront of innovation as citizen news producers, due to their agility with new technologies. But the ranks of amateur providers include representation from many different walks of life. The information distributed by citizen news producers runs the gamut from fact and opinion about current issues and events to highly personalized thoughts and accounts of individual experiences.

Despite these trends, new media's evolution in favor of greater citizen input and control has been haphazard and inconsistent both across and within formats. Citizen news producers are in some ways captives of the technologies in which they thrive. Their audiences are far more limited and specialized than those of journalists working in the traditional press. As amateurs, they often are responsible for bearing the financial and time costs of establishing and maintaining their communications outlets while they pursue occupations in other fields.

AN "OPEN PRESS" MODEL OF NEW MEDIA

As Tim Cook points out in the introductory essay, media systems can evince aspects of both "free press" and "open press" models, an insight which undoubtedly pertains to new media. A "free press" model, as espoused by Justice William Brennan and Justice Potter Stewart, implies the existence of an organized institution of the press that operates unfettered by government intervention.[12] An "open press" model, as articulated by Robert W. T. Martin, conveys the right to free expression to individuals, rather than to an institution.[13] This model posits that all people should have the opportunity to articulate their views for popular consideration. Communications technologies are considered a public good that can be used by those who desire to get their message out.

While it is clear that new media have not revolutionized American politics in the way that optimistic observers had expected, they have been moving decidedly, albeit slowly, in the direction of an "open press" model of freedom of the press. New media can facilitate opportunities for average people to express themselves freely outside of the formal institutional confines of the organized press.

The trend toward increased new media openness, however, can be taken only so far. Although the new media do not constitute an organized press due to their diversity and eclecticism, some outlets function as extensions of traditional news organizations. Television news magazines, Web versions and supplements of traditional media, and call-in programs sponsored by major networks share more of the characteristics of the "free press" model than the "open press" model. Such new media style operations are integral to large, profitable, long-enduring institutions. Audience members who participate in these channels delegate the authority to express themselves freely, as their speech is subject to interpretation and management by entrenched institutional intermediaries—program producers, anchors, and journalists. They surrender, as well, their ability to act as guardians of the public interest on their own terms.

Still, a number of developments have converged that are favorable to an "open press" model of new media. Basic assumptions have shifted about what constitutes news, focusing more inclusively on general information rather than on timely events. This change renders new media an increasingly attractive and realistic option for citizen news producers. In addition, individuals have developed greater facility with new media. They have discovered creative ways of employing new media platforms so as to maximize their technological and social advantages. New media offer lower cost alternatives to the traditional press with fewer barriers to entry. Certain new media forms, such as online sources, cable television, and low-power FM radio, readily accommodate open participation by amateur news producers. New media increasingly appeal directly to small audiences based on common values, ideologies, and experiences. Further, effective new media mechanisms have emerged that cultivate direct citizen action beyond monitoring information and expressing opinions. New media ultimately permit citizens to work on their own behalf as effective government "watchdogs." Thus, citizens today can better exploit the potential for conveying information and promoting debate than in the early days of the new media.

NEWS AS INFORMATION

Journalists for traditional media and citizen news producers operate in an environment where the definition of news has come to mean information, broadly construed. News as information has an "anything goes" quality and encompasses, under the same rubric, fact-based reporting, hard-hitting investigative journalism, and personal accounts of happenings by amateur observers. It includes opinions of professional editorialists, personal viewpoints expressed by average people, and rumors. When news is defined this broadly, the lines between reliable and unsubstantiated material—as well as between fact and opinion—become obfuscated.

This transformation, in part, has been encouraged by the efforts of citizen news producers to fill the vast new media news hole that emerged in conjunction with the proliferation of technologies and communications formats. Professional journalists working in a news industry that was increasingly motivated by profits rather than public service saw a shift in their own understanding of what constitutes news, especially during the 1980s era of deregulation. They began to shy away from traditional investigative reporting that was costly and that ran the risk of alienating the media company's financial affiliates in favor of safer, entertainment-style reporting.[14] The public's expectations about what material they consider worthwhile for consumption has shifted along with the fundamental transition from news as current events to news as information. New media are as valid news sources as traditional news media for many consumers.

Writing in 1999 about the traditional press, Robert Samuelson proclaimed "The End of News." In the 1960s, news, which was disseminated primarily via institutional print, radio, and television offerings, meant a report of recent events, primarily focused on fact-based "hard news" associated with crime, politics and government, disasters, scandals, and sports. But the news began to "soften" in response to what profit-making news organizations perceived to be most fruitful for the bottom line. Audiences gravitated toward stories that were more personalized and provided information that was helpful for advancing socially and economically. More attention was paid, first, to reporting of broad economic, social, and lifestyle trends, then entertainment and celebrity affairs, and ultimately personal services, such as how to stay healthy and invest wisely. The concentration on facts gave way to a preoccupation with analysis and opinion. News, whether in traditional or new media, has become equated with information more than timely coverage of breaking events. "The result is not simply that the news isn't what it used to be—it's now hard to say what it is," concludes Samuelson.[15] Nowadays, journalists for traditional news outlets are as likely to say that news is entertainment and storytelling as they are to claim that they are keeping people up-to-date on pressing events of monumental significance.[16]

Washington Post editors Leonard Downie Jr. and Robert G. Kaiser provide a definition of news as information that increasingly guides decisions in traditional news outlets. In characterizing "good journalism," they define news in terms of its ability to serve communities and create meaningful shared experiences:

> Good journalism—in a newspaper or magazine, on television, radio, or the Internet—enriches Americans by giving them both useful information for their daily lives and a sense of participation in the wider world. Good journalism makes possible the cooperation among citizens that is critical to a civilized society. Citizens cannot function together as a community unless they share a common body of information about their surroundings, their neighbors, their governing bodies, their sports teams, even their weather. Those are all the stuff of the news. The best journalism digs into it, makes sense of it and makes it accessible to everyone.[17]

This interpretation of the meaning of news pertains to both old and new media, with one significant difference. In the new media culture, news is *any* information that can stimulate audience interest and attention. Whether or not news contributes to the greater good of the community may be another matter.

Public perceptions of what constitutes news parallel trends in new media content, which features healthy doses of entertainment and whose connections to genuine community experience are sometimes elusive. Survey data indicate that a large proportion of the public believes that the content of news magazines, such as *Dateline* and *20/20* (63 percent), and radio commentary programs (36 percent) is equivalent to news.[18] A 2003 Gallup poll indicates that 22 percent of Americans say that political talk radio programs, such as Rush Limbaugh's show, disseminate news rather than opinion.[19]

New media have exacerbated the blurring of the lines between news and information, as well as between information and entertainment.[20] The multiplicity of communications channels has freed the media from the time and space constraints of a prior era when decisions focused on prioritizing events and issues that could be squeezed into the ever shrinking print news hole[21] or included in the twenty-three minutes of news time on network evening broadcasts. The abundant, almost limitless, opportunities to disseminate information have created the reverse problem of continually seeking a sufficient supply of material. Traditional news outlets have responded to this dilemma by endlessly recycling the same information.

Consistent with an "open press" model of press freedom, citizen news producers thrive in the new media environment, which accommodates virtually anyone with an inclination to take part in the process of producing and disseminating information. Amateur content providers are better equipped to offer information, unlike eventful news that requires advanced reporting and investigative techniques and significant resources. Conventional news format standards, such as the inverted pyramid style of newspaper journalism, do not pertain. Such an all-inclusive definition of news coupled with a more fluid environment for media access and relaxed standards for articulating information pave the way for citizen news producers to play a more significant role in the political process.

CITIZEN NEWS PRODUCERS

The increased propensity for citizens to be news publishers and producers is perhaps the most visible indicator of the new media's conformity to an "open press" model. People are more willing to create and distribute content as they gain greater familiarity and experience with new mediums of expression. As citizen voices proliferate in new media channels, they gain greater legitimacy in the political sphere.

The trend in favor of citizen news production is illustrated by the online behavior of those with Internet access (see Table 1). Of the majority of the population that has gone online (approximately 109 million people),[22] almost all have communicated using email and half of those have sent instant messages. More relevant to the production of news is the healthy proportion of people who have participated in online chat or discussion groups, have been active in online membership groups, have created Web sites and posted thoughts, and have developed Weblogs ("blogs") that others can read. An even greater number of individuals access Web-based political content, a good deal of which is produced by amateurs, including news, political information, and government Web sites, and conduct research using the Web.

Under the very best of circumstances, individuals operating outside of established journalistic circles can be purveyors of high-quality, reliable, and useful information. Amateur content providers, often informally, have developed standards of fact-checking and sourcing that, while sometimes unconventional, can be effective. Participants in political discussion boards, which often are run in conjunction with Web sites containing articles and opinion pieces, will verify information through personal sources and cross-validation with respected media. Many eyes scrutinize the same material, and discussion threads that address the accuracy of information are not uncommon. Certain participants gain a reputa-

TABLE 1.

USE OF THE INTERNET BY THOSE WITH ONLINE ACCESS

	% Ever	% Daily
SEND MESSAGES		
Send email	93%	56%
Send instant message	46%	11%
CREATE CONTENT		
Participate in chat or online discussion group	25%	4%
Take part in an online group of which you are a member	16%	6%
Create content for the Internet, build Web site, post thoughts	19%	4%
Create a Weblog ("blog") that others can read	7%	1%
GET NEWS/POLITICAL INFORMATION		
Get news	71%	26%
Look for political news/information	40%	13%
Visit a government Web site	56%	10%
RESEARCH		
Use search engine to find information	85%	29%
Search Internet for answer to specific question	83%	19%
Research for school or training	53%	10%
Research for job	52%	19%

SOURCE: Pew Internet and American Life Project, "Internet Activities" and "Daily Internet Activities," Washington, D.C., http://www.pewinternet.org/reports/chart.asp?img=Internet_A8.htm (January–December 2002), accessed March 17, 2003.

tion for being reliable, and thus the respect of the online community. Particular sites attract visitors because they are known for the quality of their information. My own experience with this scenario comes from participation in an online college basketball discussion board (hoyasaxa.com). Questionable information that is posted about the coach or a player's status is regularly debated, and fact is sorted out from fiction with surprising regularity. Egregiously incorrect information is flagged as such by the board administrator, and if it includes a vicious personal attack, it is removed from the board. Renegade board posters attempted to set up an alternative board that is free from what they perceive as censorship, but the move failed after less than a week. Yes, new media facilitate the transmission of tremendous amounts of unverified rumor, false statements, and uncivil personal attacks. It is unlikely that these practices will be curbed.[23] Yet it is far from impossible to responsibly and democratically manage information in the most open of new media channels.

The practice of traditional journalism itself may undermine the role of professional journalists. Online reporters, including those working for major news organizations, are unlikely to have any formal training in journalism. Instead, they are hired for their technical facility with Internet and other new communications technologies. Further, news organizations, responding to the cost-effectiveness of providing information and commentary, have significantly cut their investments in traditional news gathering and production resources.[24] While online news producers for established news organizations spend much of their time reprocessing content from their print and broadcast news products, they increasingly have the opportunity to make their own contributions.[25] Some of the more eye-catching aspects of online news products, such as photo galleries with gripping captions, are essentially the work of amateur journalists.

Downie and Kaiser predict that the ranks of amateur journalists will swell in the near future, propelled by the public's distrust of and dissatisfaction with the old-style institutionalized media. Citizens seeking to check the veracity of traditional news accounts and to delve more deeply into issues that are glossed over by the established press will make use of readily accessible new media technologies.[26] Younger generations of citizens who are raised on new media, have strong technical skills, and accept these channels as legitimate will likely be at the forefront of this movement. They may perceive new media as a mechanism for bypassing roadblocks to entry into the traditional media establishments. There is clear potential for the development of a cadre of citizen investigative reporters, rather than mere information purveyors.

INCREASED ACCESS

Average citizens seeking to express themselves through the traditional news media often face insurmountable hurdles. Journalists and editors can deem their story or opinion irrelevant or unimportant. Even individuals formally trained as journalists can face obstacles when attempting to break into the highly entrenched echelons of the institution.

In contrast, the technologies and the communication formats associated with new media have become more accessible to average citizens over time, bringing the new media ever closer to Martin's "open press" ideal. The first generation of "digital divide" issues are less relevant as computers become more widely available and skill requirements have declined with improvements in point and click technology. Census Department statistics indicate this basic technology gap had closed significantly by 2000.[27] In addition, there is convincing evidence that younger generations of citizens should be well equipped technically to connect with politics using computers and the Internet. As a result of the Clinton/Gore administration's initiative to have Internet access in schools and libraries, which included the $2.25 billion E-Rate program that subsidized equipment and training, 98 percent of U.S. secondary schools had been wired for the Internet by 2001.[28]

Technologies that facilitate the production of news and information are more easily procurable, less costly, and more portable. Inexpensive digital still and video cameras allow individuals to supply material to news outlets, including traditional news organizations. These devices also permit amateurs to create news products that incorporate the dramatic images of professional productions. Handheld computers allow citizens to act as reporters and supply information to both traditional and new media outlets from remote locations as they witness events unfolding.

In December 2002, the Federal Communications Commission (FCC) approved the first 255 licenses for low-power FM stations (LPFM). These one hundred–watt stations have a broadcast range of three miles and are inexpensive to equip and operate. The FCC created LPFM as a noncommercial educational service catering to nonprofit organizations with an educational and civic mission and local and state governmental and nongovernmental entities that provide public service messages. The initial goal of LPFM licensing was to offer a communications mechanism to small local bodies with shared interests—especially racial and ethnic groups with linguistic and cultural similarities, schools seeking to enrich their conventional curricula, and civic organizations that were not adequately supported by commercial, full-power radio. Political maneuvering by the full-power radio community has effectively limited the reach of LPFM to primarily rural locations.[29] Still, LPFM is providing opportunities for citizens living in remote municipalities, community and church organizations, and schools to exchange information. For example, Mountain Empire Community Broadcasting, one of the first LPFM stations, serves the communities of Potrero, Campo, and Morena Village, California, towns that lack local newspaper, television, or radio service. The five thousand residents of these towns had previously relied exclusively on bulletin boards and word-of-mouth to publicize local affairs. Rockland Family Radio in Maine is a school-based LPFM station that involves many community members in producing religious services, poetry readings, children's programming, local history shows, live music, foreign language tutorials, and international affairs programs. The Sitka Tribe of Alaska and the Cherokee Communications Council in Oklahoma are working in conjunction with Northeastern State University to use LPFM as a mechanism for meeting the needs of Native Americans whose voices have traditionally been muted on commercial radio networks.[30]

Those outside of the press establishment have increased options for participating directly in more established new media endeavors. Talk radio airwaves are becoming available to citizens and politicians in ways that circumvent established hosts' control over discourse. Lycos Talk Radio allows listeners to host their own Internet radio call-in programs.[31] Local political leaders host call-in radio shows where they address community concerns as well as entertain constituents, a trend that has developed especially in smaller markets.[32] The proliferation of local cable television networks, which can suffer from a dearth of programming options, provide citizens with platforms for addressing community affairs.

New media also provide a stage from which lower profile politicians can run for office, and are in part responsible for the proliferation of "statement candidates." These candidates may or may not have the resources to made a serious run for political office, but value the opportunity to develop name, or "brand," recognition and express their views. The large field of Democratic presidential hopefuls who contemplated runs in the 2004 campaign include "statement candidates," such as activist Al Sharpton, former senator Gary Hart, Senator Christopher Dodd, Senator Bob Graham, retired general Wesley Clark, Representative Dennis Kucinich, former Vermont governor Howard Dean, and former senator Carol Moseley-Braun, who all used cable television, talk radio, and Internet resources to promote their cause.[33]

Even "reality television," where average people can hold the national spotlight, if only for a short time, offers opportunities for citizens to voice their political views. Storylines on MTV's *The Real World* have featured young people debating political issues, such as the government's handling of AIDS policy, and defending their political beliefs, including a Latina woman who worked on behalf of Republican candidates. Fans of the program could weigh in with their views via the *Real World* Web site. HBO's *American Candidate* has showcased citizens from a variety of backgrounds campaigning for president of the United States. The "winning" candidate was able to make a nationally televised speech.

AUDIENCE COMMUNITIES

Traditional news media seek broad audiences to attract advertisers, with marketing strategies still focused on enhancing audience size. Thus, the messages dis-

TABLE 2.

AUDIENCES FOR TELEVISION, PRINT, RADIO, AND INTERNET NEWS

	% Who Regularly Use Medium		
	1994	2000	2002
Television News	81%	75%	78%
Daily Newspaper	74%	63%	63%
Radio News	53%	46%	48%
Internet News	—	27%	25%

SOURCE: Pew Research Center for the People and the Press, "Public's News Habits Little Changed by September 11," Washington, D.C., www.people-press.org/reports/display.php3?ReportID=156 (June 9, 2002), accessed March 3, 2003.

seminated by traditional media are aimed at a wider and more heterogeneous audience, which is in keeping with "free press" principles. Audiences for new media are smaller, more specialized, and more homogeneous than even the most targeted audiences for traditional media. New media audiences share core values and specific ideals. LPFM, local cable public affairs programs, and political Web sites reach community members with common interests and concerns. Localized formats such as these tend to be the most accommodating to content produced by their constituencies. The new media's ability to accommodate audience communities where members can deliberate freely is consistent with an "open press" model.

When new media were newer, they did not seriously cut into the audiences for traditional offerings. There was considerable audience overlap, as new media were supplements to traditional news and information sources, especially among political junkies. Audience members appeared reluctant to rely exclusively on untested and largely unvalidated new media for their news and information.[34]

More recent evidence suggests that new media are not only garnering greater audience attention, they also are attracting audience members away from the traditional press. The audiences for television, newspaper, and radio news have fallen off somewhat since the mid-1990s, despite a momentary increase immediately following the September 11 terrorist attacks.[35] As Table 2 indicates, more people say they rely on some form of television news than any other source, a trend that has been in evidence for the entirety of the new media era. The television audience, however, has shifted away from network news to cable offerings, a movement which has stabilized since 2000. Another steady pattern of audience use is the quarter of the population that report they regularly rely on the Internet for news. While many Internet news users also indicate that they consult print newspapers,[36] there is a growing trend toward sole reliance on online sources. This development coincides with the public's belief that the online news product is as reliable as the print press. A study conducted in 2002 by the Online News Association indicates that the public considers online news to be more reliable than national and local network television news, national radio news, and local newspapers. This perspective is not shared by working journalists, who have substantially less respect for online news sources and their colleagues who work in the genre.[37]

Table 3 gives a general idea of the diversity of sources to which individuals turn for news and information, although it largely underestimates the scope of new media offerings due to the limitations of the survey data.[38] Traditional news stalwarts, including local television news, still command sizable but shrinking audiences. Stable audiences have emerged for a variety of new media, including national morning shows, talk radio, cable news, and television news magazines.[39] Particularized offerings by both traditional and new media attract more specialized audiences. The trends in favor of increased, exclusive audiences for new media are especially pronounced for young people.[40] This indication of a generational shift in media consumption habits bodes well for the future of new media.

Some contend that the increasing segmentation of the news audience contributes to the decline of community, whereby isolated, narrowly focused conversation and knowledge networks of like-minded individuals become increasingly ignorant and intolerant of wider societal issues and concerns.[41] Yet, far from constraining discourse, nontraditional, highly concentrated communications networks create communities by connecting, and thus empowering, citizens outside of the political mainstream. As Susan Herbst documents, social groups at the margins, who lack access to political resources, including media, historically have created alternative "public spheres" to accommodate their own discourse. Nonconventional communication networks, such as the black press of the 1930s, allowed groups to organize successfully for social action.[42] Similarly, an important contribution of the Internet to political life is the creation of communities, many of which exist outside of the mainstream political radar screen.[43]

Audience segmentation also helps people to deal with the deluge of information that bombards them daily at breakneck speed.[44] Small, coherent communities of citizens can provide cues to one another for prioritizing, organizing, and ultimately managing information in ways that best represent their interests and

TABLE 3.

FREQUENT USE OF TRADITIONAL AND NEW MEDIA IN 2002

	Pew (regularly)	Gallup (every day)
TRADITIONAL MEDIA		
Local newspapers		47%
National newspapers		11%
News magazines	13%	
Local television news	57%	57%
Network television news	32%	43%
Public television news		35%
News Hour (Jim Lehrer)	5%	
C-SPAN	5%	
Spanish-language television news program	4%	
National Public Radio	16%	22%
NEW MEDIA		
Print tabloids	3%	
People Magazine	6%	
National morning shows	22%	29%
Cable news programs		41%
CNN	25%	
Fox News Network	22%	
MSNBC	15%	
CNBC	13%	
Cable talk shows *(O'Reilly)*	6%	
Cable talk shows *(Larry King)*	5%	
Television news magazines	24%	
Television entertainment show	9%	
Late night shows	12%	
Tabloid television shows	9%	
Daytime talk shows	7%	
Talk radio	17%	22%
Rush Limbaugh on Radio	4%	
Don Imus on Radio	2%	
Online news	25%	15%

TABLE 3.

(cont.)

NOTE: Specific networks or programs appear in italics.

SOURCES: Pew Research Center for the People and the Press, "Public's News Habits Little Changed by September 11," Washington, D.C., www.people-press.org/reports/display.php3?ReportID=156 (June 9, 2002), accessed March 3, 2003; Gallup Organization, "Poll Topics and Trends: Media Use and Evaluation," December 5–8, 2002.

needs. This scenario provides a democratic alternative to relying on news directors and other media establishment gatekeepers to decide what is important and what is not.

CITIZEN MOBILIZATION

Critics have pointed out that while new media provide endless opportunities for expression, they do little to help translate this discourse into meaningful political action. Because of the personalized nature of much of the communication that occurs in new media channels, as well as the emotional investment users feel when they engage in on-air and online discourse, new media leave the impression of participating without acting. Thus, some charge that new media distract people from genuine political engagement.[45]

Despite this criticism, new media's ability to facilitate political action is perhaps the biggest development in their evolution. It is also the characteristic that distinguishes new media most from the traditional press. Traditional media relegate average citizens to the roles of reader, listener, and viewer. New media not only allow people to become newsmakers and information conveyers, they also enable citizens to engage in the political process.

Steve Davis, Larry Elin, and Grant Reeher contend that the new media's activating influence has been underestimated because of the tendency for political observers to focus on established institutional structures and related behaviors. Those who lament the limited role of the Internet during the 2000 presidential campaign failed to observe the scope of online community-building it stimulated by bringing together millions of people who shared similar concerns but were separated from one another by time and space. The uniqueness of Internet communities large and small is vested in their ability to unite individuals from diverse backgrounds by transcending established social hierarchies—"a lawyer can discuss politics with a dishwasher from Denny's."[46] Internet communities that formed around the 2000 presidential campaign continued to exist after the election, and some of their members have moved beyond the realm of virtual connectivity to real world action.

The ability to coordinate among new media formats in innovative ways has enhanced their power to influence politics. Technological convergence is nothing new to the traditional media, which routinely use new media as ancillaries to their usual fare, such as Web sites that supplement news and infotainment broadcasts. Yet, the inclination of traditional news organizations to innovate is limited by their commercial imperatives, the impersonal nature of their communication networks, the size and heterogeneity of their audience base, and their orientation toward national and global reporting.

Some successful coordinated efforts facilitated by new media have been localized, grassroots, and spontaneous. New media are more willing to promote discourse and action that seriously challenge the status quo than is the traditional press, a point which is illustrated by the California recall movement that resulted in an unprecedented special election. With the aid of new media, politicians and citizens mounted a successful effort in early 2003 to recall Governor Gray Davis (D) for alleged mishandling of the state's budget. Conservative talk show hosts and Web sites run by Republican operatives, disenchanted Democrats, and antitax organizations prompted thousands of letters and email messages demanding the recall. The official Web site of the Recall Gray Davis Committee, chaired by a former state assemblyman, collected over ten thousand signatures on an online recall petition in the first ninety-six hours after its launch.[47] The talk radio and online efforts, and the word of mouth that they generated, encouraged hundreds of citizens to volunteer their time to circulate petitions and work toward a special election. Funds from large and small donors were raised to offset the estimated $2 million cost of collecting the 897,158 signatures needed from registered voters to get the measure on the ballot. A rally of several hundred people protesting outside the state capital and demanding the recall was organized online.[48] The traditional press, while not supporting the governor, tended to view the effort as futile. Every California governor for the last thirty years had been threatened with recall without resulting in ballot action. However, no recall movement had the momentum nor generated the monetary and volunteer resources produced by this new media campaign.[49] The recall prompted a gubernatorial election in which Davis was unseated by Republican Arnold Schwarzenegger.

New communications technologies and media formats are revolutionizing the ways in which political movements take shape. In the past, movements were orchestrated from organizational hierarchies that took significant time to form. New style social movements emerge from decentralized networks of previously uncoordinated groups that may be associated with a vast array of individualized concerns. Although they lack a single, identifiable leader, their high level of connectivity through communications networks allows them to quickly adapt to changing political conditions.[50] The time, place, and focus of demonstrations can be changed with relative ease. Protestors at World Trade Organization meetings in Seattle, Washington, D.C., Quebec City, and other locations used the Internet to coordinate logistics, including how to deal with law enforcement. "Books not Bombs," an antiwar protest involving 230 campuses nationwide sponsored by the National Youth and Student Peace Coalition, was organized using the Internet and regional talk radio.[51] Referring to protests against the possible war with Iraq that attracted more than eight hundred thousand people in the United States and 1.5 million in Europe, Todd Gitlin observed, "It took four and a half years to multiply the size of the Vietnam protests twentyfold. . . . This time the same thing has happened in six months."[52] The first "virtual march" on Washington, organized by moveon.org, which formed a coalition called "Win Without War," involved thirty-two groups and several hundred thousand people who flooded Capitol Hill offices with calls, faxes, and emails.[53]

PUBLIC POLICY AND THE MOVEMENT TOWARD AN OPEN PRESS

The new media system is at a critical juncture in its development, as public experimentation with new technologies is radically altering the ways in which society communicates. Public policy initiatives governing access to new technologies and their use have the potential to either promote or hinder the trend toward a more open press model. Policies can expand or limit citizen access to communications technologies, and concurrently influence the freedom of expression within these channels.

Government policy pronouncements have improved the availability of media technology on some fronts. The Telecommunications Act of 1996 states that "the Commission [FCC] and each State commission with regulatory jurisdiction over telecommunications services shall encourage the deployment on a reasonable and timely basis of advanced telecommunications capability to all Americans."[54] Implementation has focused on initiatives to provide access to computers, especially in primary and secondary schools. Even as the conventionally defined "digital divide" between technological haves and have-nots has been closing, new technology-driven disparities in access are developing. Less privileged individuals and groups find their ability to become part of the larger political discourse hindered by substandard communications technologies. A bandwidth divide is emerging, where those with access to higher speed, more powerful communications technologies have an advantage. This gap may render marginalized political constituencies unable to leave the confines of their technologically inferior ghettos as they seek to express themselves or take action. Nonprofit organizations who are at the low end of the technological curve are disadvantaged when they do not have a current arsenal of tools for educating and informing, such as the ability to process and produce multimedia content. Policy debates surround the means of making broadband technologies that support the most sophisticated uses of the Internet available to more users.[55]

Policy initiatives have also created formal impediments to the ability of new communications technologies to serve the interests of the underrepresented and disconnected. As thousands of applications for licenses poured into the FCC, an alliance of the National Association of Broadcasters and National Public Radio lobbied to stop the proliferation of LPFM, which they viewed as a threat to commercial and more established public stations. This effort resulted in the passage of the Radio Broadcasting Preservation Act of 2000, which effectively limited the power of the FCC to grant licenses to anyone other than those in remote municipalities that lack sufficient high-power access. This eliminated 40 percent of the first wave of applications for consideration and has prevented many more potential users from seeking licenses.[56]

CONCLUSION

The current communication environment is a hybrid of the old media, where traditional institutional boundaries prevail, and the new media, where individuals have a bigger stake in the action. Trends indicate that the content disseminated by traditional and new media is becoming increasingly indistinguishable, as news as information is the order of the day. Further, citizen news producers act as government watchdogs and champion healthy and diverse public debate. Thus, the privileged position accorded the institution of the media by Justices Stewart and Brennan may no longer pertain. In fact, as Charles Clark's essay points out, the idea of a distinct freedom of the institution of the press has not applied historically. Citizen news producers existed in the nation's early years apart from the institution of the press. Thus, a general notion of "freedom of expression," which encompasses both institutional and individual speech rights, is perhaps more fitting in the present phase of media development.

The evidence points clearly toward the evolving dominance of the "open press" model. New media have supported the rise of amateur reporters who disseminate news on-air and online. Individuals are increasingly inclined to use new media technologies to broadcast their own messages as well as to seek information. New media sources provide perspectives that are not represented in the established press, and have a greater propensity to buck the status quo. While new media continue to enhance communication opportunities for those who are already empowered, they also provide outlets for communities of political outsiders to form and, in some cases, develop political strength. Finally, they accommodate a politics that is less hierarchical and more widely accessible to a greater variety of constituents.

Some factors work against the new media's ability to exploit the possibilities for citizen involvement that characterize an "open press" environment. First, the undisciplined definition of news as information renders it difficult to distinguish the important from the trivial. This is a problem for old as well as new media. Further, contemporary assumptions about what passes for news do not privilege greater community values or the public good. While the scale and scope of available news/information has grown exponentially, the quality of much of it remains suspect. Without consistent, trustworthy, and efficient filers, the information glut, in fact, may cause people to stop paying attention to politics altogether.[57]

The trend toward greater audience specialization may also work against the development of political networks of individuals with shared interests. New media's tendency to appeal to specialized audience segments still speaks to persons as members of publicly visible groups. A newer development is the personalization of media experiences whereby individuals exercise control over their exposure to information, including their scheduling of media consumption. The latest generation of technological innovations, such as wearable computers, will serve to further privatize communications experiences.

In addition, new media are not routinely successful at meeting the interests of small, marginal communities, although they do a better job of this than the traditional press. While the trend is toward greater press and political openness, significant roadblocks still impede participation by many. In the current multi-tiered press system, traditional media still hold more sway than new media in generating publicity. Much new media-related political activity still occurs outside the purview of political leaders, and is even considered "fringe." The Internet promotes a kind of "stealth activism" that only becomes visible when it is covered by the traditional press. Ultimately, new media activists may have to rely on validation by traditional news media in order to gain momentum. The "virtual march" on Washington may have clogged Capitol Hill switchboards, but it received minimal media coverage considering the hundreds of thousands of people it is alleged to have engaged.

It may well be the case that as new media mature further, the constraints on their ability to accommodate citizen voices and activation will be eradicated.

The already flimsy boundaries of the institutional press are likely to disintegrate as new media assume more prominent places in the political communications arena. Thus, the pertinence of an "open press" model of free speech in the United States potentially will become even more compelling.

NOTES

I would like to thank Amanda Shoemaker for her invaluable assistance with the research for this project.

1. Richard Davis and Diana Owen, *New Media and American Politics* (New York: Oxford Univ. Press, 1998); Doris A. Graber, "Media as Opinion Resources: Are the 1990s a New Ball Game?" in *Understanding Public Opinion,* edited by Barbara Norrander and Clyde Wilcox (Washington, D.C.: C. Q. Press, 1997), 67–89.

2. For a comprehensive catalogue of hypotheses about the new media, see W. Russell Neumann, "The Impact of the New Media," in *Mediated Politics: Communication in the Future of Democracy,* edited by W. Lance Bennett and Robert M. Entman (New York: Cambridge Univ. Press, 2001).

3. Marion R. Just, Ann N. Crigler, Dean E. Alger, Timothy E. Cook, Montague Kern, and Darrell M. West, *Crosstalk: Citizens, Candidates, and the Media in a Presidential Campaign* (Chicago, Ill.: Univ. of Chicago Press, 1996); Dirk Smillie, "Talking to America: The Rise of Talk Shows in the '92 Campaign," in *An Uncertain Season: Reporting in the Postprimary Period,* by Everette E. Dennis et al. (New York: Freedom Forum Media Studies Center, Columbia University, 1992), 17–27; Edward C. Pease, "'New' Media Voices Challenging 'Old' Media Status Quo," in *The Homestretch: New Politics, New Media, New Voters?* by Everette E. Dennis et al. (New York: Freedom Forum Media Studies Center, Columbia University, 1992), 100.

4. Dan Katz, "The Plugged-In Voter: The News Has Reconnected People and Politics," *Rolling Stone,* December 10–24, 1992, 115.

5. Pew Research Center for the People and the Press, "TV News Viewership Declines," http://people-press.org/reports/display.php3?ReportID=127 (May 13, 1996), accessed March 3, 2003.

6. David A. Jones, "Political Talk Radio: The Limbaugh Effect on Primary Voters," *Political Communication* (July–September 1998): 367–82.

7. David C. Barker, *Rushed to Judgment: Talk Radio, Persuasion, and American Political Behavior* (New York: Columbia Univ. Press, 2002).

8. Diana Owen, "Who's Talking? Who's Listening? The New Politics of Talk Radio Shows," in *Broken Contract: Changing Relationships between Americans and Their Government,* edited by Stephen C. Craig (Boulder, Colo.: Westview Press, 1996), 127–46.

9. Dan Katz, "Birth of a Digital Nation," *Wired,* April 1997, 48–57. Survey results reported in this study indicate that although more than half the U.S. population had access to the Internet, only 8.5 percent of the population had any connection to politics online in 1997. A knowledge gap surrounding the political opportunities that the Internet offered and the desire to use them was linked to education, income, and occupational disparities.

10. Davis and Owen, *New Media and American Politics.*

11. The new media's emergence in the late 1980s coincided with the Gulf War and a number of high-profile legal cases, including the William Kennedy Smith trial for alleged sexual misconduct. Radio stations, who were experiencing declines in their audience for music as Baby Boomers aged, experimented with talk formats, with significant initial success. The new media became firmly established in the 1992 presidential campaign, as candidates sought to circumvent traditional media gatekeepers and get their messages out to the public through nontraditional channels. See Davis and Owen, *New Media and American Politics*; Tom Rosenstiel, *Strange Bedfellows: How Television and the Presidential Candidates Changed American Politics* (New York: Hyperion, 1994).

12. Potter Stewart, "Or of the Press," *Hastings Law Journal* 26 (1975): 631–7.

13. Robert W. T. Martin, *The Free and Open Press: The Founding of American Democratic Press Liberty, 1640–1800* (New York: New York Univ. Press, 2001).

14. David H. Weaver and G. Cleveland Wilhoit, *The American Journalist* (Bloomington, Ind.: Indiana Univ. Press, 1986).

15. Robert J. Samuelson, "The End of News," *Washington Post,* June 18, 1999, p. A 41.

16. For an example of the range of definition of news offered by journalists from a variety of traditional and new media outlets, see "It's News to Me: Journalism in the Internet Age," Symposium, Carleton College, Ontario, Canada, October 7 10, 2002.

17. Leonard Downie Jr. and Robert G. Kaiser, *The News About the News* (New York: Vintage, 2003), 6. This perspective is shared by other prominent journalists. See Bill Kovach and Tom Rosenstiel, *The Elements of Journalism: What People Should Know and the Public Should Expect* (New York: Three Rivers Press, 2001).

18. Radio and Television Director's Foundation, "The American Radio News Audience Survey," www.rtnda.org/radio (January 3, 2001), accessed March 2, 2003. Survey data collected indicate that slightly more than half of the public adheres to the old-school definition of news as current events, 33 percent equate news with information, and 9 percent consider material that is entertaining or evokes emotional reactions to be news.

19. Frank Absher, "Republican News," *St. Louis Journalism Review* (February 2002): 6. These data replicate findings of the 2001 Radio and Television Director's Foundation study indicating that 23 percent of respondents equated talk radio with news. A majority of those who consider talk radio to be news are Republicans.

20. The entertainment imperative has influenced both traditional and new media conceptions of news, as well as what kind of information is deemed a priority. In February of 2003, with the war in Iraq looming, 27 million viewers tuned in to ABC's *Dateline* news magazine broadcast of British journalist Michael Bashir's documentary about pop star Michael Jackson. This program was widely promoted on ABC's network news broadcast and was a lead story on cable news, talk radio, and in Internet chat rooms. The success of ABC's broadcast prompted copycat shows by Fox and NBC. In comparison, CBS news anchor Dan Rather's interview with Iraq's president, Saddam Hussein, on *60 Minutes II* one week later was watched by 17 million Americans. Jason Deans, "Rather's Hussein Scoop Draws 17m," *Guardian,* February 28, 2003 (online).

21. James Squires, *Read All About It! The Corporate Takeover of America's Newspapers* (New York: Times Books, 1994).

22. Pew Internet and American Life Project, "Internet Activities" and "Daily Internet Activities,"

Washington, D.C., http://www.pewinternet.org/reports/chart.asp?img=Internet_A8.htm (January–December 2002), accessed March 17, 2003.

23. Kevin A. Hill and John E. Hughes, *Cyberpolitics: Citizen Activism in the Age of the Internet* (Lanham, Md.: Rowman and Littlefield, 1998),

24. Downie and Kaiser, *News About the News*.

25. Howard I. Finberg, Martha L. Stone, and Dianne Lynch, "Digital Journalism Credibility Study" (Washington, D.C.: John S. and James L. Knight Foundation, 2002).

26. Downie and Kaiser, *News About the News*.

27. U.S. Census Bureau, "The P.C. Generation: Computer Use," in *Population Profile of the United States* (Washington, D.C.), 10–1, 10–2, www.census.gov/population/pop-profile/2000/chap10.pdf (2001), accessed March 2, 2003. There are still gaps between the proportion of people who access the Internet from home based on income level. Forty-seven percent of those with annual incomes under $24,000 use computers at home, compared to 88 percent of those earning over $75,000. Racial differences also exist, but are closing. Seventy percent of whites, 71 percent of Asian Americans, 56 percent of blacks, and 49 percent of Hispanics have home computer Internet access. Taking into account the number of people without home access who use the Internet from work or public locations, such as schools, libraries, and digital cafés, the gap in Internet use between subgroups declines further.

28. Kattina Fabos, "Searching for Educational Content in the For-Profit Internet" (Michigan State Univ., manuscript, 2002).

29. Rachel Anderson and Kevin Taglang, "Is Low Power FM Finally Finding Its Voice?" *Communications Policy and Practice*, http://www.benton.org/publibrary/digitalbeat/db041101.html (April 11, 2001), accessed March 3, 2003.

30. Ibid.

31. "Gab Fest," *Interactive Week,* April 2, 2001, 58.

32. William Wyatt, "Good Morning, West Virginia," *State Legislatures* (January 2001): 32–6.

33. Mark Leibovich, "Cable-Age Candidates," *Washington Post,* February 22, 2003, p. C 01.

34. Davis and Owen, *New Media and American Politics*.

35. Pew Research Center for the People and the Press, "Public's News Habits Little Changed by September 11," Washington, D.C., www.people-press.org/reports/display.php3?ReportID=156 (June 9, 2002), accessed March 3, 2003.

36. Jane Saul, "Newspaper's Brand Strength Gives Online Information Credibility," *Gannett News Watch,* July 21, 2000, http://www.gannett.com/go/newswatch/99/july/nw0702-1.htm, accessed March 3, 2003.

37. Finberg, Stone, and Lynch, "Digital Journalism Credibility Study."

38. Data from both the Pew Research Center and the Gallup Organization are included to illustrate the difficulty of accurately estimating the audiences for particular media. Differences in question wording may account for some of the disparities, as Pew asked respondents if they "regularly" used the medium and Gallup asked if they were "every day" users. However, some of the findings are in the opposite direction from what one would expect. Gallup found that 43 percent of the public watched network news daily, while Pew data indicated that only 32 percent were regular watchers.

39. As traditional and new media increasingly converge in style, format, and content, it has become more difficult to categorize particular media and offerings.

40. Pew Research Center for the People and the Press, "Public's News Habits Little Changed by September 11," Washington, D.C., www.people-press.org/reports/display.php3?ReportID=156 (June 9, 2002), accessed March 3, 2003.

41. Robert Putnam, *Bowling Alone: The Collapse and Revival of American Community* (New York: Touchstone, 2001).

42. Susan Herbst, *Politics at the Margin: Historical Studies of Public Expression Outside the Mainstream* (New York: Cambridge Univ. Press, 1994).

43. Steve Davis, Larry Elin, and Grant Reeher, *Click on Democracy: The Internet's Power to Change Political Apathy into Civic Action* (Boulder, Colo.: Westview, 2002).

44. Todd Gitlin, *Media Unlimited* (New York: Holt, 2002).

45. Roderick P. Hart, *Seducing America: How Television Charms the Modern Voter* (New York: Oxford Univ. Press, 1994).

46. Davis, Elin, and Reeher, *Click on Democracy,* 91.

47. www.RecallGrayDavis.com, accessed March 2, 2003.

48. William Booth, "Web Spreads California Recall Effort," *Washington Post,* February 23, 2003, p. A 07.

49. Margaret Talev, "Davis Recall Is Gaining Traction," *Sacramento Bee,* February 11, 2003, p. 7.

50. Howard Reingold, *Smart Mobs: The New Social Revolution* (New York: Perseus Press, 2002).

51. Ryan Long, "Students Pencil in Iraq Protest," www.cnn.com/2003/US/03/04/sprj.irq.college. protest, accessed March 5, 2003.

52. Todd Gitlin, as quoted in Jennifer Lee, "How the Protesters Mobilized," *New York Times,* February 23, 2003, p. 25.

53. John Tierney, "An Antiwar Demonstration That Does Not Take to the Streets," *New York Times,* www.amadorpeace.org/virtual2.htm (February 26, 2003), accessed March 2, 2003.

54. Telecommunications Act of 1996, Section 706, www.fcc.gov/telecom.html, accessed October 11, 2004.

55. Chic Smith, "Demystifying Broadband," Digital Divide Network (Washington, D.C.: Benton Foundation), www.digitaldividenetwork.org/content/stories/index.cfm?key=156 (July 2, 2001), accessed March 3, 2003.

56. Anderson and Taglang, "Is Low Power FM Finally Finding Its Voice?"

57. David Shenk, *Data Smog: Surviving the Information Glut* (New York: HarperCollins, 1997).

AFTERWORD

EMILY ERICKSON

At the close of the Breaux Symposium, the event that would ultimately launch this book, the dean, Jack Hamilton, approached me. Earlier that year, we had discussed the idea of revisiting the themes of the Hutchins Commission for a later symposium. "You know, I realized as you were speaking that we don't really need to recreate the Hutchins Commission," he said. "We just did it today." I agreed. In fact, after dusting off the 1977 *Journalism Monograph* in which legal scholar Margaret Blanchard provided a masterful treatment of the commission, I had realized the similarities and the contrasts between the two eras and scholarly groups—the Hutchins Commission and today's symposium speakers—would lend themselves to the task of synthesizing our panel's responses to Timothy Cook's original challenge: Do empirical assessments of the press suggest that the First Amendment really has engendered either Justice Stewart's "organized, expert scrutiny of government" or Justice Brennan's "debate on public issues [that is] uninhibited, robust and wide-open"? Implicit in Cook's question is a belief that the press's First Amendment freedoms may be tied to its ability to provide these outcomes. That belief was also held by the prestigious scholars who made up the Hutchins Commission and argued that press freedoms were ultimately dependent upon press responsibility.

The commission, envisioned and financed by *Time* founder Henry Luce, issued its report in 1947, proclaiming that the time had come "for the press to assume a new public responsibility." Citing shallow, conflict-driven journalism, troubling levels of ownership concentration, and an economic structure that brought the highest profit from the lowest-common-denominator content, the commission even suggested that the press—defined as the newspaper, radio, and film industries—might "provide a forum for the exchange of comment and criticism" and, if necessary, become "common carriers of the public expression" in order to ensure a diversity of viewpoints.

Nearly sixty years later, you have seen the same themes echoed in the pages of this volume.

Three scholars in the volume operate within a framework which Robert W. T. Martin described as the "free press" model of the First Amendment, which concentrates its examination on the institutionalized press, or the news media as an industry. The abundance of research done on the news media in the past fifty years stands in stark contrast to that which existed when the Hutchins Commission issued its report—which was, in short, not a lot. The field of mass communication was not old enough to be heavily researched, and the commission members took a rather journalistic approach to their own query: they examined documents and conducted confidential interviews with individuals working in newspapers, radio, and film.

Today, mass communication boasts a substantial body of research that is both theoretically and methodologically diverse. And yet definitive answers about press performance still elude us because of the complexity of the findings. We can agree, as Professor Frederick Schauer argues, that the way to conceptualize our original research question today is to consider press performance as a dependent variable and try to determine how our independent variable—the First Amendment—affects that performance. This demonstrates a more empirical orientation to the question than the Hutchins Commission took—but does that make the results any clearer?

Like the Hutchins Commission report, much in this book suggests that today's press falls short of the ideals articulated by Stewart and Brennan. Both Professors Michael Schudson and Regina Lawrence, for example, cite an entire body of social scientific research that shows an uncomfortable degree of what Lawrence calls "embedded journalism"—press reliance upon officials who keep America's newsrooms stocked with government-managed news items. Research also confirms that journalists tend to articulate a limited spectrum of ideas—a phenomenon linked to this dependency on official sources, the professional structures of news gathering and reporting, and the limited worldview shared by journalists who have a professional affinity for reporting the "conventional wisdom" surrounding a given news item.

There are, then, reasons to criticize press performance—reasons to believe that the First Amendment has secured for this nation neither an ideal watchdog nor a vibrant marketplace of ideas within our institutionalized press.

But what if our press were *not* so free? Schauer suggests that the enormous freedom afforded the press under American libel law may not engender more scrutiny or debate after all. Brennan's assumption in *New York Times v. Sullivan*—that fear of legal liability would chill speech—is not supported by Schauer's examination of the Australian press, which shows that a strong press system can and does exist under more constraining libel laws. Meanwhile, in the United States, he sees an imbalance. Under the *Sullivan* rule, Schauer argues, freedom of the press has too completely trumped the right of individuals to protect their reputations. Given this state of affairs, Schauer, like Schudson and Lawrence, concludes that industry practices and ideals are actually stronger predictors of press performance than the lack of government censorship afforded by the First Amendment.

What is surprising about this consensus, however, is that behind it lie three very different conclusions. All three scholars agree that news conventions affect the news more than laws, or lack of laws. But Schauer suggests that those news conventions—in this case, the journalistic impulse to behave as a watchdog and critic of public officials—is strong enough that it exists *whether or not* the First Amendment is there to defend journalists from subsequent lawsuits. Schudson, while citing the sociological research of the newsroom, criticizes that research for placing news into an "airless box" by emphasizing the rule and not considering the exception—the times when journalists *do* exercise their "outsider" scrutiny of people and events. And Lawrence concludes that a strong First Amendment may preclude government censorship, but it does not necessarily provide an *incentive* for the news media to aspire to either the watchdog or the marketplace of ideas ideals.

In this volume, we have an excellent piece of revisionist history in Professor Charles Clark's chapter that implicitly challenges historian Leonard Levy's now widely accepted description of the colonial press—a description that, itself, challenged prevailing historical interpretation. We then have Lawrence and Schudson arriving at somewhat different conclusions, even looking at similar evidence. And Schauer's comparative approach to the First Amendment/press performance relationship suggests that there are still many ways not just to *interpret the answer,* but to *ask the question itself.*

The research and interpretations emerging from this volume suggest that we must be precise in how we frame our inquiry. While Schauer, Schudson, and Lawrence all address the performance of the institutionalized press, two of them are concerned primarily with the watchdog functions of the press—Stewart's "organized, expert scrutiny of government." Lawrence, on the other hand, considers press performance in terms of the watchdog *and* marketplace of ideas ideals, and finds room for significant improvement in both. All three scholars operate, nevertheless, within a framework that Martin described as the "free press" model of the First Amendment—which concentrates its examination on the institutionalized press, or news media as an industry. Different questions provide different criteria and different answers. Hence, as much attention needs to be paid to the questions we ask as to the evidence we examine.

AN OPEN PRESS

Three scholars in this volume take a somewhat different approach, highlighting Martin's "open press" model of the First Amendment, which conceptualizes the press as a vehicle for all individuals to disseminate their views, historically and as we move into the future with new, fragmented forms of media.

First, Clark's essay argues that the colonial press did not resemble the free press model at all, let alone Stewart's watchdog ideal of that model. Clark describes the Boston newspapers, for example, as "willing acolytes of both the royal governor and the established clergy, to whom they owed much of their patronage." Printers instead operated in something resembling the "open press" model, printing views based on their sponsorship, not on the notion that they as printers should behave as an institution whose function is to scrutinize the government. Newspapers were, as Clark points out, only one type of media that printers published. They also printed magazines, books, and pamphlets, indeed, whatever their patrons ordered. Although the press began a transition during the Revolution—one that moved toward the free press model—it was essentially a loose collection of printers who published views of whomever would pay them.

As Clark describes the beginnings of a transition from an open press to a free press model during the Revolution, Professors Diane Owen and Lance Bennett see exactly the same process in reverse today. Bennett, whose own work has also contributed substantially to the research showing limitations of the traditional news media, argues that we are actually witnessing the "twilight" of that form, in part because it has failed to realize either the ideals of the watchdog or the marketplace of ideas functions. Both he and Owen describe how new media forms, from low-powered radio to the World Wide Web, have facilitated the reemergence of something much closer to an open press.

Although the traditional news media have a dominant presence online, for example, Owen cites the growth of a new type of press in the shape of "citizen news producers"—individuals who, although not trained news professionals, post information online that is *used* by the public as a form of news. And these citizen news producers, Owen argues, succeed in places where the traditional news media have failed. They represent the diversity of backgrounds and views that can be expressed in the American marketplace of ideas. And they offer a positive addition to that marketplace because they are free to deliver news as general information rather than timely events; they provide perspectives that may fall well outside the spectrum provided by officials and thus the traditional news media; and they can go beyond what Schudson called "the conventional wisdom" embraced by the press because they have not experienced journalistic socialization in the newsroom.

However, the vision of new media that both Owen and Bennett sketch is one that others are still reticent to crown as a triumph of the open press model. And Owen herself highlights some of the challenges facing citizen news producers. Their audiences, for example, are smaller and more specialized than those of the traditional mass media, whose coverage is ultimately still necessary for these alternative messages to be heard by the nation. And there are two sides to the independence enjoyed by citizen news producers: They are not bound by commercial pressures or journalistic conventions, but their outsider status also makes it difficult to finance their publishing endeavors and survive long enough to build a broader audience.

All three essays, whether they describe an historical manifestation or an emerging one, seem to suggest that the open press model has great potential for at least complementing the free press model. Clark argues that the paradigm of printers who served as vehicles for a variety of sponsored viewpoints succeeded quite well in realizing the ideal of a diverse and vibrant marketplace of ideas. Owen and Bennett see the same benefits in the growing citizen presence—and activism—found in today's new media, as well as potential for an enhanced watchdog function. Again, they contrast this with the failings and limitations of today's corporate mass media approach to news and suggest that a growing dissatisfaction with that approach will continue to draw individuals to the open press model emerging in today's new media.

THE FREE PRESS, THE OPEN PRESS, AND THE PRESS CLAUSE

Throughout this book, our media scholars have explicated from their various vantage points the two models described by Martin—the free press and open press models—as well as the two First Amendment ideals of the watchdog and the marketplace of ideas. Implicit in the preceding analysis—and in Cook's initial challenge—is the notion that *both* ideals of the First Amendment can be found within each model. The traditional news media as an industry can attempt to serve as a watchdog of government, as well as illuminate a diversity of viewpoints by representing fairly the marketplace of ideas—the range of opinion—in their coverage of public issues. By the same token, an "open press" made up more loosely of individual publishers (such as those with Web sites on the Internet) can also provide scrutiny of government and represent the range of debate on various issues.

In this book, criticism has been leveled at the ability of the traditional news media to realize—or even consistently aspire to—either ideal. As most of the authors have concluded, either implicitly or explicitly, the First Amendment freedoms granted to the press may or may not be a *necessary* condition to achieve the desired dependent variable, but they apparently are not a *sufficient* one. This must then lead to the next question: If the First Amendment is not necessarily engendering the best type of free press, should its freedoms be reconsidered within existing American laws? Notably, this was the specter held up to the press in 1947 when the Hutchins Commission warned the media industries of that era to improve their sense of accountability to the public—also in terms of the watchdog and marketplace of ideas ideals—or else expect their freedoms to erode with time.

The characterizations of the two First Amendment ideals by Stewart and Brennan suggest an additional point to consider. Potter Stewart argued that, in the founding fathers' perception, "a free press was not just a neutral vehicle for the balanced discussion of diverse ideas. Instead, the free press meant organized, expert scrutiny of government."[1] Brennan, in *New York Times v. Sullivan*, emphasized "a profound national commitment to the principle that debate on public issues should be uninhibited, robust and wide-open, and that it may well include vehement, caustic, and sometimes unpleasantly sharp attacks on government and public officials."[2]

As Cook noted in the introduction of this book, a close reading of the justices' words shows that Stewart was distinguishing the *free press* clause of the First Amendment from the *free speech* clause—and Brennan was consistently addressing "freedom of speech and press," thus conferring the *Sullivan* triumph upon both the press *and* speech clauses. In other words, Stewart privileged the watchdog role for the institutionalized press—the free press model—and Brennan heralded both ideals in a way that suggests he would attach them both to the free press and open press models.

What does this mean for the First Amendment and the arguments made in this book? It certainly suggests that we should consider policy and research implications not only via models and ideals but also within the architecture of the First Amendment itself.

Perhaps the first question to tackle is whether the press clause should actually protect an "organized private business," as Stewart suggested. There are several reasons to reject such a reading. To begin with, he was probably wrong in characterizing the founders' vision of the press as an organized institution scrutinizing the government. And even if he was not, the layers of conflicting historical research suggest that founders' original intent is too uncertain a notion upon which to base our current First Amendment freedoms. As for Supreme Court interpretations, the press clause of the First Amendment has only been an explicit part of its jurisprudence since 1931, when the Court ruled in *Near v. Minnesota* that the state must return Jay Near's printing press to him despite its assertion that his newspaper was a "public nuisance."[3] If we must engage in an original-intent argument, perhaps *Near v. Minnesota* is the better place to start. And if we do, it is significant to note that the first Supreme Court ruling on the press clause extended its protection *not* to a member of the institutionalized press but to a pesky outsider who happened to own a printing press. In other words, the context of that decision privileges the open press model.

Another reason to reject protecting the press as an institution is that such a reading allows the press to use the First Amendment to protect itself as a for-profit entity rather than a journalistic one. Such an approach utterly fails to enhance the ideals underlying the First Amendment and creates precisely the type of criticism of the press that is being leveled at today's conglomerate-owned news organizations.

Here, too, it is helpful to look back at the era in which the Hutchins Commission did its work, for it was also launched in response to growing criticism of the press. Cook has recalled in his introduction the crucial decades of the 1920s and 1930s when the groundwork was being laid for laws that would govern that age's "new media." It was also during this era that the U.S. Supreme Court famously resisted President Franklin D. Roosevelt's attempts to impose government regulation on American businesses that had flourished under decades of laissez-faire capitalism. The newspaper industry was resisting as well, trying to elude the new regulations, which would force businesses to respect antitrust rules, working-hour restrictions, and the imposition of labor union power. Publishers tried to argue that these regulations could not constitutionally apply to the newspaper industry without violating the press clause of the First Amendment. They were unsuccessful. In the same year that the Court began upholding Roosevelt's legislation, it ruled on *Associated Press v. National Labor Relations Board,* informing the press that the First Amendment *did not* prohibit government regulation of its purely business aspects when that regulation was applied to all other businesses.[4]

Not surprisingly, the industry's attempt to wrap its business practices in the First Amendment provided fodder for its critics, who were already speaking "almost with one voice," calling the press "a representative of established commercial interests and of the upper socio-economic class, out of step with the general population's wishes for society while reflecting the biases of its owners in its presentation of the news."[5]

Perhaps it should not be surprising when the institutionalized press—the "organized private business" side of the press—acts like any other corporate entity. Certainly history demonstrates that such a phenomenon is not new, and that the press as an industry will naturally try to harness the First Amendment for itself from time to time—just as it did in the 1920s and 1930s. But the more license it takes in trying to protect itself as an institution, the more it undermines itself. It was a year after the *Associated Press* decision that former *Chicago Tribune* foreign correspondent George Seldes leveled a critical eye at his era's publishers and famously noted that "[n]othing is sacred to the American press but itself." Such cynicism is, again, a good reason to avoid a press-clause interpretation that privileges the press as an institution.

Decades later, when Stewart gave his Yale speech, the press was being subjected to public criticism again, this time for unearthing too much objectionable government activity in Vietnam and the White House. And although Stewart's Yale speech is one of the most famous readings of the press clause, he actually described a different rationale for the free press three years earlier, when he dissented in *Branzburg v. Hayes,* arguing that the press receives its constitutional protection primarily because it serves "the broad societal interest in a full and free flow of information to the public."[6] The *Branzburg* argument sounded closer to the marketplace of ideas than the watchdog ideal he later touted. But consider the context of these two rationales. In the Yale speech Stewart was trying to defend the press's insistence on digging beneath the official, government-approved headlines. In *Branzburg* he was trying to defend a journalist's ability to gather news, even when that occasionally meant refusing to give source materials to law enforcement. Indeed, if one considers Stewart's Yale speech in combination with his *Branzburg* dissent,[7] it is possible to infer a broader concern with *both* the marketplace of ideas and watchdog ideals through a press-clause protection of *watchdog conduct.*

This is particularly useful to consider in light of the shift in recent press-clause scholarship to issues related to news gathering conduct rather than publication.[8] This shift can be attributed to the fact that many constitutional questions concerning publication have either been answered by press-clause cases like *Near v. Minnesota* or cases like *New York Times v. Sullivan,* which encompassed both the speech and press clauses. It can also be attributed to the growing number of lawsuits against the press for torts related to journalistic news gathering—torts that, unlike libel, have no associated First Amendment defenses (a trend that makes it all the more important to build on Schauer's research).

But what difference does it make if scholars or even the Supreme Court envision the press clause as protecting watchdog conduct if the First Amendment seems to have little impact upon daily press behavior? Consider a point that Schudson and Lawrence make when they describe journalistic autonomy as an exception rather than a rule. Schudson even takes this a step further, noting that reporters tend to emphasize their greatest moments of autonomy as definitive of their craft. In other words, even if their daily reporting does not always demonstrate autonomy from official sources, it is clearly part of how they *want* to see themselves, part of the philosophical ideal to which they aspire. Therefore, these exceptional moments of journalism should be aligned with the understanding that the marketplace of ideas and watchdog ideals are *also* exceptional. They are, after all, ideals. Indeed, it is likely that the press clause of the First Amendment matters more for its symbolism than anything else. It may be forgotten in the chaos of filling a daily news hole, and it may even be neglected by the news media for years at a time, but its greatest value comes from the role it has symbolically conferred upon the press.

Stewart's characterization of the press clause, while problematic in its privilege of the institutionalized press, can be read as closer to Brennan's if one considers both the Yale speech and the *Branzburg* dissent, the latter of which emphasized the "free flow of information to the public." Both, recall, were in the context of Stewart's overarching desire to protect the actions of journalistic watchdogs—one in the face of public criticism, the other in the face of government coercion. If this broader reading of Stewart is combined with a rejection of the press clause as a protector of the institutionalized press, another vision of the press clause emerges: one that seeks to protect the watchdog conduct of anyone who seeks to serve in that role, whether it is a traditional newspaper journalist or an citizen gadfly like Jay Near. It is, in short, an "open press" reading of the press clause that privileges behaviors related to the watchdog ideal of the First Amendment but also serves the marketplace of ideas ideal by explicitly opening the press clause to all citizens. It would include the citizen news producers described by Owen, as well as answering Schudson's call to enhance the role of journalists as outsiders by being triggered when the press is acting, as Schudson puts it, particularly "unlovable," pushing the government's buttons to get its news.

CONCLUSION

Of course, it is one thing to advocate a more inclusive press clause—to bring today's new media, and new citizen news producers, under the press-clause wing of the First Amendment. It is, practically speaking, a more radical proposition to suggest that the government start forcing the institutionalized press—today's corporately owned print, broadcast, and cable news organizations—to allow the fledgling new media enough space to become a full-grown open press rival to their free press industries. And it is equally radical to suggest that the government set out to give new media the same kind of policy privileges that the traditional media have enjoyed over the past century—nearly all of which have been dispensed in response to press lobbying, not the First Amendment.[9]

In 1947, the Hutchins Commission advocated the provision of "a forum for the exchange of comment and criticism" and challenged the press to "accept the responsibilities of common carriers of information and public discussion"—in order to ensure a diversity of viewpoints.[10] It was vague about how such an idea could be implemented, but certainly the specter of government intervention was there—a tacit warning. And yet nothing ever came of this threat. Since then the press has been able to boast another half-century of survival in the face of continuing criticism without the imposition of a government-mandated open press paradigm upon its features.

Are these radical suggestions just as empty today? Congress opened the door to a policy that flirted with an open press model of broadcast more than a decade before the Hutchins Commission issued its report, creating a Federal Communications Commission and giving it a mandate to regulate broadcast media "in the public interest, convenience and necessity."[11] The press, within the broadcast framework, was expected to respect the obligations of the FCC's fairness doctrine, providing a fair presentation of each side of public affairs issues. It was the grand experiment, an attempt to carve out a small space within broadcast media for the open press model. And the experiment ended in 1987 when the FCC threw up its bureaucratic hands in resignation and abandoned the fairness doctrine altogether. In the past decade, the courts struck down the last few remaining pieces of that doctrine as the FCC stood by, presumably relieved to be done with them.

Meanwhile, new media outlets began to emerge. In their accounts of this phenomenon, both Owen and Bennett argue that the new media are moving toward an open press model of the First Amendment—mostly independent of law and fueled by a growing disaffection toward the traditional press. Bennett even suggests that the "twilight" of the traditional news media is inevitable, and Owen argues that "the privileged position accorded the institution of the media by Justices Stewart and Brennan may no longer pertain."

But ironically, the open press characteristics of the new media have actually provided the rationale to allow more "freedom" for the traditional news media to pursue a course of increased ownership concentration. With all these new media outlets, the media giants argue, there is no longer a need to push for the marketplace of ideas via government policy. The Internet alone can boast the ideal's virtual fulfillment; citizen news producers are acting as watchdogs; and the fragmented characteristics of the new media make concentration of ownership necessary to the economic survival of the traditional press. Ultimately, the growth of an open press model within new media has actually *strengthened* the problematic side of laissez-faire policies toward the press, enabling traditional news organizations and their conglomerate owners to cite the First Amendment while embarking on a path that appears to be undermining both the marketplace of ideas and watchdog models. The press may not have succeeded in eluding business regulations in the 1930s, but it has been dramatically successful in achieving deregulation in the last ten years.

So, does this leave us with the legacy of the Hutchins Commission, which found a press falling short of First Amendment ideals and issued warnings that never came to fruition? Perhaps not. There is another legacy of that era which could be ours today. When the U.S. Supreme Court finally began upholding FDR's New Deal regulations in 1937 and dismantling the decades-old laissez-faire economic system, it was finally applying a "legal realist" approach to that system—considering *how* the government's lack of intervention in American business had shaped the economic landscape. This was a dramatic shift from their "formalist" approach of simply applying rules of law without considering their impact. By the time the Court began using this approach, it had been formulated, debated, and explicated repeatedly by legal scholars for decades. And the Legal Realists did more than provide a structure; they had actually *designed* it in order to dismantle the country's troubling economic doctrine.

For the past two decades, many First Amendment scholars have been hoping for a similar fate to befall the First Amendment—for the courts to begin incorporating closer scrutiny of the subtle ways that government's current laissez-faire approach to the press has hidden a media economy, set up by the government through various policies, that allows those with more money and power to dominate the marketplace of ideas. Interestingly, the Supreme Court has begun demanding empirical evidence from the government when it seeks to restrict speech or press freedoms,[12] but has remained reluctant to examine more fully the broader impact that government policies have in *privileging* the press.[13] This is where the research done on the press—notably by the scholars in this volume—has helped build a foundation of empirical evidence and policy formulations for the future.

The final ingredients—leadership that can push the scholarship into a new public policy mold and a nationwide demand to do so—were both present when the United States changed its economic path in the 1930s. In 2003, the public ire raised by further FCC deregulation suggested that such a possibility may not be so far away.

NOTES

1. Potter Stewart, "Or of the Press," *Hastings Law Journal* 26 (1975): 631–7, quote at 634.

2. *New York Times v. Sullivan,* 376 U.S. 254, 271 (1964).

3. The Minnesota law provided for "the abatement, as a public nuisance, of a 'malicious, scandalous and defamatory newspaper, magazine or other periodical.'" *Near v. Minnesota,* 283 U.S. 697, 702 (1931).

4. *Associated Press v. National Labor Relations Board,* 301 U.S. 103, 132 (1937). "The business of the Associated Press is not immune from regulation because it is an agency of the press. The publisher of a newspaper has no special immunity from the application of general laws."

5. Margaret A. Blanchard, "The Hutchins Commission, the Press and the Responsibility Concept," *Journalism Monographs* 49 (May 1977): quote at 8.

6. *Branzburg v. Hayes,* 408 U.S. 665, 726 (1972).

7. Interestingly, Stewart's *Branzburg* dissent has the unusual distinction of being explicitly applied by lower courts. Because the *Branzburg* votes and opinions were so fragmented, courts sometimes opt for White's "test" and sometimes opt for Stewart's "test" when trying to determine whether to allow journalists to refuse disclosure of notes and sources.

8. See Jon Paul Dilts, "The Press Clause and Press Behavior: Revisiting the Implications of Citizenship," *Communication Law and Policy* 7 (2002): 25–49.

9. See Timothy E. Cook, *Governing with the News: The News Media as a Political Institution* (Chicago: Univ. of Chicago Press, 1998).

10. Commission on Freedom of the Press, *A Free and Responsible Press* (Chicago: Univ. of Chicago Press, 1947), quotes on 20, 92.

11. Telecommunications Act of 1996, 47 U.S.C. 257(b) 2000. (Originally in the 1934 Communications Act.)

12. This is illustrated by, for example, the evolution of the *Central Hudson* test over the past twenty years, which ostensibly subjects government regulation of commercial speech to relaxed scrutiny—but which has increasingly edged closer to a strict-scrutiny test, including an expectation of empirical evidence that commercial speech restrictions will actually forward the government interest they seek to serve.

13. The federal courts' demands of the FCC to defend its ownership and content regulations in broadcasting—which the FCC has been loathe to defend anyway—are a good example of this.

CONTRIBUTORS

W. LANCE BENNETT is Ruddick C. Lawrence Professor of Communication and a professor of political science at the University of Washington, where he serves as director of the Center for Communication and Civic Engagement (www. engagedcitizen.org). His most recent book is the sixth edition of his seminal *News: The Politics of Illusion* (2005).

CHARLES E. CLARK is a professor emeritus of history at the University of New Hampshire. A former newspaper reporter for the *Providence Journal*, he is renowned for many books on New England history, along with his definitive work *The Public Prints: The Newspaper in Anglo-American Culture, 1665–1740* (1994).

TIMOTHY E. COOK is a professor of mass communication and political science in the Manship School of Mass Communication at Louisiana State University and holds the Kevin P. Reilly, Sr., Chair of Political Communication. An updated edition of his book, *Governing with the News: The News Media as a Political Institution*, with a new afterword, is forthcoming in 2005.

EMILY ERICKSON is an assistant professor of mass communication in the Manship School of Mass Communication at Louisiana State University. She specializes in communication law and policy, and is the co-editor of the second edition of *Contemporary Media Issues* (2004).

CRAIG M. FREEMAN is an assistant professor of mass communication in the Manship School of Mass Communication at Louisiana State University. A practicing attorney, he teaches and has written on First Amendment issues.

RALPH IZARD is Sig Mickelson/CBS Professor of Mass Communication in the Manship School of Mass Communication at Louisiana State University. A longtime director of the Scripps School of Journalism at Ohio University, he served for twelve years as editor of *Newspaper Research Journal*.

REGINA G. LAWRENCE is an associate professor of political science at Portland State University. Among her publications is *The Politics of Force: Media and the Construction of Police Brutality* (2000).

DIANA OWEN is an associate professor of political science at Georgetown University, where she is affiliated with the program on Communication, Culture, and Technology. Among the books and articles she has published is *New Media and American Politics* (1998).

FREDERICK SCHAUER is Frank Stanton Professor of the First Amendment at the Kennedy School of Government at Harvard, where he is affiliated with the Joan Shorenstein Center for the Press, Politics, and Public Policy. A second edition of his classic *Free Speech: A Philosophical Enquiry* is forthcoming in 2005.

MICHAEL SCHUDSON is a professor of communication and adjunct professor of sociology at the University of California, San Diego. His most recent book is *The Sociology of News* (2002).

JACK M. WEISS is a partner in the New York office of Gibson, Dunn & Crutcher LLP, where he represents Dow Jones & Company, Inc., the publisher of *The Wall Street Journal,* and other media clients. He teaches a seminar on the First Amendment and the media at Columbia Law School.

INDEX

Absolutist approach, 3, 6

Actual malice rule, 4, 52, 53, 66n14, 72

Adams, John, 4

African Americans, 18, 82

Alabama, 4

Alien and Sedition Acts, 4, 9, 59

Amazon.com, 19

American Media, 61

American Prospect, 82

American Weekly Mercury, 36

AmeriCorps, 78–79

Anti-Defamation League, 97

AOL-Time Warner, 114

Archibold, Randal C., 79

Arkansas, 58

Associated Press, 18

Associated Press v. National Labor Relations Board, 169, 170, 174n4

Associated Press v. United States, 4

Associated Press v. Walker, 30, 66n13

ATTAC, 127

Audience: of conventional news media, 117–23, 149–50, 152–53, 160n38; of new media, 140, 149–53, 157; segmentation of, 151, 153; technology and specialized audiences, 17, 18, 157

Aurora, 46

Australia, 13, 30, 54–60, 63, 65, 67n19, 68n41, 165

Australian, 56

Australian Broadcasting Corporation v. Lenah Game Meats, 67n25

Australian Capital Television v. Commonwealth, 67n23

Austria, 122

Autonomy: of colonial and Revolutionary press, 35–39, 46, 48; "content autonomy," 89; definition of, 35; of news media, 4–6, 15, 35–39, 41; of reporters, 13–14, 15, 171

Bache, Benjamin Franklin, 45

Bandwidth divide, 155–56

Bartnicki v. Vopper, 65n4

Bashir, Michael, 159n20

BBC, 113, 114, 123

Beauharnais v. Illinois, 66n7

Beckham, David, 117

Belgium, 122

Bennett, Lance W., 10, 14, 19, 20, 21, 74, 85n3, 93–94, 99, 109, 110, 111–37, 140–41, 166–67, 172

Bill of Rights, 46

Bimber, Bruce, 130

Black, Hugo, 4

Black press, 18

Blackmun, Harry, 7

Blacks. *See* African Americans

Blanchard, Margaret, 163

Blogs. *See* Weblogs

Blumler, Jay, 123

BMW of North America v. Gore, 68n41

Bogart, Leo, 1

Bollinger, Lee, 6, 9, 23n4

Boston Evening-Post, 38

Boston Gazette, 36, 38, 43–44

Boston News-Letter, 36, 42–43

Boston Post-Boy, 49nn10–11

Boydell, John, 43

Bradford, Andrew, 36

Bradford, William, 36, 43

Branzburg v. Hayes, 23*n*8, 25*n*42, 30, 170, 174*n*7

Breaking news, 14, 15

Brennan, William H., Jr.: and freedom of speech, 168; on freedom of the press generally, 6, 12, 16, 20, 141, 163, 172; and *New York Times v. Sullivan,* 4–5, 30, 52–53, 55, 59, 72, 91, 164, 168; and *Smith v. California,* 66*n*9; and watchdog and marketplace metaphors for the press, 87, 91, 98, 100

Britain, 11, 48*n*3, 57, 68*n*41, 115, 117

Broadcast media. *See* Radio; Television

Brooker, William, 36

Brown, Richard D., 41, 49*n*13

Brown v. Board of Education, 5

Bulgaria, 122

Bumiller, Elisabeth, 80–81

Bush, George H. W., 80

Bush, George W., 2, 76, 80–81, 88, 95–96, 97

Bush, Laura, 81

Bustamante, Cruz, 82

C-SPAN, 82

Cable television, 6, 9, 17, 114, 118, 141, 142, 149, 150, 152. *See also* Television

California, 17, 82, 154

Campbell, John, 36, 42–43, 45, 46

Canada, 11, 57

Canberra Times, 56

Censorship of the press, 37, 46, 90

Center for Communication and Civic Engagement, 123, 127

Center for Media and Public Affairs, 118

Central Hudson test, 174*n*12

Chaffee, Steven, 112

Chicago Tribune, 14, 83, 170

Citizen action, 110, 123, 125–27, 130–34, 153–55, 157

Citizen news producers, 20, 21, 112, 141, 143, 145–47, 156, 166–67, 171, 173

Citizenship models, 114–15, 125

Civil Rights Act (1990), 82

Clark, Charles E., 12, 17, 18, 20, 29, 30, 33–50, 156, 165, 166, 167

Clark, Wesley, 149

Classified documents, publication of, 30

Clean Clothes, 127

Clinton, William, 78, 87, 94, 117, 139, 148

CNBC, 17

Cobbett, William, 45

Coleman, Stephen, 123

Coleman v. McClennan, 58, 68*n*23

Colonial and Revolutionary press: and censorship, 37, 46; centrality of, in ecology of public discourse, 43–44; as "expert," 42–46, 48; Franklin on liberty of the press, 33–34; and "free press" model, 8, 9, 33, 44; and hoax, 42–43, 46; as institution, 34–35, 46–48; limited autonomy of, 35–39, 46, 48; meaning of, 10, 12, 18, 33–48; and "open press" model, 8–9, 38, 41, 44; organization in, 39–42, 47; and partisanship, 40–42, 47; and printers, 7, 8, 10, 12, 34, 36–43, 46–47, 112, 166, 167; and propaganda, 42, 43; sources for, 40, 43; state of, in 1789, 46–48

Columbia Journalism Review, 62

Columbine High School shootings, 96–97

Company of Stationers, 39

Computers. *See* Internet; Personal information networks; Technology

Confidentiality of reporters' sources, 6, 13

Conflict-oriented news, 15, 73, 79–80, 84, 94

Constitution, U.S.: Bill of Rights for, 46; ratification of, 41, 42, 44

Content autonomy, 89. *See also* Autonomy

Conventional wisdom, 74, 75–77, 84, 164, 167

Cook, Timothy E., 35, 74, 90, 95, 100, 102, 163, 168, 169

Crime, 112, 118–20, 143

Cross-national research on news media, 10, 11, 57, 115

Crouse, Timothy, 101

Curtis Publishing Co. v. Butts, 30, 66*n*13

Cyberspace. *See* Internet; New media; Personal

information networks

Cynicism of journalists, 14, 15, 73, 80–81, 84, 121, 170

Czech Republic, 122

Daily news: accidental nature of, 89–90, 99; constraints on, 91–92; and embeddedness of media, 91–92; and First Amendment ideals, 87–102, 171; government officials' relation to, 93–95, 98, 99; and professional norms, organizational routines, and official communications strategies, 92–96, 115; public opinion on, 87–88, 115; reality versus ideals of, 90–91; and rethinking the economic First Amendment, 100–102; and rethinking the First Amendment, 98–100; unexpected events and critical news, 14, 96–98, 116–17. *See also* News media

Davis, Gray, 154

Davis, Richard, 20

Davis, Steve, 153

Dean, Howard, 149

Defamation: in Australia, 55; and First Amendment, 51–52, 66n14; Kansas Supreme Court decision on, 58; against public officials, 30, 51–52. *See also* Libel

Democracy: democratizing potential of new media, 17, 19–20, 110; Ferenczi on, 76; Gans on, 74–75, 85n3; need for unlovable press in, 15, 73–84, 85n3; Tocqueville on, 73. *See also* Citizen action

Democratic National Convention (2004), 16–17

Denmark, 122

Dennie, Joseph, 50n39

Deregulation, 102, 116, 120, 121, 123, 132, 172–74

Digital divide/bandwidth divide issues, 130–32, 140, 148, 155–56, 160n27

Digital networks. *See* Personal information networks

Dodd, Christopher, 149

Downie, Leonard, Jr., 144, 147

Drudge, Matt, 82, 114

E-Rate program, 148

Eastern Europe, 122

Economic ideal of marketplace model, 90, 100–102

Edes, Benjamin, Jr., 38, 44

"Editorial privilege" around news-gathering process, 6

Education of journalists, 83

Eighteenth-century press. *See* Colonial and Revolutionary press

Elin, Larry, 153

Embeddedness of media, 91–92, 164

England. *See* Britain

Environmental issues, 96

Erickson, Emily, 163–74

Estrada, President, 127

Europe, 121–23. *See also* specific countries

European monetary unit (Euro), 122

European Union, 122

Event-driven news, 14, 15, 16, 73, 77–79, 84, 99, 116–17

Exxon *Valdez,* 96

Fairness doctrine, 7, 172

Farinola, Wendy Jo Manard, 129

Farmer's Museum, 50n39

FCC. *See* Federal Communications Commission

Federal Communications Commission (FCC), 1, 7, 87, 101, 148, 155, 156, 172, 174, 174n13

Federal Gazette, 33

Federalist, 41

Feenberg, Andrew, 129

Feingold, Russ, 83

Fenno, John, 44–45, 46

Ferenczi, Thomas, 76

Fifth Amendment, 59

Finland, 122

First Amendment: absolutist approach to, 3, 6; and advantage to already powerful, 22; and defamation, 51–52, 66n14; economic uses of, 100–102; hands-off understanding of, 2–3,

6–9, 22; origins of, 46; press clause of, 3,
168–71; and rights of readers and viewers, 6, 7,
8–9, 22. *See also* Freedom of speech; Freedom
of the press; and specific court cases
"Flaming" problem, 126
Flanagan, Andrew, 129
Fourth Amendment, 59
Fowle, Daniel, 41
Frame dominance in the news, 94
France, 76, 122
Franklin, Benjamin, 8, 33–34, 37, 39, 42,
49*n*10
Franklin, James, 8, 9, 35, 37, 38
"Free press" model: definition of, 8, 141; in
eighteenth century, 8, 9, 33, 44; and hetero-
geneous audience, 150; and institutionalized
press, 164–66; and marketplace of ideas
model, 167–68; and new media, 142; and
watchdog model, 167–68
Freedom of assembly, 34
Freedom of expression, 156
Freedom of religion, 34
Freedom of speech, 3, 5, 7, 34, 111, 168, 170, 173
Freedom of the press: absolutist approach to,
3, 6; abuse of, by mass media, 19; Brennan
on, 4–5, 6, 12, 16, 20; compared with freedom
of speech, 5, 111, 168; daily news and First
Amendment ideals, 87–102, 171; empirical
evidence on, 9–12; First Amendment text on,
3; Franklin on, 33–34; hands-off approach
to, 2–3, 6–9; historical perspectives on,
7, 8, 9–10, 12–13, 33–48; Madison on, 46; and
rights of readers, 6, 7, 8–9, 22; "secondary
image" of, 6, 9. *See also* First Amendment;
"Free press" model; Marketplace of ideas
model; News media; "Open press" model;
Watchdog model; and specific court cases
Freeman, Craig M., 29–31
Freneau, Philip, 44–46

Game framing of political news, 95
Gans, Herbert, 11, 74–75, 85*n*3

Garrison v. Louisiana, 66*n*10
Gazette of the United States, 44–45, 48
Germany, 77, 115, 122
Gerry, Elbridge, 44
Gertz v. Robert Welch, Inc., 66*n*14
Gill, John, 38
Gitlin, Todd, 155
Global Citizen Project, 123
Global Exchange, 127
Globalization, 114–17, 132–33
Goddard, William, 38
Google.com, 19, 22
Gore, Al, 76, 148
Gorgura, Heather, 82
Government officials' relation to news media,
14, 93–95, 98, 99
Government regulation: of business, 169, 173; of
Internet, 22; of media, 1–2, 21, 100–101, 169
Graham, Bob, 149
Great Britain. *See* Britain
Green, Bartholomew, Sr., 39
Gridley, Jeremiah, 44
Grosjean v. American Press Company, 23*n*13,
65*n*2
Gulf War, 159*n*11
Gun control, 96–97

Hall, David, 38–39, 41
Hallin, Daniel, 10, 11, 12
Hamilton, Andrew, 49*n*13
Hamilton, Jack, 163
Hand, Learned, 4
Harris, Benjamin, 36
Hart, Gary, 149
Hartman, Charles J., 67*n*18
Hawke, Bob, 54–55
HBO, 149
Herbert v. Lando, 23*n*8
Herbst, Susan, 151
Hershey, Marjorie, 97
Hill v. Church of Scientology, 68*n*30
Hinch, Derryn, 56

Hong Kong, 57
Hume, Brit, 94
Hungary, 122
Hunter, William, 49n10
Huske, Ellis, 49n10
Hussein, Saddam, 159n20
Hutchins Commission, 110, 163, 164, 168, 169, 172, 173

ICan (BBC), 113
Illegally obtained material, publication of, 51
Illinois, 58
Independent Reflector, 38
"Indexing" hypothesis, 10, 74, 93–94, 99
India, 57
Indian Point nuclear power plant, 79–80
Indymedia.org, 113, 129
Institutionally driven news, 15
International news, 119
Internet: and Amazon.com, 19; audience of Internet news, 150–51, 152, 157; and citizen action, 110, 125–27, 130–34, 153–55, 157; and citizen news producers, 141, 145–47, 173; and digital divide/bandwidth divide, 130–32, 140, 148, 155–56, 160n27; gatekeeping and journalism norms for, 128–30; government regulation of, 22; inclusiveness of, 129; and personal information networks, 123–25; political information on, 17, 113, 114, 125–28, 130–34, 149, 150, 158n9; radio call-in programs on, 149; reliability of information on, 128; and reporters, 14; in schools, 148; search engines for, 19, 22; statistics on, 130, 146, 158n9, 160n27; variations in access to, in different countries, 130; Web sites of news organizations, 18; and Weblogs, 15, 16–17, 18, 82, 83, 113, 126, 129–30, 141, 145, 146; and Zagat.com, 19. *See also* Personal information networks
Iraq War (2003), 87–88, 92, 95–96, 116, 125–28, 131, 155, 159n20
Ireland, 11, 122
Israel, 57

Italy, 115
Izard, Ralph, 18, 109–10

Jackson, Michael, 159n20
Journalism. *See* Freedom of the press; News media; Reporters
Journalism education, 83

Kaiser, Robert G., 144, 147
Kansas, 58
King, Martin Luther, Jr., 4
King, Rodney, 96, 99
Klinenberg, Eric, 14
Kneeland, Samuel, 37, 38
Kucinich, Dennis, 149

Landmark Communications, Inc., v. Virginia, 65n4
Lange v. Australian Broadcasting Corporation, 67n25, 68n30
Latinos, 82
Lawrence, Regina G., 14–16, 20, 71, 74, 79, 87–105, 116, 164, 165, 171
Lawsuits against the press, 170. *See also* Libel
Le Monde, 76
Legal proceedings, disclosure of, 51
"Legal realist" approach, 173
Leonard, Thomas C., 42
Lester, Marilyn, 14, 97–98
Levy, Leonard W., 9, 50n23, 165
Lewinsky, Monica, 82, 114
Libel: and actual malice rule, 4, 52, 53, 66n14, 72; under Alien and Sedition Acts of 1790s, 4, 59; Australian laws on, 13, 54–58, 59, 60, 63, 65, 67n19, 68n41, 165; chilling effect of legal liability for, 51, 60, 61, 67n18; in common-law countries, 57, 59; eighteenth-century laws on, 4, 34, 48n3, 49n13; insurance coverage for, 61–62, 63; and *New York Times v. Sullivan,* 4, 29–30, 51–65, 164–65; statistics on libel cases, 68n37
Libel Defense Resource Center, 68n37

"Liberal" media systems, 11

Liberty of the press. *See* Freedom of the press

Licensing of journalists, 51, 66*n*5

Limbaugh, Rush, 144

Long, Huey, 7

Lott, Trent, 81–82, 83

Louisiana, 7

Low-power FM stations (LPFM), 141, 142, 148–49, 150, 156

LPFM. *See* Low-power FM stations

Luce, Henry, 163

Lycos Talk Radio, 149

Madison, James, 41, 46

Mancini, Paolo, 11, 12

Market-driven journalism, 17, 117–23

Marketplace of ideas model: and autonomy as ideal, 91; Brennan on, 4–5, 6, 91, 98, 100; and conflict-oriented news, 94; daily news and First Amendment ideals of, 87, 88, 89–91, 100; definition of, 3; and democratic ideal of free expression, 90; as economic ideal, 90, 100–102; and "free press" model, 167–68; motivations for news organizations on, 98; and "open press" model, 167–68; Stewart on, 103*n*12, 170; two views of, 21, 90

Martin, Robert W. T., 7–8, 9, 33, 41, 44, 141–42, 148, 164, 165, 166

Mass media: decline of, 111–12, 115–23, 132–34, 140–41, 166, 172; digital interactive formats for, 113; functions of, 21; and market-driven journalism, 17, 117–23; profit motive of, 101, 102, 113, 115–23, 132, 143; reform efforts for, 132–33. *See also* News media; Radio; Television

Massachusetts, 35, 36–38, 41, 43–44

Masters, Chris, 56

Mayton, William T., 50*n*23

McChesney, Robert, 100, 101

McManus, John, 17

Media. *See* Freedom of the press; News media

Mein, John, 41

Melbourne *Age*, 56

Mergers, 115, 116, 118, 172–73

Metzger, Miriam, 112, 129

Miami Herald v. Tornillo, 7

Micro media, 19, 111–15. *See also* Personal information networks

Middle media, 19, 111–15, 128. *See also* Personal information networks

Mill, John Stuart, 68*n*44

Minneapolis v. Star, 65*n*2

Minnesota, 58, 174*n*3

Missouri, 58

Mobro garbage barge, 14, 96

Molotch, Harvey, 14, 97–98

Moral hazard, 61

Morris, Lewis, 37

Moseley-Braun, Carol, 149

Mott, Frank Luther, 44

Move On, 127, 131

MTV, 139, 149

Mugabwe, President, 57

Murders, 112, 118. *See also* Crime

Murrah Federal Building bombing, 97

Nader, Ralph, 76–77

Narrowing of the news, 115

National and Community Service Trust Act, 78

National Association of Broadcasters, 156

National Enquirer, 61

National Gazette, 44–46

National Public Radio, 152, 156

National security and prior restraints, 51

National Youth and Student Peace Coalition, 155

Nationwide News v. Wills, 67*n*23

Native Americans, 149

Near, Jay, 169, 171

Near v. Minnesota, 169, 170, 174*n*3

Nebraska, 58

Nebraska Press Ass'n v. Stuart, 65*n*3

Netaction, 127

Neuman, W. Russell, 17

"Neutral transmitter" model, 87–88, 103*n*7

New-England Courant, 35, 37, 38

New-England Weekly Journal, 37, 43

New Hampshire, 35, 41, 50*n*39

New media: accessibility of, to average citizens, 147–49, 158*n*9; audience of, 140, 149–53, 157; and citizen mobilization, 153–55, 157; and citizen news producers, 20, 21, 112, 141, 143, 145–47, 156, 166–67, 171, 173; conclusion on, 156–58; constraints on, 157; democratizing potential of, 17, 19–20, 110; examples of, 139, 142; and "free press" model, 142; gatekeeping for, 128–30; and news as information, 143–45, 157; "open press" model of, 20, 141–42, 148, 150, 155–58, 166–67, 172–73; and outsider news, 81–84; and personal information networks, 141; and political campaigns, 139, 140, 149; potential of, 139–40; public policy on, and movement toward open press, 155–56, 172; relations between government officials and, 14, 93–95, 98, 99. *See also* Internet; Personal information networks; Technology

New Republic, 82

New York, 41, 43, 79–80

New-York Gazette, 34, 36

New-York Mercury, 38

New York Times, 17, 57, 59, 60, 61, 78–81, 93–94

New York Times Co. v. United States, 65*n*1

New York Times v. Sullivan, 4, 5, 23*n*4, 29, 30, 51–65, 72, 91, 164–65, 168, 170

New York Times v. United States, 30

New-York Weekly Journal, 36, 37

New-York Weekly Post-Boy, 38

New Zealand, 57

News: daily news and First Amendment ideals, 87–102, 171; definitions of, 20, 144, 159*n*18; eventfulness and event-driven news, 14, 15, 16, 73, 77–79, 84, 99, 116–17; "hard" versus "soft" news, 118–20, 122, 143–44, 159*n*20; as information, 143–45, 157; institutionally driven news, 15; international news, 119; narrowing of, 115; and newsworthiness, 15

News media: audience of, 117–23, 149–53,
160*n*38; in Australia, 55–57, 60, 165; autonomy of, 4–6, 15, 35–39, 41; compared with personal information networks, 131–32; and conflict-oriented news, 15, 73, 79–80, 84, 94; constraints on, 13, 15, 74–76, 84, 91–92; and conventional wisdom, 74, 75–76, 84, 164, 167; cross-national research on, 10, 11, 57, 115; and cynicism of journalists, 14, 15, 73, 80–81, 84, 121, 170; daily news and First Amendment ideals, 87–102, 171; decline of, 111–12, 115–23, 132–34, 140–41, 166, 172; declining confidence in, 121; democracies' need for unlovable press, 15, 73–84, 85*n*3; as establishment institution, 74–77, 169–70; and eventfulness and event-driven news, 14, 15, 16, 73, 77–79, 84, 99, 116–17; functions of, 21; government regulation of, 1–2, 21, 100–101; "hard" versus "soft" news on, 118–20, 122, 143–44, 159*n*20; historical meaning of the press, 10, 12, 18, 33–48; and institutionally driven news, 14–15; international news in, 119; and market-driven journalism, 117–23; professional culture of, 74, 75, 84, 92–96, 115; profit motive of, 101, 102, 113, 115–23, 132, 143; public opinion on, 87–88, 115, 144, 159*nn*18–19; reform efforts for, 132–33; source-dependence of, 74–75, 88–89, 93–95, 98, 99, 164; Stewart on qualities of the press, 29, 30, 37, 40, 41; strategic opportunities for free expression in, 77–84; Tocqueville on, 73; trends in, 1, 117–23, 156; unexpected events and critical news, 14, 96–98. *See also* Daily news; First Amendment; Freedom of the press; Reporters; Television

"News values," 14

Newspaper Protection Act, 2

Newspapers. *See* News media

Newsweek, 119, 131

Newsworthiness, 15

Nicaragua, 93–94

Nixon, Richard, 5

Noah, Timothy, 82

Norms. *See* Professional culture of news media

Norris, Pippa, 122
Norway, 122
Nuclear power plant, 79–80

Objectivity, 94–95, 115
Ocala Star-Banner Co. v. Damron, 66*n*17
O'Connor, Sandra Day, 21
Office of National Service, 78
Oklahoma, 58, 97
OneWorld TV, 128, 129
Online News Association, 151
"Open press" model: definition of, 8, 141–42;
    in eighteenth century, 8–9, 33, 38, 41, 44; and
    marketplace of ideas model, 167–68; of new
    media, 20, 141–42, 148, 150, 155–58, 166–67,
    172–73; and watchdog model, 167–68, 171
Operational bias in news reporting, 75
Outsider news, 81–84
Outsider role of reporters, 15, 82–83, 171
Owen, Diana, 19–20, 20, 21, 109, 110, 166–67,
    171, 172

Parker, James, 38, 39
Partisan press, 10, 24*n*25, 40–42, 47
Pataki, George, 79–80
Patriot Act, 83–84
Patterson, Thomas, 10, 99
PBS, 17, 101–2
PDAs. *See* Personal digital assistants
Pennsylvania, 7, 33–37, 48*n*3
Pennsylvania Gazette, 34, 35, 38–39
Penny press, 10
Perot, Ross, 139
Personal digital assistants (PDAs), 139
Personal information networks: and citizen
    journalism, 112; compared with conventional
    news, 131–32; and digital divide/bandwidth
    divide, 130–32, 140, 148, 155–56, 160*n*27;
    examples of, 111–12; and future of public
    information, 123–24; gatekeeping and jour-
    nalism norms for, 128–30; and integration
    of information and citizen action, 126–27,

130–34, 153–55, 157; and interactive digital
    media channels, 112–13; and issue continuity,
    127; logic of, 124–25; and new information
    and personal politics, 132–34; and new media,
    141; and news from everywhere, 127–28; and
    political information, 125–26; and trust, com-
    munity, and reliability, 128. *See also* Internet;
    New media
Peterson v. Advertiser Newspapers, 67*n*20
Pew Research Center, 87–88, 150, 152–53, 160*n*38
Philadelphia Aurora, 45
Philadelphia Newspapers, Inc., v. Hepp, 67*n*19
Philippines, 127
Poland, 122
Political information on the Internet, 17, 113, 114,
    125–28, 130–34, 149, 150, 158*n*9
Porcupine's Gazette, 45, 46
Postal service, 49*n*10
Powe, Lucas, 24*n*24
Presidential election campaigns, 139, 140, 149,
    153, 159*n*11
Press. *See* Colonial and Revolutionary press;
    News media
Press freedom. *See* First Amendment; Freedom
    of the press
Printers: in colonial and Revolutionary
    America, 7, 8, 10, 12, 34, 36–43, 46–47, 112, 166,
    167; family or business dynasties of, 38, 39;
    and Stamp Act (1765), 40; types of materials
    printed by, 39, 166
Professional culture of news media, 74, 75, 84,
    92–96, 115
Profit motive, 101, 102, 113, 115–23, 132, 140, 143
Providence Gazette, 38
Public Occurrences, 36
Public opinion of news media, 87–88, 115, 144,
    159*nn*18–19

Radio: audience of radio news, 150–51; cor-
    porate conglomeration in, 100–101; federal
    legislation on, 156; historical development of,
    18; Internet radio call-in programs on, 149;

LPFM, 141, 142, 148–49, 150, 156; National Public Radio, 152, 156; talk radio, 139, 140, 144, 149, 152, 154, 155, 159*n*11, 159*n*19

Radio Broadcasting Preservation Act (2000), 156

Rather, Dan, 159*n*20

Reagan, Ronald, 14

Real World Web site, 149

Recall Gray Davis Committee, 154

Red Lion Broadcasting Company v. Federal Communications Commission, 7

Reeher, Grant, 153

Rehnquist, William, 29

Renas, Stephen M., 67*n*18

Reporters: accountability of, 13–14; and anticipatory avoidance of pressure, 11; autonomy of, 13–14, 15, 171; confidentiality of sources of, 6, 13; constraints on, 13, 15, 74–76, 84, 91–92; and conventional wisdom, 74, 75–76, 84, 164, 167; cynicism of, 14, 15, 73, 80–81, 84, 121, 170; and embeddedness of media, 91–92, 164; insider role of, 82–83; and Internet, 14; and "news values," 14; and newsworthiness, 15; online reporters, 147; as outsiders, 15, 82–83, 171; and professional culture, 74, 75, 84, 92–96, 115; relations between government officials and, 14, 93–95, 98, 99; source-dependence of, 74–75, 88–89, 93–95, 98, 99, 164

Revolutionary period. *See* Colonial and Revolutionary press

Rheingold, Howard, 127, 128

"Right to reply" in newspapers, 2, 7

Rivington, James, 41

Romania, 122

Roosevelt, Franklin D., 169, 173

Roosevelt, Theodore, 48

Roth v. United States, 4

Rove, Karl, 95

Royal American Magazine, 39

Sacramento Bee, 82

St. Amant v. Thompson, 66*n*12

Samuelson, Robert, 143

Santa Barbara oil spill, 14

Schauer, Frederick, 13, 20, 29–30, 51–68, 90, 103*n*7, 164–65, 170

School violence, 96–97

Schudson, Michael, 15, 16, 71, 73–86, 111, 115, 125, 164, 165, 167, 171

Schwarzenegger, Arnold, 154

Sciolino, Elaine, 81

"Secondary image" of press freedom, 6, 9

Securities and Exchange Commission, 61

Segal, Eli, 78

Seldes, George, 170

September 11 terrorist attacks, 2, 79–80, 87, 97

Sharpton, Al, 149

Shays's Rebellion, 44

Sheppard v. Maxwell, 65*n*3

Shield laws, 13

Slashdot (Weblog), 129–30

Smith, William Kennedy, 159*n*11

Smith v. California, 66*n*9

Snepp v. United States, 65*n*1

Sons of Liberty, 41

Sources: for colonial and Revolutionary press, 40, 43; confidentiality of, 6, 13; dependence of reporters on, 74–75, 88–89, 93–95, 98, 99, 164

South Africa, 57

Southern Anti-Poverty Law Center, 97

Spano, Andrew J., 80

Speakes, Larry, 14

Speech, freedom of. *See* Freedom of speech

Speiser v. Randall, 66*n*9

Sphere of consensus, 10

Sphere of legitimate controversy, 10

Stamp Act crisis, 34, 40, 47

Star, 61

Steele, Janet, 75

Stephens v. West Australian Newspapers, Ltd., 67*n*24

Stewart, Potter: and *Branzburg v. Hayes*, 170, 171, 174*n*7; on freedom of speech, 5, 111, 168;

on freedom of the press, 5–6, 8, 10, 12, 16, 17, 19, 20, 29, 30, 35, 37, 39, 40, 41, 95, 102, 141, 170, 172; on marketplace of ideas model, 103*n*12, 170; on qualities of press, 29, 30, 37, 40, 41; on watchdog model, 5–6, 8, 35, 39, 40, 87, 91, 98, 100, 102, 163, 165, 168, 170; Yale speech of, 170, 171

Stop the War Coalition, 125–28

Subpoena power of the courts, 30

Sullivan, Andrew, 82

Sullivan, L. B., 4, 66*n*17

Sullivan case, 66*n*12

Sutherland, George, 7

Sweden, 115, 122

Sydney Morning Herald, 56, 57

Tabloid trend in media content, 117, 139, 152

Talk radio, 139, 140, 144, 149, 152, 154, 155, 159*n*11, 159*n*19

Taxation: Bush's tax cut, 80–81; of the press, 7, 51

Technology: and citizen news producers, 20, 21, 112, 141, 143, 145–47, 156, 166–67, 171, 173; democratizing potential of new media, 17, 19–20, 110; historical perspective on, 18, 109; interactive digital media channels, 112–13; and specialized audiences, 17, 18, 157; trends in, 18, 109–10. *See also* Internet; New media; Personal information networks

Telecommunications Act (1996), 155

Telegraph, 18

Television: audience of television news, 150, 151, 152; in Australia, 55–56; cable television, 6, 9, 17, 114, 118, 141, 142, 149, 150, 152; constraints of professional culture on, 75; crime news on, 118–19; in Europe, 122; international news on, 119; and market-driven information, 117–20; and MTV, 139, 149; PBS's news programming, 17, 101–2; reality television, 120, 149; and relationship between reporters and officials, 94; "soft" versus "hard" news on, 118, 119, 159*n*20; Spanish-language television news, 18, 152; trends in, 139

Theophanous v. The Herald and Weekly Times, Ltd., 67*n*24

Thomas, Isaiah, 39

Thurmond, Strom, 81

Time magazine, 81, 119, 163

Tocqueville, Alexis de, 73

Tribune Co. v. Minnesota Commission of Revenue, 65*n*2

Turner Broadcasting System v. Federal Communications Commission, 24*n*20, 26*n*51

UCLA Internet Report, 130

UNESCO, 81

Unexpected events and critical news, 14, 96–98

United States v. Progressive, Inc., 65*n*1

U.S. News and World Report, 119

U.S. Supreme Court. *See* specific cases and justices

Valdez, 96

Vietnam War, 95, 131, 170

Virginia, 7, 14

Virginia State Board of Pharmacy v. Virginia Citizens' Consumer Council, 23*n*14

Vittachi, Anuradha, 117

Walker, James L., 67*n*18

Wall Street Journal, 17

Washington Post, 144

Watchdog model: and autonomy as ideal, 91; Brennan on, 87, 91; and colonial and Revolutionary press, 35, 39, 40, 44; and conflict-oriented news, 94; daily news and First Amendment ideals of, 87, 88, 89–91, 100; definition of, 3; and "free press" model, 167–68; motivations of news organizations on, 98; and "open press" model, 167–68, 171; in Pennsylvania Constitution, 7; Stewart on, 1, 5–6, 8, 35, 39, 40, 87, 91, 98, 100, 102, 163, 165, 168, 170

Watergate, 5, 95

Web sites. *See* Internet

Weblogs, 15, 16–17, 18, 82, 83, 113, 126, 129–30, 141, 145, 146

Weekly Rehearsal (Boston), 44

Weintraub, Dan, 82

Weiss, Jack M., 20–21, 71–72

White, Byron, 7, 17

Winship, In re, 66n9

Witt, James Lee, 79

Witt report, 79–80

World Bank, 117

World Trade Organization protests, 155

World Wide Web. *See* Internet

Yahoo.com, 22

Zagat.com, 19

Zaller, John, 85n3

Zenger, John Peter, 9, 37, 48n3, 49n13

Zimbabwe, 57

Zuckman, Jill, 83–84